BORN
in
FIRE

Facsimile of the Indonesian Proclamation of Independence, August 17, 1945.

BORN
in
FIRE

The Indonesian Struggle for Independence

*

AN ANTHOLOGY
edited by

COLIN WILD
PETER CAREY

*Published by arrangement with
BBC Publications,
a division of BBC Enterprises, Ltd.*

Ohio University Press ✻ *Athens*

Originally published as *Gelora Api Revolusi*
in 1986 by P. T. Gramedia, Indonesia

© Copyright 1986 by the British Broadcasting Corporation

Ohio University Press edition published 1988.
Printed in the United States of America.

Ohio University Press books
are printed on acid free paper.∞

LIBRARY OF CONGRESS
Library of Congress Cataloging-in-Publication Data
[Gelora api revolusi. English]
Born in fire: the Indonesian struggle for independence: an anthology/edited
by Colin Wild, Peter Carey.
    p. cm.
Translation of: Gelora api revolusi.
Bibliography: p.
Includes index.
ISBN 0-8214-0881-X. ISBN 0-8214-0882-8 (pbk.)
1. Indonesia—History—Revolution, 1945–1949.
2. Indonesia—History—20th century. 3. Nationalism—Indonesia—History.
I. Wild, Colin. II. Carey, P. B. R.
DS644.G3613 1988
959.8'035—dc19   87-31223
                                                                   CIP

CONTENTS

University describes the myths, heroes, and ancient wars which inspired the leaders of the independence movement, and shows how they in turn used these stories to inspire the people.

BY PROF. AKIRA NAGAZUMI
One of the first nationalist organizations to be established in Indonesia was, originally, more cultural than political in character. It was never a large organization numerically, yet its influence on the independence movement was profound. Akira Nagazumi of Tokyo University describes the growth and influence of Budi Utomo from its foundation in 1908 until 1935.

BY DR. A. P. E. KORVER
In the early days of this century the birth of a sense of Indonesian national consciousness coincided with a reform movement within the Islamic community. Islam was a major feature of Indonesian culture, and an aspect of the reform movement was the identification of Islam with the nation and the growing impatience with colonial status. Peiter Korver of the University of Amsterdam describes the development of Islamic thought in the early days of the independence movement, and in particular the role of Sarekat Islam.

BY DR. RUTH McVEY
Colonialism subjected the weak and the poor to the will of the strong and the rich. Within Western societies there were also great disparities of wealth and power, and there political philosophy had grown up to challenge these ancient injustices: socialism. The most potent and revolutionary form of socialism was communism, which sought to influence and control independence movements all over the world. Ruth McVey, formerly of the School of Oriental and African Studies, University of London, describes the growth of the Communist movement in Indonesia up to 1942.

BY H. B. JASSIN
The birth of Indonesian literature was closely bound up with the birth of Indonesian nationalism. H. B. Jassin, the distinguished Indonesian literary critic and historian, traces the development of the literature of revolution from its earliest stirrings to one of its greatest exponents, Chairil Anwar.

wide economic depression deepened, many people had more urgent problems to deal with. New, more moderate organizations, such as Parindra and Gerindo, sprang up, however, seeking to achieve some progress in cooperation with the Dutch. Susan Abeyasekere of the Footscray Institute of Technology, Australia, describes the activities of these cooperating parties up to the arrival of the Japanese invading force in 1942.

it was also a period of transition. Links with the past were broken, new ideas born and, in some respects, the nationalist movement progressed both because of and in spite of Japanese influence and actions. William Frederick of Ohio University describes the effects of the occupation on the country and on its independence movement.

days, a young member of Putera and the Jawa Hokokai. This man, Wangsa Wijaya, was also at Maeda's house on the night of August 16. These three people describe the dramatic events of those 3 days.

staff, and minister of national defense. Born in North Sumatra, Gen. H. Abdul Haris Nasution passed much of his boyhood in Bandung; he was far from home when, in 1942, the Japanese army landed in Java.

a voice. Harold Crouch of the Australian National University describes the relationship between these two arms of the revolution.

The final stages of the struggle, following the collapse of the Japanese authorities, is the story of the interaction of diplomacy and warfare. But behind the politicians and the professional soldiers were impatient youth urging the older generation forward with their slogan *merdeka atau mati* (freedom or death). Anton Lucas, currently Senior Researcher at Hasanuddin University in Ujung Pandang, Indonesia, describes the influence of the revolutionary youth, the *pemuda revolusi.*

When the Japanese war machine collapsed their propaganda system collapsed also. The republic seized the apparatus of the media, particularly the radio studios and transmitters. Colin Wild, head of the BBC Indonesian Service, describes how radio became a vital means of steering the fragmented elements of the revolution and keeping the outside world informed and sympathetic to the republic.

As soon as the Japanese defeat was known, their organs of propaganda lost whatever credibility they had. New media, run by the republic and its sympathizers, sprang up. One of the pioneers of the new republican media was the founder of *Harian Merdeka*, B. M. Diah, who describes how his newspaper served and survived the years of the struggle.

The new republic had many sympathizers and friends among the nations of the world. By skillful diplomacy these friends were encouraged to support the republic so that world opinion was mobilized and the road to universal recognition shortened. Ide Anak Agung, politician, diplomat and scholar, describes the role of international diplomacy in the struggle.

were soon replaced with whole-hearted support of the republican cause, and of his role for six months as prime minister of the emergency government.

A. J. Piekaar was a colonial civil servant in the Netherlands East Indies before World War II. During the Japanese occupation he was interned. He is now retired and lives in South Africa. Dr. Piekaar describes how the independence struggle looked to Dutch eyes.

Why was the struggle for independence successful? Was it due mainly to the tenacity of the armed forces, the determination of the *pemuda,* the skill of Indonesian diplomacy, or the support of other nations of the world? Was it some abstract quality, such as the spirit of the people in general, or the will of God? Four men who each played a part in the revolution, Syafruddin Prawiranegara, the late Adam Malik, Sri Sultan Hamengku Buwono IX and Gen. Tahi Bonar Simatupang all relate the factors they think were responsible for the success of Indonesia's struggle for independence.

FOREWORD

This book arises from a series of radio programs made by the Indonesian language service of the BBC External Services in London, and first broadcast in 1985 to coincide with the 40th anniversary of the proclamation of independence in Jakarta on August 17th. The main purpose of these programs was to give the BBC's very large and predominantly young audience in Indonesia an opportunity to hear this most important part of their history told in the most authoritative manner possible. I felt this could best be done by inviting a wide range of scholars to contribute talks on those aspects of the story which they had studied most thoroughly. What such a series might lack in homogeneity of style and interpretation—compared with a series by a single author—it would gain in vividness and scholarly authority. Moreover, to parade before our Indonesian listeners a cavalcade of international scholarship would encourage them in their own studies by impressing upon them the earnestness with which their story is studied, and the excellence of scholarship that is devoted to it, around the world. We hoped that the series would make a contribution to the Indonesian-language literature available to students of modern Indonesian history, in particular offering interpretative ideas which they might miss by studying the works of Indonesian historians alone.

This last thought is not a particular reflection on Indonesian historians. Even in long-established nations like Britain and France, national history is frequently interpreted in a narrow, nationalistic manner. How often are British students, for example, invited by teachers to study their history from a French or American point of view? It is a notorious fault that Europe's disastrous history of nationalistic bickering has still not driven home to us the virtue of seeing ourselves as others see us. Indonesians, whose national history is as yet so short that many people have lived through the whole of it, could, I felt, be helped to understand that history by seeing it through disinterested eyes.

Whereas to have invited only Indonesian historians to contribute to the series would have been "taking coals to Newcastle"—doing what Indonesia could do for itself—there are, nonetheless, certain aspects of Indonesia's history in which the leading experts are, not surprisingly, Indonesians. Further, the inclusion of talks by Indonesian experts was desirable to avoid the charge of attempting to foist upon the listeners a totally foreign interpretation. More important still, though 40 years and more have passed since the climax of the struggle, much of the story still reposes in the memories of those who played a role in it. Radio can bring to the microphone not just the commentator but the maker of history himself. This we were able to do in generous measure.

When the programs were broadcast, the response from the audience was massive and enthusiastic. As a result, they were compiled in book form and appeared in August 1986 as *Gelora Api Revolusi* (The Fire of the Revolution) under the imprint of Gramedia, a well-known Jakarta publishing firm. Now here is the English edition. Its core is the texts of the original broadcasts, including translations and transcriptions of the interviews, supplemented by an introduction written by my collaborator on the radio series, Dr. Peter Carey, suggestions for further reading, and photographs. There is also a new chapter, an interview with John Coast. The manuscript has been re-edited to give the whole greater consistency and readability. While this procedure has necessarily robbed the interviews of some of their spontaneity, we feel the result is superior for this printed version.

This book is neither comprehensive nor definitive. It has many shortcomings. Not every aspect of the complex story of the first 50 years of this century has been covered; no book of this size could hope to do so. The reader may also find it lacks the continuity and stylistic integrity of a book by a single author. It is unfortunately inevitable that the interviews must lack in translation, and in more formal manuscript form, the vivid authenticity of the original broadcasts. In spite of these qualifications I hope the book has the ring of authority about it.

The story itself is that of the birth of the world's fifth largest country. It may contain no single feat of human endurance so astonishing as Mao Zedong's Long March, no single character so inspirational as Mahatma Gandhi, and thankfully, no tragedy as appalling as the massacres upon the partition of India and Pakistan, yet it is the story of a struggle comparable in magnitude to that of the birth of any modern nation. It is a story that deserves to be known better beyond the shores of that beautiful and richly endowed country. I therefore hope that this book will be read not only by those who already know the story and are looking for fresh insights and perspectives, but more particularly by those new to the subject.

The production of the original radio program and the subsequent preparation of both the Indonesian and English editions of the book have imposed demands upon many people during more than three years. Those whose names appear in the book have that as their reward, which I trust they feel is some recompense. But many others, in particular members of the BBC Indonesian section during this time, deserve my gratitude, not only for the help they gave but for their forbearance when I neglected other interests in my enthusiasm for this project. Particular acknowledgment is due to Nicholas Nugent who conducted most of the interviews and to Annabel Teh Gallop who translated them into English.

Colin Wild

INTRODUCTION

We were born in fire. We were not born in the rays of the full moon like other nations. There are other nations whose independence was presented to them. There are other nations who, without any effort on their part, were given independence by the imperialists as a present. Not us, we fought for our independence at the cost of great sacrifice. We gained our independence through a tremendous struggle which has no comparison in this world.

(Sukarno, Radio Address, December 1962, on the eve of Indonesia's confrontation with Malaysia)

The Indonesian Revolution is without doubt the seminal event in the modern history of that country. Not only did it mark the coming of age of the Indonesian people and the flowering of national self-awareness, but it also left a lasting social and political legacy, one which will continue to be interpreted and reinterpreted by Indonesian historians for years to come. Virtually every aspect of modern Indonesian life—be it the relationship between army and state, the role of the president, the nature of the constitution, *pancasila* democracy, the tension between Islam and secularism, the thrust of economic development, the composition of the elite, the evolution of an "independent and active" foreign policy, the relationship between Java and the Outer Islands, and the character of Indonesian nationalism—has been molded by the revolutionary experience. Present-day Indonesians and those yet unborn will all regard themselves (and be taught to regard themselves) as children of the revolution, spiritual members of an ever-expanding *angkatan '45*, or generation of 1945.

The fact that the Indonesian Revolution, like the French and Soviet ones before it, has now entered the realms of metahistory and ideology, however, makes the task of the historian doubly difficult. How is it possible to advance a dispassionate analysis of a process which has been so deeply marked by the exigencies of modern myth-making? Can even foreign scholars, studying the event from outside the prism of Indonesian culture, escape the shadow of historical orthodoxy? The editors of the present volume, originally broadcast as a BBC radio series to celebrate the fortieth anniversary of Indonesian independence in 1985, have few illusions about the difficulties of interpreting such a complex and multi-layered phenomenon. Not only did the requirements of the original radio series impose a severe restriction on the length of the individual contributions, but the manner in which they have been arranged, spanning the period from the cultural and nationalist awakening at the beginning of the present century to the final diplomatic recognition of the Republic of Indonesia by the Dutch at the Round Table Conference in The Hague in December 1949, has tended to reinforce the established orthodoxy of an ineluctable process toward national unity and independence, a Whig interpretation of the Indonesian Revolution first advanced by George Kahin in 1952[1] and long dominant on the historical landscape.

Although there is no denying the central importance of the years up to 1949 in terms of Indonesia's political and military struggle for independence, it is arguable that the process of decolonization did not end with the formal transfer of sovereignty. President Sukarno always insisted that the Indonesian Revolution was a continuing phenomenon, one which needed to run its full course before Indonesians could truly consider themselves free of the shackles of the colonial past. Mental attitudes of inferiority to the West, engrained during the colonial period, had to be utterly transformed. Indonesians had to learn to "stand on their own feet" (*berdikari*) and develop a pride in their national identity. To be an Indonesian, in Sukarno's view, was a privilege not a burden. His actions during the late 1950s and early 1960s, when he enjoyed full executive power as president under the revived 1945 constitution, were all aimed at enhancing Indonesian self-confidence by making them masters in their own house. One by one, the political, economic, cultural, financial, and strategic ties which continued to bind Jakarta to The Hague after 1949 were severed. In 1957, the Indonesian takeover of Dutch estates and businesses marked the de facto end of the colonial economic relationship. Four years later, with the Irian Barat affair reaching its climax, interest payments on Dutch loans had been suspended, Dutch possessions nationalized, the Dutch-Indonesian "Union" unilaterally abrogated, and diplomatic relations broken. Condemned by many in the West as an impractical visionary and demagogue, Sukarno had nonetheless succeeded in carrying the decolonization process a long way towards its logical conclusion. His youthful dream of a unitary and independent republic stretching from Sabang to Merauke[2] had become a reality. It would remain for his successors to ensure that this political achievement was rendered unassailable, through educational advances, economic development, and consolidation of state power on a scale sufficient to guarantee the coherence of the Indonesian nation in the late twentieth century, a time of change more far-reaching than any previously experienced by the inhabitants of the archipelago.

If one returns to the period of the Japanese occupation (1942-45) and the physical revolution against the Dutch (1945-49), it is possible to trace this process of nation building almost back to its source. As Anthony Reid has pointed out in a recent essay,[3] Indonesia before 1942 was far less clearly or consciously a nation than most colonies, certainly less than its Southeast Asian neighbours, Burma, Vietnam, and the Philippines. Yet by 1950, when the United States of Indonesia (USI) finally merged into the unitary republic, the nation had undoubtedly become one; its development into an ever more integrated and centralized country has been inspired directly by the forces unleashed during the revolution.

The exact nature of those forces, however, has become a subject for debate among historians. Most are agreed that there was a powerful common ideal at work, particularly that of Indonesian youth (*pemuda*), which had as its object the creation of a just and prosperous society, the *negara adil dan makmur* of millenarian and socialist prophecy.[4] But the actual character of the independence struggle has been interpreted in widely different ways by Indonesian and foreign scholars. Was it a genuine social revolution or merely a war of liberation? Did new elites come to the fore or were old ones merely consolidated? Should the period principally be seen as a series of local struggles against the Dutch and their indigenous allies, or was the power of the republican center such as to impose a unity on the revolutionary experience? Who did more to ensure the survival and eventual success of the republic, the Indonesian diplomats and politicians, or the soldiers of the republican army?

For the late Nugroho Notosusanto, head of the Center of Historical Research of the Indonesian Armed Forces, the answers to all these questions were unequivocal. The Indonesian struggle against the Dutch was not a revolution but a *perang kemerdekaan* (war of liberation). A new military elite did come to the fore, but on the whole they were scions of the old *priyayi* (bureaucratic/official) families rather than *novi homines* of peasant or plebeian stock. The unity of the struggle was provided by the republican army and not the politicians in Yogyakarta. And finally, Indonesian independence was won on the battlefield not at the conference table; *perjuangan* (armed struggle) rather than *diplomasi* (diplomacy) was the key to republican survival. All these views are clearly expressed in the last volume of the national history of Indonesia, of which Nugroho was the senior editor. Here the whole period between 1945 and 1949 is subsumed under the heading of *perang kemerdekaan*, all events center on the armed struggle against the Dutch, and the terrible social revolutions of 1945-46, which led to the physical elimination of the Dutch-supported aristocratic/bureaucratic elites in many areas, are relegated to a coy footnote.[5] It is not difficult to see in this interpretation the influence of the army-dominated politics of the post-1965 "New Order" period in Indonesia. With Sukarno's fall, the civilian politicians prominent during the revolution were discredited and the PKI view of a revolution from below anathematized. The field was left open for the army to advance its own official perspective on the revolution. Thus the revolutionary nature of the 1945-49 experience came to be consistently downplayed in favor of an army interpretation which stressed the centrality of the military struggle to the unity and survival of the republic both before and after 1949. According to this view, it was the army not the civilian leadership which was the true midwife of the republic, guaranteeing its survival by beating off attacks from both the communist left (the Madiun Affair of 1948 and the PKI "coup" of 1965) and the Islamic right (the Darul Islam revolts and PRRI-Permesta secessionist movements of the 1950s and early 1960s). The civilian politicians, when they make their appearance at all in such histories, are invariably portrayed in a negative light, either negotiating away battlefield gains against the Dutch at the conference table or appeasing extremist forces for their own self-seeking ends. Furthermore, these accounts insist that it was the army rather than the civilian politicians which forged the closest links with the Indonesian *rakyat* (peasant mass) through the guerrilla struggle in the countryside, links which were later used to justify the special role of the army in civilian and military affairs when the *dwifungsi* doctrine was being crystallized in the late 1950s.

Ironically, just as this new historiographical orthodoxy was beginning to take root in Indonesia in the early 1970s, a younger generation of Western-trained historians (some of them Indonesians preparing doctoral theses in Australia and the United States) was moving away from an overarching national interpretation of the revolution, be it from a civilian- or army-dominated perspective, toward one which laid greater emphasis on the regional dynamics of the revolutionary experience. Although to date only a few of these regional studies have been published,[7] the main outlines of their arguments can be discerned in the collection of essays edited by Audrey Kahin in 1985[8] and in the aforementioned article by Reid, which provide a masterly analysis of their common themes.[9]

Briefly stated, what these regional histories share is a common vision of the revolutionary process as a series of local movements, often quite isolated from each other, but reflecting similar characteristics and concerns. First, unlike the military accounts, they tend to see the social revolutions of 1945-46 as major catalysts of the revolutionary experience. Far from being bloody aberrations or devious, communist-inspired distractions from the anti-Dutch struggle, they are thought to have represented the resolution of tensions which had been building since the 1930s, tensions gravely exacerbated by the suffering of the Japanese occupation period. In areas such as Aceh, eastern Sumatra, Banten, and the Tiga Daerah (Three Regions) zone of north-central Java, members of the feudal aristocracy or local village elite who had been directly associated with the harsh requisitioning policies of the Japanese or who had earlier cooperated with the Dutch, were either publicly humiliated or brutally murdered along with their families.[10] More Indonesians probably lost their lives or suffered torture at the hands of their fellow countrymen during these tragic months than were killed in the whole guerrilla struggle against the Dutch. Here the Indonesian Revolution had much in common with its French and Soviet predecessors.

Appalling though this may be to present-day Indonesians, many of whom have lived through the more recent trauma of 1965-66, the social revolutions of 1945-46 must be recognized, according to these histories, as an integral part of the revolutionary climacteric. Not only do they provide the key to an understanding of the struggle between rival elites in Sumatra and Java, and the intergenerational conflicts which fuelled the evanescent *pemuda* revolution of these years, but they also throw open a window on a world suddenly cut loose from its moorings—a world in a "time of tremblingness" (*jaman kegelisahan*) in Sutan Syahrir's evocative phrase[11]—in which violence ruled supreme and the heady fusion of Islam, Marxism, and millenarianism seemed to herald a new egalitarian day. By mid-1946, this radical challenge to the revolution had been contained, but its ideal of *sama rata sama rasa* (brotherhood and equality) continued to resonate in the hearts of many long after the physical revolution had ended. In this way the dragon's teeth of the great PKI party of the 1950s and early 1960s were sown. Most important, the social revolutions shattered the link with Indonesia's "feudal" past, leaving the way open for a new national identity to be forged amid the hardships of war and the shared experience of anti-colonial sacrifice.

The second point which these regional histories insist on is the weakness of the republican center throughout the revolutionary period and the importance of local support for regional elites. The short-lived Japanese occupation (1942-45), which imposed an artificial isolation on the regions through the emphasis on economic autarky and the administrative division between the 16th Army (Java), 25th Army (Sumatra), and the Navy (eastern islands), is regarded as having been of fundamental importance. Far from having been a drawback, this isolation, it is argued, prevented any resentment of Javanese leadership taking root in the Outer Islands prior to 1945. On the contrary, the reestablishment of contact between the regions after the sudden Japanese surrender is seen to have been a positive experience which enhanced the popularity of the infant republic.[12] Rival elites in the provinces tended to look to the center for support in the resolution of their conflicts in the early months of the revolution, support which was invariably thrown in on the side of the conservative nationalists, be they scions of old *pangreh praja* (administrative elite) families in north-central Java and eastern Sumatra, or the newly-dominant *ulama* (religious scholars) in Banten, Aceh, and West Sumatra.

Even the army, lauded by Indonesian military historians as the living symbol of national unity, is viewed by the regional historians as having derived its strength largely from its local links. Again the Japanese period is seen as crucial, for the highly devolved battalion structure of the PETA (Fatherland's Defence Force) in Java is regarded as the precursor of the autonomous regional units which fought against the Dutch in the revolution. Indeed, one of the major themes of the post-revolutionary period is the gradual integration of these local units of the TNI (Tentara Nasional Indonesia; Indonesian National Army) into a unified command structure, a process which could be said to have begun just prior to the Madiun Affair in September 1948 and reached its fruition after the regional revolts of 1957-58.[13]

Both Indonesian military historians and Western-trained scholars are, however, agreed that the Dutch policy of trying to surround the republic with puppet federal states based on regional sentiments played directly into the hands of the nationalists. Not only did it destroy the legitimacy of regionalism, but it also increased sympathy in the regions for the embattled republic. As Reid has pointed out,[14] no policy could have been better designed to promote Indonesian unity, and its legacy has continued to shape Indonesian political thinking until the present day.

There are only a few echoes of this major historiographical debate between the Indonesian military historians and the Western-trained regional scholars in the present volume. The late Nugroho, although approached on several occasions by the BBC to contribute to the original series, declined to cooperate. Indeed, he was the only Indonesian to publicly voice reservations about the series, perhaps out of pique that the orthodox army line of a "war of liberation" had been passed over in favor of a concentration on the civilian politicians and the diplomatic struggle.[15] Ironically, it has been left to a Western-trained historian, Harold Crouch (Chapter 27), to give an assessment of the balance between *perjuangan* and *diplomasi* in the present volume, and to officers of an older generation, Djatikusumo (Chapter 14) and Nasution (Chapter 23)—neither of them particularly sympathetic to Nugroho—to provide personal accounts of the genesis of the TNI and the military experiences during the early months of the revolution. At the same time, the regional perspective has been largely ignored except in the interviews with Mara Karma (Chapter 24) and Syafruddin Prawiranegara, the head of the emergency government in Sumatra in 1948-9 (Chapter 35). The two Western-trained scholars qualified to discuss the "social revolutions" of 1945-46 and the regional dynamics of the revolution, Anton Lucas and Anthony Reid, were both required to address other themes in their chapters (28 and 31).

Space has not permitted the wider range of contributions which might have done justice both to the regional aspects of the revolution and the equally important post-1949 decolonization process in Indonesia, but the editors will feel disappointed if all that has been achieved here is just another sycophantic celebration of Indonesian "national history," another textbook which, suitably purged of embarrassing comments, can take its place in the sanitized syllabi of Indonesian high schools and universities. Although nearly all the contributors were basically sympathetic to the Indonesian struggle for independence, every effort was made to include as broad a spectrum of views as possible, views which range from those of ex-*pemuda* like Adam Malik (Chapters 12, 18 and 37) to senior army officers like Simatupang (Chapter 37), from journalists like B.M. Diah (Chapter 30) to men at the center of political events like Ide Anak Agung Gde Agung (Chapter 31) and the Sultan of Yogyakarta (Chapter 33). Similar efforts were made with the foreign contributors, who include economic and political historians as well as experts on the literary and cultural background of the revolution, a background still much in need of further research. Here too the stress was on the multi-faceted nature of the revolution. We hear from zestful republican enthusiasts like John Coast (Chapter 26), as well as from former colonial servants like A. J. Piekaar (Chapter 36), from pro-Indonesian socialists like Shigetada Nishijima (Chapters 16 and 18) and friends of the republican leadership in Yogyakarta like George Kahin (Chapter 34). British, Dutch, Japanese and American participants thus take their place alongside Indonesian eyewitnesses in a book which aims to enliven the historical narrative with illustrations culled from the recollections of those who had the privilege to be part of the events they describe. Indeed, if this book has any claims to originality at all, these will reside principally in the contributions made by contemporaries, men and women whose recollection of the dramatic days of the revolution were still fresh when this volume was in preparation.

Peter Carey★

★Thanks to Dr. J. van Goor of the Rijksuniversiteit te Utrecht, the Netherlands, for many suggestions used in writing this introduction.

END NOTES

1. George McTurnan Kahin, *Nationalism and Revolution in Indonesia* (Ithaca: Cornell University Press, 1952).

2. Sabang is an island off the northernmost tip of Sumatra and Merauke is a town on the southeastern coast of Irian Jaya (Indonesian New Guinea), close to the border with Papau-New Guinea. Sukarno used them as shorthand terms to indicate the vast geographical spread of Indonesia and its territorial boundaries. See Cindy Adams, *Sukarno. An Autobiography As Told to Cindy Adams* (Indianapolis; Bobbs-Merrill, 1965), p.4.

3. Anthony Reid, "The Revolution in Regional Perspective," in J. van Goor (ed.), *The Indonesian Revolution. Papers of the Conference Held in Utrecht, 17-20 June 1986* (Utrecht: Utrechtse Historische Cahiers, Rijksuniverseit Utrecht, 1986), p.196.

4. Reid, "The Revolution," p.197.

5. Nugroho Notosusanto (ed.), *Sejarah Nasional Indonesia*, Vol. VI (Jakarta: Departemen Pendidikan dan Kebudayaan, 1976), p.39, n.103.

6. Nugroho Notosusanto (ed.), *Sejarah*, pp.29-72, 142-52.

7. Apart from the older works by John Smail, *Bandung in the Early Revolution, 1945-1946. A Study in the Social History of the Indonesian Revolution* (Ithaca: Cornell Modern Indonesia Project, 1964); and Benedict R. O'G. Anderson, *Java in a Time of Revolution, Occupation and Resistance, 1944-46* (Ithaca: Cornell University Press, 1972), which concentrate on Bandung and Surakarta respectively, the only recently published monograph on the Indonesian Revolution at the regional level is Anthony Reid, *The Blood of the People. Revolution and the End of Traditional Rule in Northern Sumatra* (Kuala Lumpur: Oxford University Press, 1979).

8. Audrey Kahin (ed.), *Regional Dynamics of the Indonesian Revolution. Unity from Diversity* (Honolulu: University of Hawaii Press, 1985).

9. Reid, "The Revolution," pp. 183-99.

10. Reid, "The Revolution," pp. 190-94.

11. Sutan Syahrir, *Our Struggle*, trans. Benedict R. O'G. Anderson (Ithaca:

Cornell Modern Indonesia Project, 1968); and see Anderson, *Java in a Time of Revolution,* p. 11.

12. Reid, "The Revolution," p. 196.

13. On this process of military unification, see Ruth McVey, "The Post-Revolutionary Transformation of the Indonesian Army," *Indonesia* 11 (April 1971), pp. 131-76; and 13 (April 1972), pp. 147-82.

14. Reid, "The Revolution," p. 196.

15. Susanto Pudjomartono, "Bung Karno di Radio London," *Tempo* (27 April 1985), p. 25.

1

*

The Dragons Stir

MERLE C. RICKLEFS

The Indonesian revolution and the anticolonial movements which led up to it are crucially important episodes in Indonesian history. But the revolution and its antecedents did not arise solely because of Indonesian events; they were also linked to processes and events in the wider world. Before examining this world context it is necessary to comment briefly on a particular aspect of the Indonesian setting, in which the myth of 350 years of Dutch rule often gets in the way of historical analysis.

Nowhere in Indonesia did the Dutch rule for 350 years. The oldest permanent Dutch settlement was at Ambon, which the Dutch ruled from 1605 until the Japanese took it in 1942. That is less than 340 years, and of those the British ruled from 1796 to 1803, and again from 1810 to 1817. Jakarta (Batavia) was ruled from 1619 until 1942 (or 1949) for a total of 323 or 330 years. Semarang was held by the Dutch from 1708 for a period of 234 years. These are long periods of rule, but they apply only to enclaves, not to large tracts of Indonesian territory or large numbers of Indonesians.

Large-scale political, economic, and military control of Indonesian land and people was achieved by the Dutch no earlier than the nineteenth century, and in many areas less than a century ago. All of Java was effectively ruled after 1830, and Minangkabau after the end of the Padri War in 1838; but Lombok was only conquered in 1894 and

South Bali in 1908, less than 80 years ago. And when was Aceh conquered? Certainly not in 1873 when the Dutch first attacked, nor in 1881 when the Dutch first said they had won, for resistance continued into the early years of this century; some Acehnese never admitted defeat.

It was not 350 years of Dutch rule, then, and when one speaks of Indonesian anticolonial or revival movements—the Islamic reform movements of the early years of this century or Budi Utomo, for example—one should remember that at the same time peoples of Aceh, Bali, Nusa Tenggara, Sulawesi Selatan, Mentawai, and elsewhere were still resisting initial Dutch conquest.

With these circumstances in mind, we may look at the world context of Indonesian affairs in the nineteenth century, moving for convenience's sake from the Islamic perspective to the non-Islamic. Many nineteenth-century Indonesian Muslims were aware of being part of a world-wide *ummat Islam,* or Muslim community. Many also knew that the nineteenth century was a time of crisis throughout the Islamic world, as European powers conquered Islamic societies and as the Ottoman empire, the main symbol of unity in the Sunni world, disintegrated. To many Europeans and Muslims these events suggested that Islam was somehow weaker than and inferior to the Christian world of the West. Between about 1830 and the first ten years of the twentieth century, the British annexed Aden, Cyprus, Egypt, and Sudan, and ruled millions of Muslims in India. Russia conquered areas around the Caspian Sea and divided Persia into spheres of influence with the British. The French conquered Algeria and set up protectorates over Tunisia and Morocco, the latter being shared with Spain. Italy conquered Libya in 1911. And, as we observed above, the Dutch were conquering Indonesia while the British were moving into Malaya. Many Indonesians thus saw their troubles as part of this wider phenomenon; some, for example, prayed for an Ottoman victory in the *perang Rus* of the 1850s, when the British and French sided with the Sultan and defeated the Russians in what modern historians call the Crimean War.

In the Middle East, Islamic reform movements developed in response to the European imperial onslaught. The leading figures there were Jamal ad-Din al-Afghani, his student Muhammad 'Abduh, and 'Abduh's student Muhammad Rashid Rida. Al-Afghani was motivated throughout his life largely by a hatred for British imperialism as he had observed it in India. This drove him to an attempt to use Western knowledge, which he saw as the strength behind European imperialism, to revive and unify the forces of Islam, but without destroying the essential unity of Islamic society.

Thus the roots of Islamic modernism, as it came to be called, were to be found in anti-imperialism. To this were added doctrinal explanations of Islam's apparent decline relative to Europe. The four *madzhabs* (schools of law), said the modernists, had caused Islam to become rigid and out-of-date; the *bab al-ijtihad*, the gate of reasoning, must be reopened so as to return to the original purity of God's words as found in the Qur'an and Hadith, which would not be found to be inconsistent with modern science. Islamic modernism explained the conquest of Islamic lands by Christian powers in terms of a Muslim departure from the original truths of Islam, and it offered a solution: revive and purify Islam, embrace modern scientific learning, and unify Muslims in and across nations against the imperialists.

All of this was relevant to nineteenth-century Indonesians. Minangkabau people were particularly important in the version of Islamic modernism which arose in Indonesia. Shaikh Ahmad Khatib was a Minangkabau who became *imam* of the Shafi'i *madzhab* at the Masjid al-Haram in Mecca, and many Indonesian religious reformers were his students. His cousin Shaikh Tahir Jalaluddin, who lived until 1957, became a close friend of Muhammad Rashid Rida in Mecca. In the first years of this century Islamic modernism "took off" in Minangkabau, particularly under the leadership of Shaikh Muhammad Jamil Jambek and Haji Rasul. Shortly thereafter it appeared in Java, where leadership was first exercised by the Arab community in Batavia. Soon, however, the pace was set by Muhammadiyah, founded by Kyai Haji Ahmad Dahlan in Yogyakarta in 1912. In the 1920s, Islamic modernism began to spread outside Java and Sumatra. All of this was part of a wider process in the Islamic world, arising from analysis of the shared problem of European conquest and offering solutions in religious revival, reform, and unity.

But the modernist movement also provoked conflict. Many devout Muslims did not accept the modernists' view of the *madzhabs*. One group of these opponents, responding also to the abolition of the Caliphate and the Saudi capture of Mecca, established Nahdatul Ulama (NU) in 1926. For many years there was conflict between the modernists and the so-called *kaum tua* and *kaum adat*, the "older generation" and supporters of tradition. There were also groups who doubted that

purified Islam was an appropriate philosophical basis for a new Indonesian national character; the Taman Siswa schools of Ki Hajar Dewantara were the clearest example of this view.

The point is that all of this religion and cultural conflict, part of a
much wider world phenomenon among Muslims seeking freedom
from imperialism, led to self-examination and cultural renewal, which
in turn became powerful antecedents to the Indonesian Revolution.

In the non-Islamic world there were also important events which
contributed to Indonesia's gathering revolutionary forces in the first
decades of this century. Non-Islamic Asia was reawakening, often on
the basis of the same principles as Islamic modernism, for many Asians
wished to borrow Western science and technology while maintaining
an indigenous cultural and religious base. Japan's revival, modernization, and rise to the status of a major world power in the years after
1868 provided the clearest example of this. In 1899 the Dutch recognized this new status by giving Japanese equal status with Europeans in
the Netherlands East Indies. But there are other examples. The Chinese
Revolution of 1911 was important for its immediate impact on Chinese
living in Indonesia and its more indirect influence on Indonesians. The
Philippine Revolution of 1896 to 1901 was also an important event
though it is unclear how much Indonesians were aware of or influenced by it at the time.

Ironically, as much as the rise of European imperial power was an in-
centive to reform and revival in Indonesia and elsewhere, the apparent
decline of Europe in other respects also encouraged anti-colonialism.
European rationality and science had been exaggerated by many conquered Asians—Kartini's letters provide examples of this—but when
these supposedly rational nations tore each other to bloody shreds on
the battlefields of World War I many Asians who were in a sense Westernized were encouraged to look again to their own cultures for spiritual values they now found lacking in the West. For some the Bolshevik Revolution in Russia in 1917 seemed to offer new hope, but again
there was much exaggeration and ignorance concerning events in Russia, and much disillusionment later.

From all these local and international circumstances arose the various anticolonial, nationalist, religious, "secular," revival, reformist, and
revolutionary leaders and organizations which ultimately contributed
to the Indonesian Revolution. They were not united; often they were in
bitter conflict. But collectively they moved Indonesia forward in im-

portant ways and made possible a broadly-based resistance to the common Dutch enemy.

Yet none of these could have overthrown Dutch rule by themselves or even together, for Dutch rule was deeply and firmly entrenched. The Dutch successfully resisted pressures for reform from the Indonesians and failed to follow the example of other colonial rulers such as the Americans in the Philippines or the more cautious British in India. World War II—a calamitous episode whose origins lay far from Indonesia—was also part of that world context without which it is hard to see how the Indonesian Revolution could have occurred. Although many of the revolution's roots, perhaps even the most important roots, were indigenous to Indonesia, without the specific world context in which it occurred Indonesia's struggle for freedom would not have been what it was; perhaps it could not have developed or succeeded at all.

2

*

Myths, Heroes, and War

PETER CAREY

Every nation is the creation of the imagination; it derives its strength from the consciousness of its citizens. Thus long before the independent state of Indonesia became a reality after World War II, the idea of such an entity had to take root in the hearts of its citizens.

Four elements were central to the growth of this national awareness in Indonesia. First, there was the increasing use of the Indonesian language as a vehicle for political communication and discourse. Indonesian had been adopted by most political organizations in Indonesia in the second and third decades of the twentieth century, and was reflected in the famous Sumpah Pemuda, or Youth Oath, of October 1928, which referred to one Motherland (*Tanah Indonesia*), one People (*Bangsa Indonesia*) and one Unifying Language (*Bahasa Persatuan, Bahasa Indonesia*). Second, there was the role of a recently created national history, astutely manipulated by Indonesian nationalist leaders for political purposes. Third, there were the powerful images from Indonesia's animist past, such as the buffalo head symbol of Sukarno's early political party, and the rich archetypes of the Javanese shadow-play (*wayang*) which were frequently alluded to by Javanese orators like Dr. Cipto Mangunkusumo, H.O.S. Cokroaminoto, and Sukarno. Finally, and perhaps most important, there were the popular expectations of impending liberation by the Japanese, which were generally associated with the Joyoboyo prophecies.

Prince Diponegoro—a contemporary drawing.

Courtesy of Musium Kota, Jakarta.

Although the existence of magnificent Hindu-Buddhist monuments in Java had occasionally reminded the Indonesian people of their glorious past, it was not until the late nineteenth and early twentieth centuries that the scale of this legacy was truly realized. This was largely due to the painstaking labors of Dutch scholars such as J.L.A. Brandes, H. Kern and N.J. Krom, whose researches helped to shed new light on the pre-Islamic period in Indonesia. The discovery and translation of the unique *Nagarakrtagama* manuscript, found by Brandes during the Dutch expedition against Lombok in 1894, was particularly important. The idealized picture it presented of the famous East Javanese empire of Majapahit—at the height of its influence under the fourteenth-century King Hayam Wuruk and his astute prime minister, Patih Gajah Mada—gave a powerful boost to the self-confidence of Javanese cultural organizations like Budi Utomo, (founded in 1908), which were dedicated to the moral regeneration of the Javanese people. More than that, it established beyond doubt that long before the arrival of the Europeans, large areas of the archipelago had been bound into a loose federation under Javanese suzerainty. Gajah Mada's well known Palapa Oath, in which he swore to abstain from a favorite food until he had subdued all the other islands in the Indonesian chain, was a powerful symbol of Java-centric supremacy.

Soon after the completion of the *Nagarakrtagama* translation, which appeared in stages between 1905 and 1914, the publications of French historians Georges Coedès, Gabriel Ferrand, and others brought to light the existence of a great Sumatran trading empire known as Srivijaya, which had flourished several centuries before Majapahit and had enjoyed an even wider influence. This helped to soothe non-Javanese feelings and instill in educated Indonesians a new-found pride in their pan-archipelagic past. At the same time, the memory of the great leaders and fighters of the nineteenth century such as the Acehnese Teungku Cik Di Tiro, and the Javanese Pangeran Diponegoro, lived on in the minds of the people. Biographies of these figures, written during the Japanese period by Muhammad Yamin and others, had a great impact in literate circles. It was thus natural that when elite fighting units were set up to resist the Dutch during the period of armed conflict between 1945 and 1949, they were given the names of such men. In fact, each area of Indonesia used local heroes to galvanize the military energies of the people: Imam Bonjol in West Sumatra, Siliwangi in West Java, Senapati in Central Java, Narottama in East Java, Damar Wulan in

Madura, Hasanuddin in South Sulawesi, and Pattimura in the Moluccas.

In addition to these *pahlawan nasional*, or national heroes, potent images from Indonesia's animist past were employed in the nationalist struggle. Particularly prominent here was the wild buffalo (*banteng*), whose head was adopted as the symbol of Sukarno's Perserikatan Nasional Indonesia (PNI) and was nearly included, after independence, in the design of the national flag. A crack paramilitary organization in the Surakarta area during the early years of the revolution was also known as the Barisan Banteng. This was an especially fitting name for a corps largely composed of young men (*pemuda*), for the buffalo had been the traditional symbol of youthful strength and virility. Thus young warriors had drunk the blood of slaughtered buffalo to heighten their courage before battle, and, as a test of their magical physical powers (*kadigdayan*), they had been trained to crack the skulls of enraged buffalo with a single blow of their bare fists.

Even more important than images from the Indonesian past in arousing a spirit of heightened courage among the people, was the popular belief in the prophecies (*ramelan*) attributed to the twelfth-century king of Kediri, Prabu Joyoboyo. These had foretold the main historical eras through which Java would pass until the Javanese solar year 2000, cycles of prosperity (*jaman emas*) alternating with times of madness and depravity (*jaman edan*). For centuries these prophecies had sustained the Javanese people, whose expectations of a better tomorrow were buoyed by Joyoboyo's prediction that a messiah figure, known as Erucokro, would arise and lead them from abject oppression to the promised *jaman emas*. In the early twentieth century, particular attention began to be paid to a certain passage in the prophecies which foretold that at the very darkest period, the so-called *kiyamat kubra*, help would come from a dwarf-like, yellow-skinned people, who would conquer Java, but whose rule would only last as long as a maize seed took to flower (*saumuring jagung*), or about three months, after which they would return to their country and Java would again be ruled by its own people. With the bestowal of European legal status on the Japanese in 1899, and the stunning Japanese victory over Tsarist Russia in 1905, the passage in the Joyoboyo prophecies relating to the yellow people from the north was linked ever more closely in the popular mind to the Land of the Rising Sun. The Japanese, for their part, encouraged these beliefs and, after their attack on Pearl Harbour on 7 December 1941, dropped leaflets from the air announcing to the Indonesian people that the imperial armies would soon land and "fulfill the prophecy of His Majesty Joyoboyo" by driving out the Dutch. They made no mention of the latter part of the prophecy, which talked of the short duration of their rule, though Indonesians knew full well that the Japanese stay in Indonesia would be brief; if not the three months of the maize flower, then perhaps the three years during which the maize seed retains its germinative capacity.

All these prophecies and images had great potential in undermining Dutch authority and imbuing Indonesians with a greater sense of their own dignity. But it was largely due to the efforts of one man that this came about as it did. That man was, of course, Sukarno. A brilliant orator and demagogue, he was able to marshal the glory of the past to give Indonesians a sense of purpose for the future. "[What] are the ways of promoting nationalism? How do you bring it to life?" he enquired rhetorically in his 1930 trial speech, answering that there were three steps: "First, we show the people that they have a past, a glorious past. Second, we increase the people's consciousness that they have a present, a dark present. Third, we show the people the rays of the future, shining and clear, and the means to bring about the future full of promise."

He alluded at length to the Joyoboyo prophecies in the same speech, and stated that one day a Pacific war would break out, which would herald Indonesia's liberation. "We have no way of knowing when [this war] will erupt; we don't even know where the center of this explosion will be. We only know that. . . at some moment a Pacific war is certain to break out." Steeped as he was in an understanding of *wayang* lore, he also used the imagery from the Javanese shadow-play to great effect in his public orations. Time and again he reiterated the theme that the Dutch were foreign ogres (*buta Sabrang*) or members of the evil Kurawa faction, seemingly strong, but destined to be defeated by the peerless Pendhawa warriors (*satria*), whose kingdom they had treacherously stolen. It was up to the Indonesian people, he told his enthralled listeners, to emulate the self-control of the Pendhawas and prepare themselves for the final battle with the Dutch which would inevitably come, just as it had in the classic known as the *Mahabharata*.

These examples struck deep chords in the hearts of his Javanese followers, although they were occasionally criticized by Sukarno's non-Javanese colleagues like Hatta and Syahrir, who did not share his sense of the potency of political images and the power of prophecy. They were too rationalist and too Westernized in their outlook to grasp the need for imaginative inspiration which Sukarno sensed instinctively. The Indonesian people, in turn, looked to him rather than the pragmatic Hatta or the astute Syahrir, as the promised leader, the long-awaited messiah figure predicted in the past by Joyoboyo. Just as earlier crowds had gathered round Sukarno's mentor, Cokroaminoto, whose name seemed to have the ring of the messianic Erucakra about it, so in the late 1920s thousands flocked to hear Sukarno's spell-binding oratory and looked upon the red membership cards of his PNI party as amulets (*jimat*) guaranteeing their place in the *jaman emas*. Sukarno himself played on these millenarian hopes by talking of independence as a "golden bridge" (*jembatan emas*) which would lead to a glittering future, although the exact economic and social arrangements which would underpin that golden tomorrow were always left vague.

On another level, Sukarno acted as the great synthesizer, seemingly able to reconcile the most divergent strands of the national struggle, just as earlier the legendary god-kings of Indonesia had represented the primordial oneness and cosmic unity in their own persons. The famous words of the Indonesian national motto, *Bhinneka Tunggal Ika*, (separate yet one), found their echo in Sukarno's ceaseless striving to merge opposites, as in his brilliant essay published in 1926, "Nationalism, Islam, and Marxism," which formed the basis of his political thought until the end of his life. Indeed, it was this ability to seemingly reconcile the irreconcilable and to project an image of unity which made Sukarno the greatest living embodiment of the Indonesian nationalist struggle. A born visionary and leader, he was able to evoke the messianic prophecies, the potent archetypes of the *wayang*, and the memory of Indonesia's glorious past, to give twentieth century Indonesians a new sense of their own identity and purpose.

3

*

National Awakening

AKIRA NAGAZUMI

May 20 of each year is called Hari Kebangkitan Nasional or the day of national awakening, as all Indonesians know. On this day, most Indonesian newspapers print an article about Budi Utomo, the first Javanese national organization. The year 1908 looks so remote and the name of the organization sounds so vague that their significance may be overlooked. Yet the Indonesian people continue to see Budi Utomo as the symbol of their national awakening.

Budi Utomo is not only known as one of the earliest national organizations in Indonesia, but also as one of the longest lived. Born as a student organization in Jakarta (Batavia) it survived until 1935, when it merged with a few other organizations into the Partai Indonesia Raya (Greater Indonesia Party), abbreviated Parindra. One may wonder, however, where the symbolic significance comes from. Even at its peak the Budi Utomo membership amounted only to 10,000, rather a small number compared with that of the Sarekat Islam, for example, which exceeded 360,000 already in 1914, reportedly even reaching 2,500,000 a few years later.

Like many of the nationalist movements all over the world, Budi Utomo held two seemingly contradictory ideals: awareness of the common cultural heritage on the one hand, and the urge for modernization on the other. What was meant by "common cultural heritage," however, was pre-Islamic Javanese culture and excluded from its scope

The founders of Budi Utomo photographed in 1907, a year before the organization was formally set up.
Courtesy of Arsip Nasional, Indonesia.

the more pious Muslim Indonesians of West Java and many other parts of the island. Furthermore, the common people were not very much encouraged to participate in Budi Utomo, its members being largely from the *priyayi*, a class of native officials from the traditional aristocracy and well-educated groups. Therefore, the activity of Budi Utomo was generally limited to the field of education and culture. It petitioned the colonial government to establish schools and scholarship systems, and then undertook to do so on its own. Although it later became more politically oriented—even radical during the first half of the 1920s—for the most part Budi Utomo remained only moderately progressive, almost always cooperating with, if not submitting to, the colonial government. In this way, Budi Utomo could neither be called a people's organization, nor an all-Indonesian one. Why, then, was it so popular?

When one looks back from the 1980s, it seems difficult to imagine how great the impact of world events was on Javanese intellectuals at the turn of the century. Information from abroad was neither abundant nor well-balanced, and was often checked by the colonial government. Yet the news of the Boxer Uprising in China, the Boer War in South Africa, and the Russo-Japanese War occupied the headlines of at least one journal named *Retnodhoemilah*, edited by a certain Wahidin Sudirohusodo in Yogyakarta since 1901. He was then 48 years old. A graduate of the native medical school which had been established in Jakarta in 1851, he was engaged in the medical service in the Yogyakarta area, and worked hard at enlightening the local population. Acutely aware of the grim realities of the struggle for survival among the nations of the world, he emphasized the spread of education as the only solution. Not only did he propose in his journal that a scholarship system be set up for promising native youths, but he himself launched a campaign for its establishment after having resigned as editor on the pretext of ill health.

Although his campaign was anything but successful, his enthusiasm greatly impressed two medical students, Sutomo and Suraji, who visited him during his stay in Jakarta at the end of 1907. To their classmates these students proposed the formation of an organization not just for the scholarship system but for the enlightenment of their compatriots. The name of the organization, Budi Utomo, was reportedly taken from Sutomo's remark upon hearing Wahidin's indefatigable zeal for the campaign: "it is a good deed and points out supreme wisdom [*keutamaan budi*]." The concept of *budi* in the Hindu-Buddhist context would mean the supreme wisdom which gives balance and harmony to all kinds of fragmentary knowledge of a human being. As the name suggests, the ambitious stance of the students during the first months gradually gave way to a more moderate guideline of "harmonious development." The leadership of the organization also shifted to elderly native officials during the period between its May 20 meeting and its first general assembly on 3-5 October 1908. At this October congress the more progressive persons became disappointed with the irresolute and inefficient attitude of the Budi Utomo leaders toward modernization. Those dissidents broke away and formed their own organizations: both the Sarekat Islam and the Indies Party started to function in 1912. The former especially attracted pious Muslims, and it could be called the first popular movement in Indonesia. The latter, on the other hand, could be called its first political party aiming at self-determination.

The impact of the birth of Budi Utomo was not limited to these two organizations. The top native Javanese officials were motivated to organize their own association, the Regentenbond, or Bupati's Union. Budi Utomo also gave an impetus to the foundation of many ethnically-based organizations inside and outside Java. Such religious movements as Muhammadiyah also came into being under the influence of Budi Utomo, the formation of which acted as a catalyst on an Indonesian society in a state of fermentation.

Because of Budi Utomo's moderate and levelheaded nature, the colonial government gave credit to it, sometimes describing it as "an adopted child of the Ethical Policy." However, the adopted child never blindly obeyed its father, and indeed often admonished him at critical moments. For instance, it was Budi Utomo which raised the issue of establishing a parliament for the Netherlands East Indies on the occasion of debate over the establishment of a native militia during World War I. Although the Volksraad or People's Council which was set up in May 1918 was far from a real parliament, its Budi Utomo representatives made an effort to express their frank opinion to the government. In other words, the organization did its best for the betterment of the Indonesian society within the given situation.

The friendly relations between Budi Utomo and the enlightened elements of the colonial government, however, deteriorated when it became increasingly clear that reform under colonial rule certainly had its limitations. Having become suspicious of the government's intention toward reform, the younger and more radical elements of Budi Utomo held the reins for a few years after 1921, supporting, for example, the strike of native government pawnshop workers in 1922. The repressive measures taken by the government against the unsuccessful communist revolts in 1926 and 1927 put an end to a quarter century of the Ethical Policy. From then onward Budi Utomo returned to its previous dormancy, which its leaders called *mundur mapang* or withdrawal. The organization disappeared in 1935 when it became part of Parindra. Although the president of the new party was none other than Sutomo, one of the two medical students who had been inspired by Wahidin Sudirohusodo, one could no longer expect much activity from it.

With all its shortcomings, Budi Utomo did represent the initial aspiration of the Javanese people toward awakening, and, for that matter, that of all Indonesians. Virtually every prominent leader of the Indonesian nationalist movement during the early decades of this century had at least some kind of contact with this organization.

Now that the historical building of the celebrated medical school, first called the Dokter Jawa School and later known by the Dutch abbreviation STOVIA, has been completely restored to the condition of 1908, it is worthwhile to visit this building at the Gambir district of Jakarta. Standing on the cool stone floor of the *pendopo* or main hall, the visitor feels as if he had just heard an echo of Sutomo's loud voice, announcing that first meeting on the morning of 20 May 1908.

4

*

The Islamic Movement

A.P.E. KORVER

In the early years of this century, an influential Islamic reform movement took root in Indonesia and became an intrinsic part of the contemporary struggle for nationalist self-identity (*pergerakan*) in the archipelago. Inspired by modernist Islamic thinkers like Muhammad Abduh (1849–1905) and Jamal al-Din al-Afghani (1839–97) in the Middle East, the Indonesian reform movement strove to do away with many of the local traditions and beliefs which in the course of time had been grafted onto the core of the Islamic religious system, clouding the force and simplicity of the Prophet's original teachings. It also tried to bring Islam more into harmony with the modern worldview and the challenges posed by Western scientific discoveries. The important Arab minority of immigrant Hadhramis and modernist Islamic thinkers, authors, and journalists from West Sumatra were primarily responsible for spreading these reformist ideas in Indonesia.

The Al-Jam'iyat al-Khairiyah (Association of the Good) (founded 1906), Sarekat Islam (founded 1911), and Muhammadiyah (founded 1912) were the principal organizational motors of the Islamic reform movement in Indonesia between the years 1911 and 1921. Both the Al-Jam'iyat and the Muhammadiyah were orientated mainly towards educational projects rather than politics during this period. From the political point of view the most influential organization was Sarekat Islam (SI), which was not only by far the most important branch of the

Islamic reform movement in this decade, but dominated the whole Indonesian nationalist movement until the early 1920s.

Dynamic and multi-faceted, Sarekat Islam was the first mass movement in modern Indonesian history, subtly combining the political appeal of later nationalist parties such as Sukarno's PNI, with the social, economic, and cultural programs of other Islamic reform organizations. In this respect, Sarekat Islam stands as an important example to other developing countries currently striving for regeneration, an example which so far has not been emulated with any degree of success.

Sarekat Islam was founded in Surakarta in 1911 by a youthful and energetic batik trader, Haji Samanhudi, as a commercial and cultural organization to provide protection for indigenous Muslim traders against Chinese competition in the traditional textile trade. Almost immediately it won a mass following among the local Javanese population of Surakarta, and soon spread to other parts of the island. On the eve of World War I it counted numerous followers in the outer islands, especially Sumatra and Kalimantan. Contemporary political commentators compared its growth to a prairie fire, and it struck fear into the hearts of conservative Dutch administrators and their educated Indonesian subordinates. The progressive Governor-General A.W.F. Idenburg (in office, 1909–16) and his immediate advisers sympathized to some extent with the movement, whose ideals regarding Indonesian national development appeared similar to their own. They also very astutely blunted its potential as a political organization by only recognizing the local branches of SI and refusing to permit the existence of a strong central committee.

In 1915 Sarekat Islam reached the peak of its popularity with a membership close to the half million mark, the greatest numbers being in South Sumatra (Lampung), Southeast Kalimantan (Banjarmasin), and Jakarta Residency. This shows clearly that Sarekat Islam was by no means confined to Java like most of the other movements. After 1915 the dynamic growth which had marked the early years of Sarekat Islam began to wither, however, especially in the social field. The development of Sarekat Islam after 1915 thus passed ineluctably into the realm of "political history," the most important event of this period being the struggle within the movement between the leftist radicals of the "Red" SI (*Sarekat Merah*) and the Islamic moderates of the "Green" wing of the organization known as the *Sarekat Hijau*. This internal contest ended in 1921 with an open break between the two factions and the expulsion of the "Reds" from the movement; most joined the Indonesian Communist Party (Partai Kommunis Indonesia, PKI), which had been founded the previous year.

Among the many activities of Sarekat Islam in the social, economic, religious, and political fields, certain ones stand out. The stress on "mutual help" (*gotong royong*) loomed large, for example, in the movement's social organization and contributed powerfully to the immense popularity of Sarekat Islam among the poorer sections of the Indonesian population. An instance of this sort of mutual help was the assistance given to the family of a deceased member. On these occasions, members of the local chapter were obliged to help the relatives of the deceased with the funeral expenses, to participate in the *selametan*, or religious feasts held in honor of the departed, and to accompany the bier to the place of burial.

Economic activities were also much in evidence during the first years of Sarekat Islam. These mainly took the form of different types of cooperatives founded under SI auspices to enable members to maximize their commercial potential in the face of continuing competition from Chinese and other foreign Orientals, principally Indians and Arabs. Small shops (*toko*), street stalls (*warung*), trading and transport companies, tailoring outfits, and batik workshops were all organized along cooperative lines by SI members during these years, and some were notably successful.

Achievements in the religious field were more modest, consisting mainly of the promotion of schools and educational curricula with a strong modernist Islamic basis, but even here the SI was able to cater to some of the inexhaustible demand for education at the grass roots level of Indonesian society at this time.

Last but not least, Sarekat Islam had ambitious political goals. These dated from the very inception of SI as an organization, but they were not trumpeted too loudly in the early years, since before 1916 indigenous political organizations were not officially allowed in the Netherlands East Indies. Prominent among the political activities of the movement was the systematic gathering by SI members of the many social and economic grievances of ordinary Indonesians, especially in rural areas. SI leaders not only elicited lists of these grievances from their members, but also took pains to bring them to the attention of the colonial authorities. In this way, SI functioned as a sort of unofficial parliament or forum for airing popular discontent, before anything of that nature actually appeared in Indonesia. Furthermore, in the very early stages of the movement the main leaders demanded a greater measure of political independence for Indonesia from Holland. As one of these leaders trenchantly pointed out in 1916, "it is no longer proper that the Netherlands East Indies be governed by the Dutch in the same way estates are controlled by a landlord."

Sarekat Islam achieved few of its political goals, mainly because of defective organization at the local level and the lack of trained cadres. Failure on the political front was one of the reasons for the decreasing popularity of the movement after 1915. But it would be wrong to conclude from this that SI had no lasting impact on the popular imagination. To the contrary, it acted as a catalyst, awakening the masses to the reality of their position in colonial life. SI made ordinary Indonesians acutely conscious, for the first time, of their social and economic under-development compared to the privileged groups in colonial society like the Europeans and the Chinese. It also inspired them to do something for themselves to change the situation. In this context, SI is of immediate relevance to the condition in which Indonesia finds itself today when every effort is being made to modernize and regenerate the country to cope with the fierce challenges of the modern world.

Who were the principal leaders of this remarkable movement? Many names come to mind, but two stand out above all others: the founder of the SI in Surakarta, Haji Samanhudi, and the charismatic H.O.S. Cokroaminoto, who was primarily responsible for transforming the movement into a mass party after 1912. Cokroaminoto's lambent personality has often eclipsed the more modest figure of Samanhudi, who passed quickly from center stage. Yet the astute Samanhudi was in many respects much more representative of the style of local SI leadership in the organization's formative period. This style owed much to the activities of young Indonesian entrepreneurs who, notwithstanding their pronounced economic individualism, also had an eye on the social needs of the broader masses of the population. The social activities of the local branches of the SI owed much to their inspiration and example.

As for Cokroaminoto himself, he was the most important leader of Sarekat Islam, and also became one of the most important leaders in the entire history of the Indonesian nationalist struggle. Endowed with exceptional personal qualities, he was a man who stood head and shoulders above his contemporaries, combining the roles of orator, journalist, politician, and diplomat. With seemingly inexhaustible energy, he gave his heart and soul to the movement. Most important of all he was a democrat to the backbone, striving for both Indonesia's national independence, and the improvement of the lot of the ordinary Indonesian man and woman. Certainly he made a profound impression on his contemporaries, in particular the young Sukarno, who boarded with his wife in Surabaya while attending the local Dutch high school and was betrothed for a time to his daughter, Utari. In his autobiographical memoirs Sukarno referred to Cokroaminoto as his "mirror" and his first model in the arts of oratory and political leadership.

Despite its brief period of success as a mass political organization, Sarekat Islam left an abiding legacy. For a time after 1912, it succeeded in igniting the tinder of popular discontent throughout the archipelago and seizing the imaginations of the downtrodden masses. Like a sudden prairie fire, however, the first impetus of the organization was soon exhausted. Early dynamism gave way to disappointment and cynicism as it became clear to adherents that the organization could not wring any lasting political concessions from the Dutch colonial masters. Nevertheless, the SI was an important historical phenomenon. For the first time, it succeeded in breaking through the ethnic and regional divisions of Indonesia so carefully fostered by the Dutch to facilitate their hold over the archipelago. It also set a shining example of what might be achieved in the realm of social and economic organization if the Indonesians were able to work together in local, cooperative frameworks. Sarekat Islam's appeal echoes down the decades and speaks directly to contemporary Indonesians and their aspirations for a better spiritual and material future.

5

*

Early Indonesian Communism

RUTH McVEY

In 1916, at its first national congress, the Sarekat Islam discussed the question of combining Islamic principles and socialism. Already, very early in the development of the Indonesian national movement, socialism had come to be the symbol for a modernity opposed to that of imperialism, a modernity that would bring colonial peoples social justice, prosperity, and independence. Much of the responsibility for introducing this idea lay with a small group of Dutch Marxists who were living at that time in the Netherlands East Indies. In 1914 they had formed the Indies Social Democratic Association, usually known by its Dutch initials ISDV. They then had to decide whether to limit their propaganda to the European workers in the colony or bring the socialist message to the Indonesians as well. The moderates wanted the former, the radicals the latter; the radicals won.

But how to propagate socialist ideas among the Indonesians? The ISDV had only a handful of members, all Europeans, who had little real knowledge of Indonesian society. Henk Sneevliet, leader of the radical wing, urged that they try to gain influence in an Indonesian association that did have a hold on the population, which could then transmit the new teachings to the masses. The Sarekat Islam was the obvious choice, for it commanded a greater popular following than any other group. The SI was also receptive to radical ideas at the time, for World War I had cut the Indies off from Europe, with dire consequences for the export economy and for Java's supply of rice. The unpleasant aspects of capitalism and imperialism were thus particularly visible to Indonesians. The Sarekat Islam as a whole became more resentful of colonial rule, and some of its more radical younger members were attracted to the socialist message and joined the ISDV. They did not leave the Sarekat Islam to do so; at that time there was no party discipline, and a person could belong to as many political associations as he pleased. The major communist leaders of the colonial period—Semaun, Darsono, Tan Malaka, Musso, Alimin—all had begun their political careers in the Sarekat Islam. Indonesian adherents of the ISDV came to form a bloc within the Sarekat Islam, which by 1917 was already so powerful that the established SI leadership became alarmed. The leftist center of strength was Semarang, where the SI branch was pretty thoroughly under ISDV control. That of the main SI leadership was in Yogyakarta, so that people often spoke of the rivalry between "Red" and "White" SI as the quarrel between Semarang and Yogyakarta.

The rapid rise of Marxist influence reflected not only worsening economic conditions but also an increasingly tense relationship between the colonial government and the Indonesian political movement. News of the Bolshevik Revolution in Russia and the European revolutions which accompanied Germany's defeat in 1918 shook the colonial government and encouraged a revolutionary spirit among the Indonesians. For a time the government made concessions—the formation of the Volksraad was the most important—but as the European revolutionary wave receded and conservatives in both the Netherlands and the Indies felt stronger, the colonial authorities restricted drastically the possibilities for Indonesian political activity.

All the Indonesian parties suffered under this, but the radical socialists were least badly hurt. They benefitted in the first place from the increasing bitterness felt by Indonesians, which turned more of them to think of revolution. They also benefited from the fact that Indonesian leaders who were frustrated in political activity turned their attention to labor unions, and initially at least the government encouraged this in the belief that it was less dangerous to colonial rule. As the socialists were already heavily involved in labor activity, centered on Semarang and Surabaya, this put them at the heart of the action. The ISDV by no means dominated the labor scene, however; the first two major Indonesian strikes—the sugar workers in 1920 and the pawnshop workers

in 1922—were not led by Marxist unions. But perhaps that, too, benefitted the radicals, for the government and employers took such a stern
stand against the strikes that they ended disastrously and discouraged
all but the far left. After 1922, only the communists were seriously involved in labor activity.

Another inadvertent benefit of the regime's repression was that most
of the Dutchmen who had founded the ISDV were expelled from the
Indies. This made possible a smooth transition from Dutch to Indonesian control of it. In May 1920 the transfer was formalized by giving
the ISDV a new, Indonesian-language name. It became the PKI, standing at first for Perserikatan Kommunist di India and later, from 1924,
for Partai Komunis Indonesia. The substitution of "Communist" for
"Social-Democratic" merely confirmed what had always been the case,
that the movement was in the hands of its revolutionary wing.

The PKI was the first Communist party to be established in Asia beyond the borders of the former Russian Empire. At the end of 1920 it
voted to join the Communist International, or Comintern, which had
recently been formed in Moscow as a forum and executive center for
Communist parties around the world. The PKI leaders saw no conflict
between this and participation in the Indonesian independence movement. Like the Sarekat Islam, the party was national but not nationalist; that is, it was conscious of a national identity but did not take an
Indonesian national state as its supreme goal. Indonesian parties at this
stage of political development were "national" in the sense of being Indonesian, but they were mostly founded on a regional-cultural basis,
like Budi Utomo and Pasundan, or looked to universal principles like
the SI and the PKI. The Sarekat Islam took a keen interest in Pan-
Islamism and the Chalifate movement, and the PKI participated in the
Comintern, but for both groups such activities were distinctly periph-
eral to their Indonesian concerns, and the PKI never subordinated itself
to the International in the way in which many Western Communist
parties did.

This did not prevent international attachments from becoming an issue, for anti-communist SI leaders accused the PKI of putting world
revolutionary interests above Indonesia's, and the PKI charged that the
Sarekat Islam was devoting itself to Pan-Islamism and not to the plight
of the Indonesian people. What was really at stake in this argument,
however, was a struggle for power within the movement. The SI was
in a very difficult position, for as the principal Indonesian organization

it faced the brunt of government suspicion and retaliation. As the chances for meaningful political participation narrowed, and as labor unions met with repeated defeat, SI leaders began to look for a basis of activity that would hold popular loyalties but also avoid confrontation with the government. Greater emphasis on religion seemed the best possibility, and the chief "White" SI leader, Haji Agus Salim, urged movement in this direction and a break with the PKI. Leftist strength was now growing dangerously within the Sarekat Islam, for though many people were leaving the SI in discouragement, those who remained were becoming more radical. Economic depression was now adding to the people's misery and to labor unrest, and it seemed the communists, if left alone, might come to dominate the movement. SI chairman Cokroaminoto was loathe to break with the PKI, as he believed—quite rightly—that unity was essential to the strength of the independence movement. For some time he resisted his colleagues' demands that the Sarekat Islam impose "party discipline"—that is, that they refuse to allow members of other parties to belong to their association—but eventually relations with the PKI leaders became too bitter for even Cokroaminoto to bridge. In 1921 the central executive of Sarekat Islam adopted party discipline, and in 1923 it was applied to the local branches as well. The communists were thus expelled and now, for the first time, began to develop as a mass movement on their own.

The break between the PKI and Sarekat Islam gravely weakened the independence struggle. Heretofore the SI had been a mass movement both in the sense of reaching the common people and in the sense of involving a significant part of the population. Now, however, a great many SI members were disillusioned and withdrew from politics altogether. What was left of the SI divided into "White" and "Red" branches, with the Red SI groups adhering to the PKI, which renamed them Sarekat Rakyat and made them its main mass organization. The communists won the contest with the "White" SI leaders in the sense that most SI members went over to them, and the Sarekat Islam itself ceased to be important politically. The PKI emerged as the most popular Indonesian party and the leader of the anti-Dutch struggle, but it led a greatly weakened movement.

As the leader of the anti-colonial struggle, deprived of the SI's shelter, the PKI now had to face government repression directly. The authorities used the PKI's popularity to accuse the Indonesian opposition as a whole of stirring up a naive populace with ideas that were alien and unnatural to them. The people, they declared, should be kept free from politics. The atmosphere in the Netherlands itself had grown very much more conservative, so that little was left of the Ethical Policy, which had permitted the early development of the Indonesian movement. Whatever action they took, PKI leaders found themselves liable to arrest; yet what had attracted the bulk of the Sarekat Islam following to them was the fact that they represented a militant challenge to the Dutch, and people would lose interest if action were not taken.

The greatest pressure came from the labor unions, for the depression was causing both the state and private firms to cut wages and lay off workers. The railroad workers, whose union, the VSTP, was a mainstay of communist support, pressed for a strike against plans to cut the wages of the lowest-paid workers. The union and party leaders hesitated, for they knew the government would use a strike to crush the labor movement; but the workers were desperate and demanded action, and eventually the leaders conceded. The railroad strike of 1923 was the greatest labor action taken in the colonial period; it was also the last, for the government took firm steps to crush it and assumed new powers that restricted Indonesian political activity even more severely.

In spite of the strike's defeat and the imprisonment or exile of many leftist leaders, the Communist party increased in strength during the following year and began to spread significantly beyond the urban proletariat and outside Java. The effect of the government crackdown, combined with suffering caused by the depression, made many people angry rather than discouraged, and they came to the PKI in protest. But what they expected from the communists was revolutionary action; they saw that nothing less than the overthrow of Dutch rule would bring a real solution, and they were too desperate to heed arguments for patient preparation. At the same time, the PKI had lost most of its more experienced and moderate leaders, and increasingly the movement fell into the hands of hotheads whose desire for a revolution far exceeded their ability to organize one. At the end of 1924 the party took a decision in principle to prepare for revolution. During the next year and a half the PKI came increasingly under the influence of anarchist impulses, denying the realities of power in favor of a blind will to revolt. Increasingly, too, the movement became influenced by older modes of protest, so that it took on some of the aspects of a traditional movement of rebellion. The cities and the proletariat, its original base of support, gave way to the countryside and smaller towns as the focus of agitation. There was a strong Muslim element in this ferment, for in spite of the quarrel between the PKI and Sarekat Islam leaders there was at this time little feeling that communism and Islam were incompatible. Such leaders as Haji Misbach in Central Java and Haji Datuk Batuah in West Sumatra attempted to combine the teachings of Islam and communism, and when the PKI revolt broke out—in November 1926 in Banten and January 1927 in Minangkabau—it was in two of the most fervently Muslim areas of Indonesia, whose farmers, artisans, traders, and religious leaders as well as workers felt they could no longer bear the burdens of colonial rule.

The rebellion was an act of despair rather than a credible attempt to seize power: "We thought it better to die fighting than to die without fighting," as one of the PKI leaders later told the Comintern. It was easily crushed by the government, for communist organization had by then been so thoroughly undermined by police action and anarchist pressures that the revolt was uncoordinated and local in character. Nonetheless, it was proof of widespread and deep Indonesian discontent. The government, however, did not respond to the warning with reform. Instead, reflecting the reactionary atmosphere of the time, it unleashed massive repression. The PKI was destroyed in the process; a concentration camp was set up in a remote part of West Irian, Boven Digul, and many rebels and communist cadres ended their lives there. Political activity was still further restricted, so that it was almost impossible for Indonesian leaders to spread critical ideas legally. The people themselves were discouraged; the uprising's defeat made them skeptical that any movement could save them from oppression, and they refused their loyalty to new leaders. As a result of police intervention and popular indifference, even those organizations which aimed to attract the masses after 1927 remained basically parties of the elite. It was only after the conquest of the Dutch regime by the Japanese in 1942 that the common people were to return to the political scene.

In spite of its failure, the Communist movement in the colonial period did have a lasting impact on Indonesian politics. We can see this in the continuing strong influence of Marxist concepts and the goal of socialism, in the emphasis on an approach through the common man rather than the elite, and in the early prominence of labor organization. Enough people had been impressed by these ideas and by the party's fervent if hopeless struggle against colonial rule to influence the development of nationalist parties after 1927 and to make possible a resurgent Indonesian communism in 1945.

6

*

The Literature of Revolution

H.B. JASSIN

The birth of Indonesian literature cannot be separated from the struggle of the Indonesian nation. This is because Indonesian literature not only arose as a means of aesthetic expression, but was also used by early Indonesian writers as a medium for national struggle.

Language—the means through which literature is expressed—plays a key role in any discussion on the birth, growth, and development of literature. Hence even today there is still no agreement about when literature in Indonesian should begin to be called "Indonesian literature," because Indonesian was only officially declared the national language on 18 August 1945. But Indonesian literature was really born long before that, and before the proclamation of independence of the Republic of Indonesia a day earlier. Its birth coincided with the growing use of Malay throughout the archipelago. Malay had played an important role as a lingua franca between the different tribes and peoples in the region since the fourteenth century, when inter-island trade was able to flow freely because the inhabitants of every island and the people in every port could understand Malay.

Throughout the region, Malay was used not only by traders but also by *ulama*, Muslim scholars, to propagate their religion. It was not uncommon to find these missionaries making use of various forms of literature, and eventually, directly and indirectly, literature in Malay started to play a role in society. Figures like Abdullah bin Abdulkadir

Munsyi enriched the Malay language, and its usage in society was reinforced at the end of the nineteenth century with the advent of mass printed media like newspapers, magazines, and books.

Following Abdullah bin Abdulkadir Munsyi's death in 1854, the next development in literature was the birth of the "Indo" (Eurasian) and Sino-Malay literatures. While Indo literature can be regarded as the product of Western literary influence, it was Sino-Malay literature which exhibited characteristics that heralded the beginnings of a true Indonesian literature. The founding of Budi Utomo in 1908 and the establishment of Komisi Bacaan Rakyat (Bureau for Popular Literature) gave an added impetus to the development of an Indonesian literature. With the national awakening, people began to look ahead, spiritually and intellectually, towards a free Indonesia. Moreover, the new Bureau for Popular Literature inevitably helped to increase literacy. And with the rise in literacy, the first works in the history of Indonesian literature were born: the novels *Azab dan Sengsara* (*Torment and Misery*) by Merari Siregar and *Sitti Nurbaya* (a girl's name) by Marah Rusli, published in 1920 and 1922, respectively.

These first novels clearly awakened and stimulated national consciousness amongst the people, especially through characters like Datuk Meringgih and Samsulbahri (both from *Sitti Nurbaya*). Symbolizing the older generation, Datuk Meringgih was a figure worthy of admiration, especially for his defense of the people's rights against the plundering colonialists. On the other hand, Samsulbahri symbolized the younger generation, and he inspired young Indonesians to believe that through hard work and diligent study they could realize their ambitions.

The widespread use of Malay as an everyday language throughout the archipelago contributed greatly to the growth and unity of Indonesian nationhood. The sense of sharing in a common fate, with common trials and tribulations, increased the solidarity of race, fatherland, and language, as described by Muhammad Yamin in his poem "Bahasa, Bangsa" ("Language, Nation"), published in the journal *Jong Sumatra* in February 1921. Its second verse says:

> *Born into a nation with its own language,*
> *Surrounded by family on left and right,*
> *Brought up in the wisdom of the Malay land,*
> *In its grief and joy, and its sorrow,*

Its feelings of solidarity fuse
In its beautiful and melodious language.

The swearing of the Sumpah Pemuda or Youth Oath on 28 October 1928 demonstrated both a realization that for ages past the Indonesian people had possessed one homeland and had been of one nation, and an affirmation that they would embrace Indonesian as their language of unity. After the Sumpah Pemuda this language of unity, Malay, entered a new era in which it developed rapidly in the fields of science, literature, and philosophy, and acquired the new name of "Indonesian." As an everyday language, Indonesian captures and expresses the emotions, thoughts and feelings of the common people. When spoken by intellectuals, it satisfies the linguistic requirements for use at national and international forums, and it is also capable of serving as a scientific language. In literature it can be used beautifully and succinctly by writers as a medium of expression. This is clearly illustrated in S. Yudho's poem "Bahasaku" ("My Language"), which reflects the range and power of Indonesian as the language of unity, which draws together the Indonesian nation because it reflects the spirit of that nation:

> *My language,*
> *Messenger of my feelings,*
> *Illustrator of my sorrowing soul,*
> *Binder of the desire for unity,*
> *Spreader of the new spirit.*
> . . . . . .
> *My language,*
> *Hidden within you,*
> *Has indescribable strength,*
> *To soothe spiritual ills*
> *And refine the character.*

Nationalist sentiment in Indonesia arose not only in political and diplomatic circles, but also blossomed in literature. Among the writings of politician and writer Muhammad Yamin is the poem "Indonesia Tumpah Darahku" ("Indonesia My Fatherland"):

> *Indonesia is the name of my fatherland*
> . . . .
> *I think of the country and its people*
> *A family for all time*
> *Full of the good fortune of its numerous*
> *histories.*

Writers cherished dreams of independence, and they believed in it as a concrete reality that would one day be achieved. Muhammad Yamin wrote:

> .... *we are of one blood and one nation*
> *our fatherland is Indonesia*

which firmly states his belief that independence will be achieved and that all the Indonesian people will join together to struggle and construct from the beautiful islands of Indonesia a free homeland for themselves. In 1921 Mohammad Hatta also wrote symbolically about the independence of Indonesia:

> *See the beautiful colors in the east*
> *Dawn rises, day breaks.*

In the 1920s Balai Pustaka published a number of novels by writers such as Abdul Muis, Nur Sutan Iskandar, and even Adinegoro, which implicitly fostered Indonesian national consciousness. This awareness received an extra boost when Sutan Takdir Alisyahbana's novel *Layar Terkembang (Unfurled Sails)* appeared on the literary scene. In this novel the importance of national unity is expounded in dialogue between the principal characters, young people who are activists in educational and political movements. The speeches and advice given by these characters made Indonesians aware that they possessed a nation, a fatherland, and a language. The dynamic and fighting spirit of the characters boosted the confidence of the Indonesian people in their capacity for self-reliance. This attitude is exemplified by Tuti, a girl who strives for the progress of her sex by leading a women's movement, an organization whose aim is to create a "new image" for Indonesian women. With this novel, Sutan Takdir Alisyahbana lit the flame of the struggle in many Indonesian breasts, especially among the young and educated. The characters in this novel were the ideal prototypes of the "warriors" who would one day free Indonesia from the hands and shackles of her colonizers.

The novels, poems, and literary essays published in the 1920s and 1930s clearly stimulated desires for an independent and free nation. The ideas expressed in Sutan Takdir Alisyahbana's *Layar Terkembang* had in fact already been formulated in his article "Towards a new society and culture," first published in 1935 in the journal *Poejangga Baroe*, at the opening of which he wrote:

"In speaking of a new society and culture, what we are referring to, of course, is the society and culture of Greater Indonesia, as envisaged in the minds of all the inhabitants of these islands who hope for a fitting place for their country and their people alongside other countries and peoples......"

The underlying philosophy of the works of the Balai Pustaka and Poejangga Baroe writers influenced those who followed them. In spite of a literary revolution in form and content, they were still linked to earlier writers by a thin line: the "spirit of the struggle" and the "spirit of Indonesia." The arrival of the Japanese aroused a desire in Indonesians to prove that they could stand on their own feet and could fight to free themselves from their colonial bonds. Idrus's expressive and satirical sketches clearly show how this national consciousness was heightened by the mental and physical suffering the people were subjected to at that time. Even more strikingly, Chairil Anwar's daring and honest poetry expresses brightness and revival. His poem "Siap Sedia" ("Ready"), dedicated "To my generation" (he clearly meant the youth of Indonesia), contains several stirring lines about unity and integrity:

> *Your blood will flow till the very end*
> *But we will leap in to replace you*
> *And continue working toward a Victorious Society.*
> *......*
> *Friends, friends*
> *And we rise with awareness*
> *Piercing right through our hides*
> *Friends, friends*
> *We'll swing our swords towards the Bright World!*

The years of the physical revolution, 1945 to 1949, were difficult ones for the whole Indonesian nation. In literature, however, those years gave birth to pithy poems and short stories, stimulating and definitely not lacking in bite. Chairil Anwar's poem "Diponegoro" clearly, courageously, and confidently reflects the feelings of all Indonesians in wishing to tear down the old and build up the new, victorious Indonesia. Diponegoro was the symbol of a national struggle that knows no retreat, a struggle which reaches out and touches every Indonesian:

> *In this age of revival*
> *You live again*
> *And admiring embers burst into flames*

Right out in front you wait
Untrembling. Your foes are a hundredfold
A sword in your right hand, a kris in your left
Shouldering a spirit which can never die

The next verse reflects the feelings of the Indonesian nation in its entirety:

Forward
This front isn't drummed in to battle
Conviction is its sign for attack
Once to be meaningful
Then to die
Forward
For you, Oh country
Prepare the fire
. . . .
Forward
Attack
Assault
Assail

7

*

Education and Revolution in West Sumatra

TAUFIK ABDULLAH

When the young *ulama* or Muslim scholars, better known in West Sumatra as the Kaum Muda or Younger Generation, launched an Islamic
reform movement in the second decade of the twentieth century, they
also suggested a solution to a potential conflict between Islamic law
and Minangkabau inheritance law, which is matrilineal. They reem-
phasized what had been pointed out before (and had even been officially recognized in several places): that there was a clear distinction
between earned property, that is, property obtained through one's efforts, and inherited property, which was passed down through the female line. Inherited property had to be regarded legally as *waqaf*, that is,
wealth donated for religious or community use. Such wealth could not
be interfered with except in special cases. In other words, this form of
property should continue to abide by existing laws of inheritance.

Apart from being a realistic legal solution, this proposal put forward
by the Kaum Muda *ulama* displayed two other characteristics. First, it
appeared to prove that by applying the principle of *ijtihad*, meaning the
direct use of the intellect to interpret the Qur'an and the Hadith, a
"new" legal concept could be revealed. These young *ulama* did not
need to follow the old *ulama*, who were inseparable from the *adat* system (system of traditional law), but neither did they have to accept the
views of their own teacher, Syekh Ahmad Khatib, who disparaged
Minangkabau inheritance law by calling it an accursed system. Second,

this solution revealed the Kaum Muda's high level of awareness of their social and cultural environment. These reformers had been influenced by Pan-Islamic thinkers, but their solution was a demonstration of their belief that, at a time when the expansion of Islam had reached an impasse, it was essential that social realities be allowed a voice if Islamic utopianism was to be fostered. In other words, Islamic ideals, which were universalist, and social realities, which were local and ethnic in nature, were inseparable. With this belief, the Kaum Muda *ulama* showed that they were *orang siak*, a term applied to students of religion who, having returned from their foreign travels, would now devotedly serve the Minangkabau realm. Efforts to reform religion did bring about social conflict, but the Kaum Muda *ulama* could not be accused of having become alienated.

So these reforms, inspired by the ideals of Islamic cosmopolitanism and of rationalism, had first been adapted to local needs. After this initial innovative step, the program carried out by the Kaum Muda *ulama* did not differ substantially from that of Islamic reform movements elsewhere. By dealing with matters which were clearly *khilafiyah*, or debatable within the framework of Islamic law, they showed that they were eschewing the *taqlid* approach of blind acceptance of traditional religious interpretations, which relied on the orthodox authorities. Although they stressed that religion should be purified from all forms of *khurafat* or superstition, a contamination which they believed was due to taking the *taqlid* approach, they also emphasized that not all reforms needed to be categorized as *bid'ah syariah*, or (controversial) Islamic legal reforms. *Bid'ah lughawiyah*, linguistic evolution, was a very natural process, and was indeed highly commendable, as long as the reforms introduced never contravened *aqidah*, or the tenets of faith. Here, too, we can see the prominence given to the intellect, yet at the same time acceptance of the absolute standing of the Qur'an and the Hadith. Thus the reformists had turned religion into an ideological basis for social change.

With these thoughts in mind, educational reforms were introduced and schools established. To encourage these initiatives, various organizations were formed and support given to publications. These educational reforms had two main features. First, schools were divided into graded classes and general subjects included in the curriculum of the religious schools. Second, general schools equivalent to the HIS (Hollandsch-Inlandsche School or Dutch-Native School) were set up, with an Islamic foundation. HIS Adabiah, founded in Padang in 1912, was the first general school based on Islam. This school was set up by H. Abdullah Ahmad with the help of merchants and civil servants. The first religious school to use the new system was the Diniyah School in Padang Panjang, founded in 1915 by Zainuddin Labai el-Junusi. The system was also used by the Surau Jembatan Besi, better known as the Sumatra Thawalib (General Organization of Students of Sumatra) after 1918. Sumatra Thawalib was directed by Syekh Haji Abdul Karim Amrullah. Of no less importance was the Sekolah Diniyah Putri (Diniyah Girls' School) founded in 1921 by Rahmah el-Yunusyah in Padang Panjang.

Coming at a time when the desire for learning was increasing and the Dutch government was either unwilling or unable to widen its network of schools, the new-style schools set up by the Kaum Muda expanded quickly. This expansion increased rapidly in the 1930s, when the political movements for independence were also becoming increasingly active. In 1933 there were about 600 of these new types of schools scattered about, at both primary and secondary level, with about 70,000 pupils. All of these students had completed three years at *volksschool* or village school. Compared with the 32,286 pupils in 189 government and subsidized schools, and the 824 pupils in 35 private schools, the figures for Kaum Muda schools are really quite impressive. They are especially significant considering that these figures do not include senior students who had entered colleges such as the Islamic College. Besides these there were 589 "untouched" religious schools owned by the Kaum Tua or Older Generation, with 9,285 pupils.

Apart from taking in pupils who had completed their village schooling, a more important function of the Kaum Muda schools was to provide an alternative to the traditional and Western educational systems. For this reason, political activity tended to increase every time the government interfered with the organization of education. This happened in 1928 when the Kaum Muda *ulama* and their network of schools defied the so-called Guru Ordonansi (Teachers' Ordinance), and again in 1932, when the government tried to enforce what was commonly referred to as the Ordonansi Sekolah-Sekolah Liar (Wild Schools Ordinance). Because this educational system was of such strategic importance, the government frequently raided these schools, and individuals they were suspicious of were banned from teaching.

Apart from a few social conflicts which were probably caused by

these educational reforms, two other processes can be directly attributed to the influence of the Kaum Muda reform movement. In the first
place, an increasingly strong role was played by organizations, which
even threatened the personal authority of the *ulama* in social and political matters. Second, there were growing attempts to seek a new identity and a political ideology appropriate to it. These two trends
emerged at a time when the true significance of the hierarchical nature
of the colonial relationship was being increasingly realized, and at a
time when people were becoming intensely aware of social diversity
and sharing a common fate with other regions. Friction between these
various trends resulted in the Silungkang Incident, also frequently referred to as a communist revolt, which broke out in 1927. This incident was the climax of a chain of events, starting with the influence of
Sarikat Rakyat (the People's Union) among students at the Sumatra
Thawalib, which resulted in the expulsion of Syekh Haji Abdul Karim
Amrullah from the school which he himself had founded. Anti-
capitalist and anti-infidel fervor had narrowed the scope for the creation of the good and blessed society preached by the *ulama*. In this
context, the political behavior and wishes of the Perhimpunan
Muslimin Indonesia (Association of Indonesian Muslims, Permi), set
up by the young non-communist leaders of Sumatra Thawalib, can be
explained. Proclaiming the slogan "Islam and nationalism," Permi put
itself forward in 1932 not just as a radical and non-cooperative party
influential mostly in West Sumatra and other parts of Sumatra, but also
as a bridge over the current of discord between "Islamic" and "nationalist" parties. Whatever the prospects of this initiative might have been,
everything was forced to a halt by the colonial government.

At one stage, a very exciting concept was the use of the "Minangkabau stamp." This meant that something which came from outside, had
to be 'Minangkabau-ized' first. Using this idea the Sarikat Rakyat—
that is, the PKI—began to expand their influence; the same concept
was used even more effectively by Muhamaddiyah. As Permi saw it,
however, the problem was no longer simply one of adaptation, but of
spreading ideas originating in the "Minangkabau realm," which they
wanted to disseminate in the Indonesian context.

With this last development, we can finally appreciate the strategic
importance of the role played by the first generation of Islamic reformists. Starting with an awareness of social realities, the solutions they
proposed did not only concern aspects of religion in the narrowest

sense, but directly tackled wider problems such as colonialism and maintaining a sense of identity. The ideas expounded by Permi clearly demonstrate how new-found self-confidence and sense of identity had given birth to a high degree of intellectual creativity.

The foundation laid by the Kaum Muda was not the only alternative put forward for Minangkabau social and cultural development. Right up until 1958, when the PRRI rebellion headquartered in Bukittinggi, took place, the dynamic influence of the thoughts and political behavior of the Kaum Muda was still being felt. State ideology, Indonesian nationalism, and political systems and patterns of behavior could only be recognized and accepted if they were seen to pass the test of "Islamic-ness" and "Mingangkabau-ness." And this was how a national tragedy occurred. Undoubtedly, historians, politicians, and sociologists will produce lengthy analyses of all this. But for those of us who experienced it, a lesson was learned.

8

*

Taman Siswa and the "Wild Schools"

ABDURRACHMAN SURJOMIHARDJO

Political opposition to the regulations concerning the supervision of private schools was highly successful in 1932 and 1933. This opposition was closely connected with the Taman Siswa schools and their leader, Ki Hajar Dewantara, who was the key figure in the people's resistance towards restrictions on educating their own race.

After the emergence of nationalist movements, an important item on the agendas of nearly all the political and cultural organizations was the education of their own people in a nationalist spirit. Although the principles and methods of that education were Western, they were adapted for use in an educational system based on Islam and on Javanese culture, with an Indonesian perspective. The best example of this was the Taman Siswa educational institute, founded in 1922 by Ki Hajar Dewantara, who was then still known as Raden Mas Suwardi Suryaningrat. The basic principle was to allow in elements of modern Western culture, which could then be tested and have extracted from them only what was needed to supplement Indonesian culture.

Between 1913 and 1919 Ki Hajar Dewantara had lived in Holland as a political exile, after his activities in the Indische Partij had been banned and the governor-general had invoked his extraordinary powers. In the Netherlands, Ki Hajar Dewantara studied Western education systems, especially the free education being developed by figures such as Jan Lighthart and Maria Montessori. He also studied the sys-

Abdurrahman Surjomihardjo (left) with Colin Wild in the office of the BBC Indonesian Service, Bush House, London, looking at the publicity booklet published to accompany the original broadcasts called "Gelora Api Revolusi" on which this book is
based.

Courtesy of the BBC.

tem of education practiced by Rabindranath Tagore. Whenever Ki Hajar Dewantara had the opportunity in the Netherlands, he was an active
speaker and writer, and when he eventually returned to Indonesia he
carried with him the idea of enriching his own culture with valuable
aspects of foreign cultures which had been "nationalized." He con-
ceived of a nationalist education system controlled by the thoughts,
spirit, and environment of its own people, absorbing only the good
from foreign cultures into its own culture. One of his aims was to create a sense of identity by upholding education based on *among*, which
meant the bringing up of children emphasizing their individual capa-
bilities, both physical and mental.

Ki Hajar Dewantara refused any government subsidy, as he wanted
to stay completely independent in his work. He felt that Indonesians
should set up their own schools. His educational ideas gave birth to a

movement that grew rapidly in both size and popularity, until in 1931 opinions were voiced in Dutch circles that unless a review of government education was carried out immediately, Taman Siswa schools would dominate the scene within a decade.

Governor-General de Jonge strongly opposed private education for Indonesians, as he saw in it a radical branch of the political movement whose aim was national independence. He announced legislation for the supervision of private schools. These were preventative laws; requests for permission to teach could be rejected on the suspicion that the said teaching might prove threatening. This ordinance concerning what the Dutch termed "wild schools" was officially enacted on 1 October 1932. The same day, Ki Hajar Dewantara sent a telegram of protest to the governor-general, warning him that "We will probably be forced into organizing the strongest possible nonviolent opposition." Three days later he sent a communique to leaders of all the nationalist movements, explaining the stand that Taman Siswa would take.

This Wild Schools Ordinance produced an extraordinary reaction amongst Indonesians. Within a few months of Ki Hajar Dewantara's telegram, various organizations—both those that cooperated with the colonial government and those that did not—had arranged protest meetings. Indonesians opposed the ordinance because it restricted Indonesian children's already limited opportunities to study, and denied the rights of Indonesians to teach and study. Various newspapers carried items about the steps taken by Indonesian nationalist parties and associations. To the nationalist movement, the ordinance posed a serious threat to the principle of freedom of education in nationalist circles. Everyone saw the withdrawal of the Wild Schools Ordinance as the only way to remove this threat. Thus they decided to continue their opposition, and each person was expected to do his duty.

Indonesians were determined to assist Ki Hajar Dewantara's action by giving both moral and material support. One consequence of the ordinance was the emergence of a startling feeling of unity. The Teachers' Council of the Perguruan Kebangsaan Indonesia (The Indonesian Teachers' Institute) in Jakarta decided to take the same line as Taman Siswa. Budi Utomo and the Palembang branch of Pasundan stated their opposition to the restrictions. Mohammad Hatta proposed that firm action should be taken. The students' organization Persatuan Pemuda Pelajar Indonesia (Indonesian Students' Union, PPPI) concluded in a motion that the aim of the ordinance was to keep the people in ignorance, and proposed that the ordinance be abolished. Both Arab and

Chinese groups at a joint meeting in Surabaya also rejected the ordinance and agreed to support Ki Hajar Dewantara's action.

What would happen with the expanding opposition if the ordinance were finally reintroduced as planned on April 1933? People would not request special permission to teach, even if that permission were certain to be granted by the colonial government. People would be forced either to close the schools or to continue teaching without permission. The latter action would result in the prosecution of those concerned. Fines incurred would not be paid and a large proportion of teachers, both male and female, would be jailed. Volunteers would replace these victims, but they would incur the same fate. Orderly education would no longer be possible, and this would lead to an intolerable situation. Thousands of teachers, and hundreds of thousands of pupils' parents, would be prepared to sacrifice themselves if the government did not realize how serious and determined were the people whose sense of justice had been wounded.

Pewarta Deli described the situation as being of educational value for all Indonesians. From various sides protests rolled in. The PPPKI (Permufakatan Perhimpunan Politik Kebangsaan Indonesia or Union of Political Associations of the Indonesian People) decided on mass action. Partindo (Partai Indonesia or Indonesian Party) would strongly increase its resistance to imperialism. PSII (Partai Sarikat Islam Indonesia or Indonesian Islamic Union Party) issued a statement which was actually a guide for organizing "spontaneous" meetings, and this was followed by general action on the part of its branches in various places such as Ujung Pandang, Gorontalo, Pare-Pare, and South Sumatra. PGHB (Persatuan Guru Hindia Belanda or Netherlands East Indies Teachers' Union) demanded that the ordinance be altered. Finally, Muhammadiyah organized a conference in Yogyakarta and stated its total disagreement with the Wild Schools Ordinance. News also spread that although schools in Minangkabau areas had not yet been obstructed, the situation there was very tense.

On 25 December 1932, general meetings of the men's and women's branches of Permi were held in Padang Panjang in West Sumatra. Both the men's meeting and the women's meeting were broken up within a few minutes of starting. The women's meeting was dispersed as it was discussing the meaning and overtones of the word "wild," while the men's meeting was broken up as its leader was speaking about "the Indonesian nation which is not yet independent."

The tension reached its climax at the end of 1932, when two prominent conferences were held within a short space of time. The first was a conference of senior Minangkabau *ulama*, who regarded the ordinance as an attempt to exterminate Islam, and accused the government of being biased in favor of the Christians. They were determined to carry on a life-or-death struggle for Islam and set up a committee for action under the leadership of Haji Abdul Karim Abdullah. Fears about restrictions on religion were very widespread in Minangkabau, as Dutch Resident van Heuven reported. He wrote that systematic efforts launched by the government to explain to the populace that

"[the government explanation that] 'the ordinance is not intended to obstruct religion'. . . . did not succeed in defusing the spirit of resistance inspired by what they regarded as an 'attack' on their personal freedom. The government, on its side, explained how unlikely it was that it would launch what the Minangkabaus called an 'attack,' but here the government was up against the Islamic view—which probably got political support—that every effort to increase knowledge, obviously including education, was beneficial to religion and its development. The ordinance has encouraged the formation of a united and realistic political front, whose meetings are held in a very angry atmosphere."

The second conference was that of Budi Utomo, the association regarded as being the most faithful to the nationalist cause, at which it was confirmed that if the Wild Schools Ordinance was not withdrawn by 31 March 1933, the association would pull out all its members from various representative bodies, close its schools, and give financial support to the victims of the nonviolent opposition.

On 11 January 1933 a meeting was held in Pangeran Tejokusumo's house in Yogyakarta, attended by representatives of various organizations. They stated their opposition to the Wild Schools Ordinance and decided to try and prevent the implementation of the ordinance in the principalities. During the meeting it was noted, among other things, that the education organized by the Dutch was purely to satisfy their need for civil servants, and was not intended to raise the cultural standards of the people of Indonesia. The Muhammadiyah representative declared that the Wild Schools Ordinance contravened God's will. God had commanded mankind to study, without any stipulations about the skill of the teachers, the nature of the premises, or anything else. The Wild Schools Ordinance obstructed private schools, thus it also obstructed God's command. Ki Hajar Dewantara stated that Dutch education in the principalities had actually increased illiteracy, because it had been the custom in this area that parents had an obligation to teach their children, but under the ordinance parents were barred from teaching. The meeting concluded with the view that the supervisory nature of this ordinance obstructed the progress of private schools and lessened the people's initiative to set up their own schools; and rulers in the principalities were urged to prevent the enforcing of the ordinance in their domains.

In an attempt to calm the situation, the government issued a circular which guaranteed that permission to teach would only be refused in those cases "where there was good reason to fear that the nature of the teaching and the actions of those concerned could lead to a disturbance of law and order." This circular was very vague. Freedom of education would not be impeded, but there were still restrictions which could be interpreted very broadly: "as long as there is no threat to the peace." The plan did not succeed in defusing the situation, and the nonviolent opposition continued. Also, Ki Hajar Dewantara, who suspected that Taman Siswa schools would be regarded as the "exceptions" referred to in the circular—although this matter was never clarified—continued with his attempts to defend freedom of education and teaching for all.

On 1 January 1933 Pasundan organized a conference which arrived at the decision that if the Wild Schools Ordinance was not withdrawn, then Pasundan would recall its members who sat in the Volksraad and withdraw them from this council on 21 March 1933.

On 3 January 1933 a Committee To Defend Indonesian Education was formed in Jember to fight the Wild Schools Ordinance. Its thirteen members each represented distinct groups. It sought volunteers to replace teachers who fell victim to the Wild Schools Ordinance, and collected funds to replace schools closed down by the Dutch government and to support the families of victims. The newspaper *Berita Betawi* criticized one of the reasons given by the government for the ordinance, namely that all private schools should fulfill certain health conditions. If the ordinance had been announced for reasons of health, why hadn't an ordinance been announced for villages, places where health care really was neglected? So the newspaper concluded that the order was essentially political in nature, and was intended to abolish all schools funded by the people.

The Partai Rakyat Indonesia (Indonesian People's Party, PRI) took a different path from the mainstream of opinion after holding a meeting to oppose the Wild Schools Ordinance on 22 January 1933. Unlike the other organizations, the PRI did not support the nonviolent opposition. Such opposition meant resigning from all government positions and withdrawing from all councils, and according to the PRI, could even be stretched to cover such things as nonpayment of taxes, forbidding children from going to government schools, and so on. Moreover, the only body identified with the ordinance was the Volksraad, and because the Volksraad had accepted the ordinance, it was only the Volksraad which deserved to be boycotted. Also, with the initiative proposed by Wiranatakusumah, which sought to block implementation of the ordinance, the PRI felt it was not yet necessary to carry out opposition. What was more, the PRI saw itself as a radical but parliamentary organization. It did not approve of the methods of various other organizations, since it believed these methods to be in conflict with parliamentary principles.

Nearly all important Indonesian parties stood behind Ki Hajar Dewantara, who was regarded as a national figure. Everywhere local committees were set up, comprising representatives from PSII, PNI Baru Taman Siswa, Muhammadiyah, Budi Utomo, Partindo, Istri Sedar (Conscious Wives), and Permi. This heralded the start of much closer cooperation and promoted feelings of unity and a common destiny, which the colonial government tried to thwart because it could only survive if its enemies were fragmented. On 5 February 1933 meetings were held everywhere to discuss a motion which stated that the intention of the imperialists was to obstruct the progress of the Indonesian nation. This could not be expressed in refined language. A more detailed announcement said that further meetings would follow. In response, the ordinance was suspended temporarily by the government.

Ki Hajar Dewantara issued a declaration halting the nonviolent opposition, but he stressed that supporters' responsibilities were not yet over. Indonesians had to be constantly alert and vigilant for signs in future legislation that could herald new threats to private education. He was correct in this, for eight months later a new ordinance was introduced which continued the repressive system. Yet in the long run Ki Hajar Dewantara's action can be said to have achieved something important. He had proved that it was possible to unite Indonesian movements, as long as the thing to be defended was clearly of value to the entire Indonesian nation.

9

*

The Press

ULRICH KRATZ

If you walk through the main streets of any Indonesian city you will see that they bear the names of prominent personalities who have distinguished themselves in the struggle for independence. Names such as H.O.S. Cokroaminoto, Haji Agus Salim, Sam Ratulangie, Danudirja, Setyabuddhi, Ki Hajar Dewantara, and Cipto Mangunkusumo are familiar to every school child. What is special about these names, however, is that they were all in the forefront of the development of a national press, a press which was destined to play a crucial role during the physical struggle for independence in the late 1940s.

During the independence struggle, Indonesian leaders needed to explain the young republic's point of view not only to the Indonesian people but also to the wider international community. The press and radio performed that vital task. The importance which these leaders attached to being able to speak directly to the Allied commanders, their governments, and the world at large can be seen from the fact that some Indonesian newspapers even carried articles, editorials, and revolutionary poetry in English.

As events were to prove, the press was able to carry out its task with resounding success, skillfully surmounting the many obstacles that were put in its way. Among the more practical difficulties were shortages of funds and paper, outdated equipment, and problems with distribution; censorship, surveillance, and persecution by the Dutch were obstacles of a more political nature. Despite all these obstructions, however, the national press proved itself indomitable. Many journalists showed courage of a high order and suffered privations in the execution of their duty. Some even paid with their lives.

Admittedly, most publications had a short life; they would nevertheless reemerge, frequently under a different name and at a different place but with the same staff and an identical appearance and political concept. Newspapers and periodicals were published in the most unlikely places and under the most improbable circumstances, and it is regrettable that our record of the activities and involvement of the press during the period of the physical revolution is so incomplete. The few personal recollections and the archival holdings in the main libraries in Yogyakarta and of the National Library in Jakarta, however, bear proud witness to the many-faceted activities of the Indonesian press in these years.

At the national level, Jakarta, Yogyakarta, and Surabaya were the main publishing centers, but other places soon rivalled their importance as the military front between the Dutch and republican forces fluctuated. In West Java, for example, Bandung, Bogor, Cirebon, Garut, Sukabumi, and Tasikmalaya all had dailies, monthlies, and weeklies. In Central Java we know of the publication of papers of Klaten, Magelang, Purwokerto, Semarang, Surakarta, and Tegal. Apart from Surabaya, East Java boasted publishers in Bojonegoro, Jombang, Kediri, Lumajang, Madiun, Malang, and Mojokerto.

But it was not only in Java that journalists and the press participated actively in the struggle. Papers were produced locally in a number of towns in Sumatra. Most prominent, of course, was Medan, but towns such as Banda Aceh, Bukittinggi, Padang, and Palembang also had newspapers. In Kalimantan, both Banjarmasin and Balikpapan saw the publication of pro-republican papers despite the fact that the area was under Dutch control. The same holds true for the Moluccas and the whole of the Dutch-inspired state of East Indonesia (Negara Indonesia Timur, NIT), though to a more limited extent. The smaller number of papers in eastern Indonesia should not be seen as a barometer of the prevailing political attitude, but more as a reflection of the smaller number of inhabitants and hence of readers. Research into the role of the press in this part of the archipelago, however, has hardly begun.

The press had already played an important part in the development of nationalism and in the shaping of a national identity prior to the

declaration of independence and the ensuing physical revolution. In
fact, the development of the press had gone hand in hand with the development of the nationalist movement as a whole. The one is un-
thinkable without the other, though the development of the press long
predates the rise of the Indonesian nationalist movement in the early
twentieth century. But here a careful distinction should be made between the Dutch-dominated press of the mid- to late nineteenth century and the indigenous press of the early 1900s.

Prior to the introduction of the repressive Printing Press Regulation
of 1856, the press in the Netherlands East Indies consisted mainly of
official organs of the colonial administration or exclusive carriers of
advertisements. An enterprising Dutchman in 1849 wanted to found a
newspaper in Batavia. He was offered a free voyage back to Holland at
the expense of the government if he would refrain from pursuing his
plans. This illustrates the attitude of the colonial authorities to any kind
of liberal press, and their view of the media as makers of public opinion.

After 1856 the newly emerging press was initially controlled finan-
cially and editorially by Europeans, but gradually European editors
and journalists were joined by members of other groups of colonial society with similar commercial interests and education, the Indos (Eurasians) and the Chinese. Unlike the purely Dutch-language press,
however, their publications to a large extent used Malay as their medium of communication. The growing nationalism of the *totok* (new-
comer) and *peranakan* (native born) Chinese community further
encouraged the development of a Chinese-language press side by side
with the Chinese-Malay press. These three varieties of press activity
came to an end only after independence.

Although many of the early ethnic Indonesian publishers and journalists began their careers in journalism as printers, proofreaders, and
typesetters in the service of the Dutch, Eurasian, and Chinese-Malay
press, it was not until the beginning of this century that they began to
take over the ownership and editorial direction of their own Malay-
language press. And it appears that the establishment of a true indigenous press was conditioned by much the same factors which led to the
foundation of the influential Sarekat Islam. *Medan Prijaji*, founded in
Bandung in 1907, is generally considered to have been the first Indonesian newspaper. Its motto was "Forerunner of public thought"
(*pengawal fikiran umum*) and it was led by R.M. Tirtohadisuryo. Mean-

while, Abdul Rivai had already started his own career in journalism, and Abdul Muis, today much better known for his novel *Salah Asuhan*, was soon to become one of the contributors to *Oetoesan Hindia*, *Oetoesan Melajoe*, and *Kaoem Moeda*.

Space does not permit a complete listing of all those who distinguished themselves in journalism, or all the important periodicals of those days. There were many; indeed we could argue that there were too many. Nationalism and the number of periodicals grew together. The colonial authorities tried to control them. Editors were often imprisoned or sent into exile outside Java for expressing their support for the nationalist cause so trenchantly. In addition, chronic financial difficulties dogged most Indonesian publications. Some ceased altogether because readers became lax about paying their subscriptions. The situation was made even worse by the proliferation of newspapers and periodicals. Every political movement and party had to have its own mouthpiece. In 1909 E.F.E. Douwes Dekker, who used the name Dr. Danudirja Setyabuddhi, listed 34 periodicals of this kind. A 1923 survey lists a total of 107 indigenous periodicals. Three of these were published in Arabic, the others in Malay and Malay-Chinese. About one quarter of the journals are identified as being of specialized religious or technical interest. All of them carry a label in accordance with their editorial policy. Thus, *Darmokondo* wore the label "liberal," *Neraca* that of "radical," *Oetoesant Hindia* that of "radical Sarekat Islam," and *Pantjaran Berita*, published in Medan, that of "Batak national."

Nationalist feelings and aspirations were not only expressed in the Malay-language press, however. Already, at a very early date, Abdul Rivai had contributed to the Dutch language press in the Netherlands itself. Later, Indonesians studying in or exiled to Holland set up their own newspapers. Most famous of these was the organ of the local Perhimpunan Indonesia, *Indonesia Merdeka*, which first appeared in 1924. The vast majority of the readers of *Indonesia Merdeka*, however, lived not in the Netherlands but in the Netherlands East Indies, where distribution was carried out in a clandestine fashion. Nationalists in the colony voiced their grievances too in Dutch-language journals. There were periodicals such as *Jong Sumatra* and *Jong Java*, together with others published by the various study clubs. After the infamous Press Ordinance of 1931, however, when restrictions on the press were tightened even further, some journals like *Timboel* protested by ceasing to publish in Dutch and publishing in Malay instead.

The arrival of the Japanese in 1942 did little to ameliorate the difficult situation which the Indonesian press had faced in the pre war
period. If anything, matters took a turn for the worse. The Japanese
closed down the majority of periodicals and immediately began to ex-
ert tight political and editorial control over those papers which they allowed to continue under new names. Under Japanese rule the press
was completely prevented from any kind of political propagandizing
other than that which supported the Japanese. Nevertheless, as the occupation wore on, many journalists managed to propagate the cause of
nationalism while ostensibly pretending to further the Japanese war effort. In a way which was not quite in accordance with the original intentions of the Japanese, the period of occupation had beneficial aspects
too. The total ban on the use of Dutch and the emphasis put on the Indonesian language (emerging from Malay) was instrumental in boost-
ing the development and use of this language in all spheres of modern
life and society. Needless to say, the use of one language considerably
furthered the feeling of solidarity and unity among the diverse ethnic
and linguistic groups of Indonesia.

The most prominent newspaper during the Japanese period seems to
have been *Asia Raya*, published in Jakarta, although *Soeara Asia* of Surabaya appears to have printed more copies. *Asia Raya* ceased publication
in 1945 after the Japanese surrender, when the Japanese, who had been
charged to maintain law and order until the Allied forces arrived,
refused to publish the proclamation of independence. As an act of defi-
ance the entire Indonesian staff of *Asia Raya* resigned.

The first republican newspaper seems to have been *Berita Indonesia*,
which appeared on 6 September 1945. *Merdeka* started printing on 1
October 1945, under the editorship of B.M. Diah. In other towns, too,
Indonesian journalists soon took over. Bandung saw the publication of
Soeara Merdeka, and Semarang *Warta Indonesia*. *Soeara Rakjat* came from
Surabaya and *Kedaulatan Rakjat* from Yogyakarta. Apart from a few
journalists who worked for newspapers set up by the returning colonial administration, it is clear that most Indonesian journalists
throughout the archipelago were united in their opposition to a return
of the Dutch. Naturally, however, there was a difference in tone between papers published in republican territory and those which were
issued in the Dutch enclaves.

Beside newspapers, there were other important press bodies such as
news agencies like the Arabian Press Board (later the Asian Press

Board), run by Indonesian citizens of Arab descent. This body was especially effective in drawing international attention to the republic's cause in the Middle East. Its members were constantly subjected to harrassment by the Dutch authorities, a sacrifice which soon earned the Asian Press Board official recognition by the government of the republic. Later the Asian Press Board merged with Antara, the national press agency, which the late Adam Malik helped to found in 1937. Censored by the Dutch and banned completely by the Japanese, who imprisoned its staff in Nusakambangan, Antara played a very important role after the proclamation of independence, first from Jakarta and then from Yogyakarta, as the voice of the government of the republic.

The crucial role of the press in those important years, though generally acknowledged, is unfortunately still not fully documented. While the role of the press from the beginnings of the national movement to the defeat of the Japanese has been recorded in great detail, the documentary evidence for the vital and unquestioned contribution of the press to the ultimate success of the revolutionary struggle is far less comprehensive. This of course is a reflection of those confused days when the nation was concentrating on the immediate task of the physical struggle. It would be sad, however, if in the course of time the record of the contribution of the press to national independence had been left largely to the private memories of those directly involved.

10

*

Sukarno, the PNI, and Perhimpunan Indonesia

JOHN INGLESON

On 4 July 1927 a small group in Bandung announced the formation of the Perserikatan Nasional Indonesia, or PNI. Its chairman was a young engineering student from the Bandung Technical College, Sukarno. Over the next two and a half years the PNI was the most active nationalist party in the colony. At its peak in December 1929 it had about 10,000 members and its influence extended throughout the towns and cities of Java and beyond to Sumatra and eastern Indonesia.

With the exception of Sukarno, most PNI leaders were young men who had been educated in the Netherlands in the early 1920s. While in the Netherlands they had joined the Indonesian students' organization, Perhimpunan Indonesia. Led by Mohammad Hatta, a young economics student, they watched the rise and fall of first Sarekat Islam and then the PKI and determined to create a new nationalist party based on neither Islam nor communism. On their return to Indonesia they formed study clubs in Surabaya, Bandung, and other cities in Java. Sukarno was a young student in 1924 when he joined the General Study Club in Bandung and came into contact with nationalists such as Cipto Mangunkusumo and Iskak Cokrohadisuryo. It was from the General Study Club that the PNI was born.

In Perhimpunan Indonesia and in the study clubs in Bandung and Surabaya there was a strong belief that the nationalist movement must be more united than it had been in the past if it was to pose a real threat to the Dutch. Sukarno himself was deeply affected by this atmosphere and at the end of 1926 published an important series of articles entitled "Nationalism, Islam, and Marxism." In them he argued that the Islamic, Marxist and nationalist movements in Indonesia had a common aim of resisting Western capitalism and imperialism, and that the three streams of political activity must unite in the struggle against the common enemy, the Dutch. The communists were destroyed after their uprising in November 1926, but for the rest of the colonial period Sukarno continued to argue for unity between Islamic and secular nationalists.

He did not succeed in this aim. A nationalist federation—the Permufakatan Perhimpunan-Perhimpunan Politik Kebangsaan Indonesia, PPPKI—was formed in December 1927, but was never very strong. Islamic nationalist parties such as Sarekat Islam in Java and Persatuan Muslim Indonesia in Sumatra continued as separate parties. There were also many other nationalist parties, almost all of which were regional organizations. However, the major parties after 1927 were the PNI, and later the Partindo and PNI Baru, known as non-cooperating parties because they refused to sit in the colonial parliament, the Volksraad, arguing that it had no real powers.

In 1928 and 1929 PNI leaders worked hard to create a strong organization and develop a mass party. Hundreds of well-organized meetings were held and great excitement was generated wherever PNI leaders spoke. An emotional atmosphere was created in the meeting halls; PNI flags—red and white, with a buffalo head in the middle—were everywhere, and the red and white national color scheme was carried onto the podium. Often patriotic songs were sung by the audiences before the arrival of the main speakers.

Sukarno was the PNI's major drawcard. He was a brilliant speaker. His speeches were full of basic nationalist ideas expressed in simple language his audiences could understand. He used popular myths and local folklore, especially *wayang* stories, to embody the nationalist ideas of the PNI. One of his central messages was that before independence could be achieved the Indonesian people had to achieve inner spiritual freedom. Spiritual freedom would be obtained, he believed, when the Indonesian people overcame their sense of inferiority and their psychological dependence on the Dutch. In his speeches and in his writings

Sukarno urged his people to be proud of their cultures and their past achievements, and to work together to create an independent Indonesian nation.

Youth organizations were heavily influenced by the PNI. One of the most important and best-remembered events in the history of the national movement was the second Indonesian Youth Congress held in Batavia on 26 and 27 October 1928. Delegates made a solemn pledge of loyalty and devotion to one nation, one culture, and one language. The final session of the Youth Congress saw the inaugural performance of the patriotic song, "Indonesia Raya." The solemnity of the recitation of the Sumpah Pemuda (Youth Oath), the raising of the red and white flag, and the singing of "Indonesia Raya" made a deep emotional impression on the youth present.

The Dutch colonial government was so concerned by the popularity of Sukarno and by the growth of the PNI that on 29 December 1929 it arrested hundreds of central and branch leaders. Sukarno, Maskun, Gatot Mangkupraja and Supriadinata were brought to trial at the Bandung District Court on 18 August 1930, charged with spreading propaganda likely to disturb public order. All were convicted, with Sukarno sentenced to four years jail, Gatot to two years, Maskun to twenty months, and Supriadinata to fifteen months.

Sukarno used the trial to make a lengthy speech explaining the nationalists' aim and methods. It was a clever tactic because the colonial government could not prevent Court proceedings from being published. Under the title *Indonesia Menggugat (Indonesia Accuses)*, Sukarno's defense speech was eagerly purchased by thousands of Indonesians who were deeply influenced by his critique of imperialism and his strong argument for Indonesia Merdeka, an independent Indonesia. It was a brilliant speech, delivered with humor, energy, and passion, and aimed at stirring the nationalist spirit in his fellow countrymen.

The arrest of Sukarno and other PNI leaders brought the PNI's activities to a halt. After their conviction the party was dissolved and a new party took its place: the Partai Indonesia (Partindo) under the chairmanship of Sartono. It was, in reality, the PNI under another name.

Sukarno had stressed the importance of public meetings, of arousing an emotional commitment to Indonesian independence and of mobilizing the masses as soon as possible in order to seize it from the Dutch. As he watched the drama of 1928 and 1929 from the Netherlands, Mohammad Hatta became increasingly critical of the way in which Sukarno was leading the PNI. He wanted the PNI to develop a strong organization and politically conscious cadres first, and only slowly evolve into a mass party. Only in this way, he argued, could a nationalist party survive Dutch repression. He was not surprised when Sukarno and other PNI leaders were arrested in December 1929, and publicly urged new tactics on his friends in Indonesia.

Hatta encouraged the development of an alternative nationalist party to Partindo. In December 1931 the Pendidikan Nasional Indonesia (known as the PNI Baru) was formed in Yogyakarta. Hatta himself returned to Indonesia in August 1932, after an absence of just over ten years. Sukarno had been released from jail on 31 December 1931 and in August 1932 joined Partindo. Partindo continued the style of the old PNI, with a heavy emphasis on large rallies, stirring speeches by Sukarno, and an effort to confront the Dutch with a large mass party as quickly as possible. The PNI Baru concentrated on recruiting and educating a well-disciplined cadre and building an organizational structure. Hatta worked closely in the PNI Baru with Sutan Syahrir, a fellow Sumatran with whom he had worked in Perhimpunan Indonesia in the late 1920s. They shared a democratic socialist commitment and an international outlook, though they were temperamentally very different people. Hatta saw the PNI Baru as a more radical party than Partindo in its social and economic thinking, with its more systematic approach to social and economic change involving the creation of collectives and cooperatives. More importantly, by concentrating on building a core membership which would be active in schools, cooperatives, and trade unions, he believed that they were laying the foundation for a better-disciplined party capable of surviving colonial repression and at some future date able to blossom into a mass party leading the people to independence.

The areas of disagreement between PNI Baru and Partindo leaders were at times bitterly contested and were permanently to affect relations between the people in the two parties. In the end, however, neither party survived the second government crackdown. In August 1933 Sukarno was again arrested and Partindo effectively banned. In February 1934 Hatta, Syahrir, and the entire PNI Baru Central Executive were arrested and that party also effectively banned. Hatta, Syahrir, and other PNI Baru leaders were exiled to Boven Digul, in what is now Irian Barat, and Sukarno was exiled to the island of Flores.

Although the secular, non-cooperating nationalist movement was repressed by the Dutch, a great deal was achieved in the seven years after 1927. An intense pride in an Indonesian political and cultural identity was developed among tens of thousands of people who joined the PNI, Partindo, or the PNI Baru, attended a nationalist meeting, or simply heard of the idea of Indonesia Merdeka from friends or neighbors. It was now impossible for any Indonesian political group to be regarded as nationalist unless it advocated complete independence and the creation of a united nation. The symbols of nationalism were also firmly rooted: the red and white flag and the "Indonesia Raya." Finally, nationalists became committed in these years to the development of one national language, *bahasa Indonesia,* as a means of unifying the diverse ethnic and linguistic groups in the country. Sukarno and Hatta had become established as key political leaders, and when the Japanese invaded in 1942 the two men were once again able to take over leadership of the nationalist movement and lead Indonesia towards independence.

11

*

Cooperators and Noncooperators in the 1930s

SUSAN ABEYESEKERE

There could scarcely be a greater contrast of periods in modern Indonesian history than that between the 1930s and the immediately succeeding eras of occupation and revolution. In fact, the years 1935-1942 are so out of keeping with the earlier flamboyance of the noncooperating nationalists and the later stormy period that they are only too likely to be forgotten.

The combination of economic depression and government repression had a crippling effect on Indonesian politics, an effect which lasted throughout the 1930s. In general the Indonesian population accepted the hardships of the crisis years fatalistically. There were no uprisings. The Dutch adviser for native affairs reported in 1935, "Among the peasantry, resignation increases with suffering." Few could afford to become involved in politics, especially when the government's crackdown on Indonesian parties made politics such a dangerous business. After 1934, stricter police vigilance and legal restrictions on the rights of association and assembly prevented Indonesian parties from attracting a mass following. Throughout the period, politics was the affair of the well-educated, the aristocratic, and the relatively well-to-do. The largest political party, the PSII (Partai Sarekat Islam Indonesia) had only about 12,000 members in 1940, and most were much smaller. Many individuals who had previously been politically active retreated into social, economic, or educational activities. It is significant that the biggest and most successful Indonesian protest of the Depression years was the campaign against licensing private schools, which in the 1930s catered to more Indonesian children than did state-run and -subsidized schools.

In the period 1935-1942, Indonesian parties adopted moderate, parliamentary tactics. Only nonpolitical organizations and parties which cooperated by agreeing to seek representation in the Dutch-created representative councils were guaranteed even a modicum of immunity from police interference. And the only relatively free forums for political expression were the representative councils. Thus the only means the nationalist movement had for bringing about reform was by exerting influence on the Dutch directly, not by organizing mass support.

Some of the political leaders of the period were genuinely convinced that something could be achieved by moderate methods. Mohammed Husni Thamrin, the leader of the nationalist group in the Volksraad, was a skilled parliamentarian who believed that useful work could be done in the representative councils. Much of the membership of the Parindra, to which Thamrin belonged, were by nature in favor of moderate, nonpolitical methods. They were mainly Javanese aristocrats who were engaged in welfare work to improve the social and economic position of ordinary Indonesians. Bridging the social and political wings of the party was its great president, Dr. Sutomo. From Parindra's formation in 1935 to Sutomo's death in 1938, the party and its leadership appeared less interested in direct political activity than in promoting organizational unity among nationalists and in involving the elite in the development of the country. Sutomo is reported to have said:

> We must deserve freedom before we can justly aspire to it. For even if we should be free tomorrow, what use will our freedom be to us if we are not in a position to utilize it to further our own welfare?

For very different reasons, the leaders of the new leftist cooperating party, Gerindo (Gerakan Rakyat Indonesia, Indonesian People's Movement), founded in 1937, were also dedicated to conciliatory methods. The central leadership of Gerindo consisted of international socialists, deeply affected by the world struggle between fascism and democracy, which they regarded as the most urgent issue of the day, overriding even the need for Indonesian independence. Meetings of Gerindo in Batavia and Surabaya concentrated largely on attacks on fascism, seen in rather theoretical terms. For instance, at a public meeting in Batavia in 1938, Amir Syarifuddin urged the audience to choose between fascism, which he said "glittered but knew no righteousness," and democracy, "which was weak but based on justice and happiness." The audience of 1000 shouted in reply, "We would rather have democracy." Gerindo's anti-fascism could also be directed at specific targets, such as Japanese intervention in China.

Just as the strictly political aims of the parties were restrained, so too were their social and economic aims. Although all parties were anxious to eliminate foreign economic domination, they did not try to spell out the social and economic shape of an independent Indonesia, since that was thought to be in the still distant future. No one spoke of radical social reform.

The first significant attempt to exploit the new moderation in Indonesian politics after 1935 was the Sutarjo Petition of 1936. As president of the Indonesian civil servants' organization, Sutarjo was not a member of a nationalist party, although he was a self-confessed nationalist. He introduced into the Volksraad a petition requesting the Dutch parliament to grant political autonomy to Indonesia. Although the petition received sufficient support from both Indonesian and European members to pass through the Volksraad, a public campaign in its favor gained no help from the major nationalist parties, and the rejection of the petition by Holland raised little outcry. At the time, it appeared that the cooperating nationalist movement was still finding its feet and was slow to grasp the opportunity for reform which Sutarjo might have offered; after all, his was the only proposal for fundamental political change to be initiated in and accepted by the Volksraad.

Yet the Petition did help to stir the nationalist movement from the apathetic defeatism in which it had been languishing since the noncooperating movement had been paralyzed. In May 1939, all the main Indonesian nationalist parties, secular and religious, united in a political federation called Gapi (Gabungan Politik Indonesia), which almost at once undertook a campaign for a fully representative, politically powerful Indonesian parliament. Moreover, Indonesian nationalists began introducing motions for piecemeal reform in the Volksraad, where previously opposition members had restricted themselves to criticism of government policy.

The nationalist movement's new enthusiasm for political reform can be attributed mainly to the turn of events overseas. By the late 1930s the international situation provided Indonesians with a new source of hope, namely that the threat of war would cause their rulers to seek their support. By May 1940, when the Germans overran Holland, nationalists felt certain that the Dutch must see the need to win Indonesian cooperation by making political concessions.

It was Dutch immovability in the face of these developments which forced many nationalists back into the personal feuding and feeling of helplessness that dominated the 1930s. The Dutch had several reasons for ignoring Indonesian demands. They were not impressed by the size of the nationalist movement, which they had taken such care to isolate from the masses, and now that the nationalist movement had been steered into a moderate path, the Dutch felt it could be safely ignored. The Dutch were also not as anxious about the international situation as Indonesians anticipated. The Dutch government underestimated the threats first from Germany and then from Japan. On both counts they thought they could remain neutral and avoid invasion. Even if they had feared defeat, it is unlikely that the colonial authorities would have been driven into the arms of the nationalists, whom they scorned and mistrusted. The most the Dutch would promise was to consider constitutional reform after the war was over.

Many Indonesian nationalists had only reluctantly adopted moderate tactics after 1935. Faced with continued Dutch intransigence, nationalists felt that even in what were apparently promising circumstances—outside threats accompanied by conciliatory Indonesian overtures—they could achieve nothing. It is not surprising that many abandoned the effort altogether. In December 1941, when the government at last agreed to hold consultations with the nationalist movement about defense, the Muslim parties refused to come to the conference table. Like many other Indonesians, they had decided to leave everything to the Japanese.

Since the early 1930s, Indonesians had been looking abroad for a solution to their problems, yet there is very little evidence of joint Indonesian-Japanese plans to overthrow the Dutch regime, even as late as 1942. Although this is surprising in view of Indonesian disillusionment with the Dutch, it is more understandable when one considers the caution on the part of the Japanese in committing themselves to the Pacific war, and the caution which had been instilled into Indonesians through their experience with Dutch repression. The arrest of Thamrin in January 1941 was the most notable case involving suspected collaboration between Indonesian nationalists and Japanese expansionists, yet even on that occasion no evidence was produced to prove treason. As the Dutch were uncomfortably aware, however, only leftist Indonesian and Chinese newspapers were unfavorably disposed toward the Japanese. And in the last months before the Japanese occupation, there was widespread reference to the Joyoboyo prophecy about the overthrow of white rulers by yellow men. While not actively helping the Japanese, Indonesians were preparing to welcome them.

As the Japanese forces swept through the archipelago, many of the nationalists who had sought in vain to cooperate with the Dutch now confidently anticipated recognition by the Japanese as Indonesia's legitimate leaders. The demoralizing influence of years of Dutch repression on the caliber of these nationalists was revealed when in March 1942 the chairmen of PSII and Parindra, intoxicated by the prospect of power, began to quarrel over the composition of the imagined new government. Contemptuously, the Japanese thrust them aside. When finally governmental prizes were distributed, the Japanese reached back into the past to award them to Sukarno and Hatta, those survivors of the noncooperating tradition. Once more history had thwarted the cooperating nationalists in their pursuit of power.

12

*

The Making of a Revolutionary

An interview with

ADAM MALIK

I first became active in the Indonesian nationalist movement after Sukarno was arrested in Bandung. Around this time, a wave of apprehension swept through Indonesia, because his arrest also meant the banning of the Indonesian National Party (PNI). Like other young men at that time, I wasn't very happy with the colonial government's action. Consequently, everywhere in Indonesia, including my town, youth movements sprang up, beginning with Indonesia Muda (Young Indonesia) and a host of local groups. At that time, I was heavily involved with the working class, because where I was in Pematang Siantar, there were large numbers of plantation coolies, or contract coolies as they were known in Sumatra. Their lot in life was full of suffering, and I used to go to the plantations twice a month so that I could experience for myself the suffering of these plantation coolies. That's why I set up a local workers' movement and a local farmers' support group. Then these were banned, so we changed course and formed a general organization, a sort of social, mutual aid movement. I did this with my friends in Pematang Siantar. After that, we agreed that we could no longer stick to lightweight movements, we ought to enter politics. That's why my friends and I set up a branch of Partindo, which was led by Sartono. This Partindo was created after Sukarno's PNI was disbanded. I worked in the Pematang Siantar branch of Partindo, and stayed active until, about a year later, drastic measures were taken by the colonial government.

At that time, because the colonial authorities felt threatened by Partindo's progress, they issued a regulation called the Vergaderverbod (Prohibition of Assembly), which forbade the gathering of five or more people. If 5 of us were to gather, whether in a coffee shop, or in a house, or in the street, we could be arrested for breaking the law. My instructions under these circumstances were to visit the branches so that even if Partindo were banned, communications would be kept open. Thus I was a kind of travelling messenger, and I went all over the place. And when, for example, I went to Sibolga or Padang Sidempuan, I avoided summoning five people at any one time, and instead stayed in one place and summoned them one by one. But spies controlled by the Dutch secret police, the PID, reported that on such-and-such a night on such-and-such a date I had received a certain number of people. Even though they had not all come together, it was still seen as contravening the regulation. So when I had returned to my base in Pematang Siantar, I was summoned before the magistrate there and sentenced to two months, which was the maximum sentence. I got two months, and each of the five friends also got two months; they had been asked one by one whether it was true that at such-and-such a time and on such-and-such a date they had been at Adam Malik's place. "Yes, it's true," each replied. But they hadn't come together. They didn't lie, and they really had seen me at the time in question. This was seen by the presiding official of the trial, the Dutch *kontrolir*, as breaking the law, so I was refused a defense, sentenced immediately to two months, and put into prison straight away. There I was given a change of clothes: convict clothes, which in those days had spots on them. We all changed our clothes and were put right to work carrying sand. In the evenings, it was sweeping and cleaning, real convict chores. I did that for two months. After I emerged from those two months in jail, I naturally did not feel any desire to give up the struggle. This was despotism, and I regarded the laws against assembly as violating the aspirations of this nation.

Because I had been sentenced to jail I no longer felt at ease in Pematang Siantar. It was too small a place, and my family, especially my parents, were obviously upset, for they saw that I was considered. . . . well . . . . people who had been imprisoned were generally despised. So together with some of my friends, especially with the journalist Sipahu-tar, I decided to cross over to Java to ask the Central Committee of Partindo why there had been no further action. On my way to Jakarta, I met the head of the party, Sartono, at his home in Bogor. From my discussion with him, I got the impression he had become rather ner-vous about facing up to the Dutch action, so much so that he even asked me, "Why did you come? We will get into trouble because the Dutch are collecting evidence to arrest more people to send to Boven Digul." This reply of his really broke my heart. I discovered that my leader was a coward who did not dare to face up to the situation. So I didn't visit him again, and while I was in Jakarta I sought contacts with other organizations.

At that time I was introduced to the movement known as Partai Re-publik Indonesia (Party of the Republic of Indonesia or PRI) which was illegal, and was led by Tan Malaka from abroad. By coincidence, I was staying with Yahya Nasution, one of the coordinators of the PRI in Jakarta. Through him, my point of view became more and more changed, to the extent that even I was no longer openly active; I didn't want to move openly, but I helped them secretly. This was in 1935 or 1936. When the colonial authorities first arrested PRI people in Singa-pore, Kalimantan, and Palembang, and organized raids throughout In-donesia, about forty to sixty people were picked up, including Yahya Nasution.

In fact I wasn't directly connected with this movement, but I was implicated through Yahya Nasution since I regarded him as one of my own family. So I was also arrested, but when I was interrogated by the Dutch, there was no evidence against me and I could not be held for longer than approximately ten months, then I was released. The others had been caught with pamphlets in their possession, and at that time, one pamphlet per person was already sufficient to send them to Digul. Since I didn't have one, the Netherlands East Indies government had no excuse to exile me to Digul, but could only detain me for a time. So they were sent to Digul and I was free in 8 or 10 months. But we had already agreed that even if they were all sent to Digul, those left behind had to continue the struggle. Consequently, when I left prison I sought out the old leaders of Partindo, which had been disbanded long ago, and we got together to think about setting up a new movement. This new movement was called Gerakan Rakyat Indonesia (Indonesian Peo-ple's Movement) or Gerindo. The situation at that time was so critical that we were forced to change our attitude rather suddenly and cooperate with the Dutch, just as a tactic. Gerindo, of course, was not the same as Partindo or PNI, but nearly all its members were ex-Partindo or ex-PNI. Thus Gerindo spread throughout Indonesia very quickly. It was then that Sipahutar—the one from Pematang Siantar—and I went to meet Sumanang and Armijn Pane to set up a national press bureau. That is how the Antara News Agency was founded in 1937, after I had been released from jail. We set up Antara with the aim of helping the independence movement which had started with Gerindo. In Gerindo, I also sat on the Central Committee in Jakarta, which was led by Gani, Wilopo, and others; Syarifuddin also joined in. With this arrangement, the party managed to function continuously almost until the occupation of Holland in the war.

During the war in Europe the situation here in Indonesia was also extremely heated. The Dutch tried various means to get Indonesians to support the war against the Japanese; we in Gerindo had already accepted the principle of cooperation, so we obviously could not disobey the colonial government. But we did try illegally to organize forces so that if the Japanese did come, we would not assist the Dutch in resisting them but would just be passive, since the war was a concern of the Japanese and the Allies. Of course there were suggestions from the Dutch Communist Party and also from the Comintern that the socialists, communists and other parties—what was called in France the "popular front"—should unite. Its influence was felt here, though by this time we had already seen that we could not cooperate with the Dutch against the Japanese. Nor could we take action, due to the regulations valid at that time, but there was still some scope for activity. We condemned fascism, like the Dutch who opposed German Nazism, but we didn't want to get involved in movements started up by the Dutch.

This method worked until war broke out, but then we were dealt with! I was arrested and exiled to Sukabumi, then taken to Garut, then to Nusa Kambangan. The plan was to transfer us to Australia, but while we were in Cilacap waiting to leave, the ship which was to take my friends and me—over 300 of us—to Australia, was bombed by the Japanese. So, we could not be taken to Australia. We were freed when the Japanese landed at Cilacap and freed all political prisoners. So that is how I became involved in the independence movement, until the time the Japanese arrived.

13

*

The Great Depression

WILLIAM O'MALLEY

It is late July in 1931, on the road leading north out of Yogyakarta into Sleman. Alongside the road a man is sitting, whimpering to himself, his life in ruins. Long ago, when he was still a youth, he had been recruited to go to work on the great plantations in East Sumatra. The government had said that the conditions there were acceptable. The company had promised him better wages than he could ever earn in Sleman. As one of hundreds of thousands of coolies in the Dollar Land of Deli, he had labored long and hard, clearing the jungle and planting and tending crops which the plantation would export. But when the company had to cut costs in 1931, he was simply dismissed and sent back to Java. His vast experience and his years of loyal service counted for nothing. He had returned to his old village, but found that he had no family left there, and no one knew him anymore. No one could take him in. He had been misled, betrayed by the new world of big business, and there was no place for him any longer in the old world of the village. He had little money, no job, no home, no security. No future. How could things have gone so wrong for him and so many others like him? How could they have gone so wrong for the Netherlands East Indies?

In the three decades before 1930, doors had been opening for many Indonesians. For those few at the top, there was a growing number of positions as doctors, lawyers, professionals, and even high-level civil servants in the colonial administration. For those with some education, there were openings as clerks, police officials, teachers, and workers in shops and business offices. There were also jobs for manual laborers. They could work on sugar plantations in Java. There was a need for labor on tobacco, rubber, coffee, and tea plantations both in Java and in the outer islands. And there were various opportunities in the growing cities and towns. As the colony modernized, and particularly as its government and economy grew, it was possible for some Indonesians to take part in that process, and even to prosper. But in the 1930s they learned that involvement with the modern economy meant involvement with its problems as well.

In 1929 the economies of Western Europe and the United States of America were plunged into a serious depression, a crisis that soon spread to most other countries. Across the world, economic institutions collapsed. Trade declined dramatically. Banks closed their doors. Factories shut down. The jobless stood in line in the streets for food.

The Netherlands East Indies was distant from North America and from Europe, but her economy was one of the hardest hit. As a colony, she had adapted herself to provide raw materials for the factories, and food for the tables, of the advanced countries. When the markets of those countries shrank in the 1930s, Indonesia's economy entered a time of great trouble, a time of economic despair that was to last for almost ten years. Prices fell very quickly. Wages were cut. Jobs, either in government or in the private sector, became scarce. Planned projects had to be abandoned, and companies and stores went bankrupt. Altogether, it was a tremendously difficult time, a difficult time shared by almost all Indonesians.

For Indonesian officials, both the old aristocracy and those who had more recently come into the expanding government service, the depression brought reductions in salary, early retirements, and threats of widespread dismissals. Morale in the administrative corps plunged, not only because of what was happening to officials in their jobs but also because of the increased difficulties they had in meeting their responsibilities at home. Many of them had large families—parents, brothers and sisters, nephews and nieces—to support, and obligations as well to finance the expensive educations of their children and of other family members. Under the depressed conditions, they were forced further into debt, and many were compelled to sell family heirlooms and property in an effort to pay off their debts.

Shopkeepers, merchants, and traders saw their businesses decline. They had goods that were wanted and needed, but potential customers no longer had money to make purchases. For a short time it was possible to extend still more credit, but as years went by with no improvement in the economy, many traders went bankrupt and their families had to give up their dreams of continued education and advancement.

Indonesians who had moved out of their villages also found themselves in trouble during the Depression. In general, those who had gone to urban centers to work in construction, transportation, and manufacturing had done fairly well in the good times, holding better jobs and earning more money than they could have in farming. But in the 1930s, their employers took no responsibility for them, they were released from their positions, and they were forced to choose between two humiliating alternatives. They could stay on, frustrated, in the cities, scrambling for any low-paying, temporary work that came up, while their families experienced the misery of urban poverty, or they could return to their villages, hoping that some work and some food would be available to compensate them for the disgrace they felt at returning home in need.

But perhaps the greatest victims were people like the man on the roadside in Sleman, who had chosen to work in the plantation sector. Plantation laborers usually came from among the poorer villagers, and before the 1930s they would return from their years of hard work with good clothes, gold coins, and stories of their unusual experiences. But during the Depression there were few joyous homecomings. The lucky workers were those who could stay on with the plantations, even though their wages were greatly reduced. Some tried to move off the plantations and live as farmers nearby, but there was difficulty in obtaining good land, and years spent taking orders as a laborer were no preparation for farming on one's own. Most of the dismissed coolies had no choice but to return to their old villages, hoping that they could fit in again. But this was not easy. They had come from overcrowded areas in the first place. They had nothing to offer but their labor. And the rural economy in Java was already under strain in the 1930s. Land taxes were still high, prices for agricultural products very low. And there were few chances to earn cash from jobs other than farming. People writing about the period often point out that the village communities were able to provide for the economic refugees in the 1930s, but this ignores the distress, the difficulty, the embarrassment, and the unhappiness that resulted as hundreds of thousands of penniless people were dumped back into villages when the modern economy collapsed.

In these times of stress and confusion, where could people turn for assistance and for direction? The colonial government had since 1900 acted as the protector of the people. It had greatly expanded the number of schools, erected hospitals and improved medical care. People's banks had been established, a labor inspectorate investigated working conditions, and councils were set up to incorporate Indonesians' views into laws as they were made. But in the 1930s, as government revenues fell, many of these services were reduced. What is more, time after time, the government took the side of European business against the interests of the people.

In Java, much of the cash flowing to people in the countryside came from the sugar industry. The factories hired thousands of people full time. The cane was planted on wide stretches of land rented at good prices from the Javanese. And during the harvesting and planting campaigns, hundreds of thousands of farmers found wage employment for a few months. But when the sugar industry met with severe troubles in the 1930s, the government acted to help the companies and ignored the plight of the people. Factories were closed, but no concern was given, or compensation paid, either by the companies or the government, for long-time employees who were released. Low-level government officials persuaded landowners to reduce the agreed-upon rents the companies had been paying them for their land. And those who had grown to depend upon part-time employment in sugar were rendered jobless, without the cash they needed to buy clothes or salt, to pay taxes, or to purchase seeds for farming on their own.

In Sumatra and Kalimantan, where Indonesian farmers had planted rubber trees to compete with the foreign-owned plantations, the government also acted on behalf of big business. Plantations were allowed to continue to operate at a profit. But in order to cut back on production by small farmers, a tax was placed on people's rubber. Then this tax was raised until Indonesians were barely receiving any money at all for their rubber. Finally, in December 1935, the government was taking 95% of the people's rubber income in taxes, leaving farmers with only 2 cents for every kilogram they collected. Hunger riots then broke out among rubber farmers in Siak. But when a high Dutch official investigated the affair and said that the tax was unjust and amounted to stealing from the people, he was dismissed from the service. The government continued to protect the plantations.

Throughout the colony, international trade policies were pursued which hurt almost all Indonesians. For over five years during the Depression, the Dutch government kept prices for Indonesia's exports artificially high on world markets, by keeping the guilder at an artificially high value. This continued until 1936, long after their major competitors had devalued their currencies, thus hurting sales and eliminating jobs for Indonesian producers and workers. At the same time, the government strengthened ties with manufacturers in Holland, and as a result Indonesian consumers had to buy more expensive goods from the mother country instead of cheaper products made elsewhere.

As in sugar, rubber, and trade, so too in manufacturing, in transportation, in credit distribution, in education, and in many other fields the Indies government followed policies that offered little or no support to Indonesians. Between 1900 and 1930, it had seemed that the colonial government was prepared to protect its subjects, but the years after 1930 clearly showed that in the eyes of the government business interests were more important than people, and the Dutch economy took precedence over the Indonesian economy.

If distressed Indonesians could not turn to the government for help, who could explain their fate to them and suggest steps they could take to improve their condition? Nationalist political figures tried. The situation was fertile soil for the seeds of revolutionary nationalism. But the 1930s was not an easy time for revolutionary politicians. The police were active and suspicious, government spies numerous. Meetings were frequently broken up; newspapers were easily banned. Under those conditions, radical nationalists could make little headway in trying to tell people that colonialism was responsible for all their ills. Important leaders—Sukarno, Hatta, Syahrir, Iwa Kusumasumantri—were sent into exile, and parties such as PNI, Partindo, and PNI Baru were strangled. Nationalist politicians and parties who did not openly confront the Dutchmen—people such as Dr. Sutomo and Husni Thamrin, parties such as Parindra and Pasundan—were able to continue their work and to speak to and on behalf of large numbers of ordinary Indonesians. Through such men and parties, attempts were made to improve the condition of the people. Cooperatives and peasant associations were formed. Credit systems and self-help projects were started. And educated persons began to see it as their duty to help illiterate people when they came into contact or conflict with the government. In Yogyakarta, Pangeran Soeryodiningrat, a brother of the sultan, established the PKN, a popular political party which tried to reduce taxes, oppose the sugar planters, and unite farmers so that they could improve their market positions. Such organizations were not always in complete agreement with the more radical parties, but the essence of their message was the same: "We have to depend on ourselves." For that was the lesson that many Indonesians finally came to learn through the Depression, that in difficult times they could not rely on European employers, or European officials, or on colonial government policies to protect them. Indonesians had, instead, to stand up for themselves and to work together to help each other.

Few people in the archipelago escaped the effects of the Depression. Pepper growers in Aceh, rice growers in Lombok, and coconut growers in Halmahera suffered alike. Traders in Surabaya, villagers in the Moluccas, hunters and farmers upriver in Kalimantan all had their lives affected. Older people had to pawn their precious belongings in order to live. Working people lost their jobs and their pride. Children sacrificed their opportunities for education. The Depression might well have been the first historical experience that all Indonesians shared, and they shared a powerful sense of misery and helplessness. In the Depression many of them had it made clear to them that colonialism as a system was opposed to them, and that the colonial government did not exist to defend them. When the Japanese arrived in 1942, intending to put an end to European colonialism, Indonesians made no effort to defend the Dutch government. For under the impact of the economic crisis in the 1930s they had learned that the colonial government was not their government and they were going to have to stand on their own. It was an experience they never forgot.

14

*

The Beginning of an Army

AN INTERVIEW WITH

LIEUTENANT GENERAL G.P.H. DJATIKUSUMO

I was born in 1917, during World War I, but it was our parents' generation who had decided at the end of the last century that, besides working on the political and diplomatic fronts, we should also form an
armed force. The problem was, from whom should we learn military
skills and where should we obtain weapons? It just so happened that in
1905 Japan won its war against Tsarist Russia, and with this the myth
that the white races could not be defeated by non-white races was destroyed. So Indonesians started thinking about how it would be if we
learned from and obtained weapons from the Japanese. It was quite
clear the the Dutch colonial government would never allow this and
would obstruct this plan in every way possible. Then World War I
broke out, and this new development showed that the Netherlands
East Indies could not be defended without the help of indigenous Indonesians. So Abdul Muis, a journalist and at that time a member of
the Volksraad, organized a petition to the queen which requested the
formation of a militia for Indonesians. By coincidence, among the
group who went to Holland to present the petition was my uncle, so I
knew how the mission went. The queen promised that the petition
would be considered, and a school for officers was opened in the area
of Jakarta then called Meester Cornelius (now Jatinegara), where one
of the first to graduate was Urip Sumoharjo, later our military leader.
Then the Dutch also opened a military academy in Breda, Holland.

72

(They already had a school for officers in Alkmaar; my older brother was in the third class to graduate from that military academy.) Then the Dutch started replacing their mercenary German soldiers from Bavaria with Indonesians, at first with Javanese, then with men from Maluku and Minahasa, and finally with men from Timor.

In 1936 it was hoped that I would enter the military academy in Breda, but I refused, because I found it too difficult to swear allegiance to the Queen of the Netherlands. So I didn't go to that school, but to another in Delft. However, after World War II had begun to flare up and the Netherlands was occupied by the Germans, the Dutch opened a branch of the Breda Military Academy—which had been closed because of the German occupation—in Bandung. They also opened a school for reserve officers, which I entered as a reserve officer. Not for long, though, because before eight months were up the Japanese landed. We fought a battle which lasted for eight days, and after that the commander in chief of the KNIL (Koninklijk Nederlands Indisch Leger or Royal Netherlands Indies Army), General Terpoorten, disbanded the KNIL, and thus all the officers who had sworn an oath of allegiance to the queen felt released from that oath. What we learned from those eight days of fighting was how not to organize a war, and how not to fight a battle. It was an important experience. The KNIL had probably never been organized or trained to fight a war against troops with as much experience as the Japanese had had in China.

After the Japanese arrival, efforts to form an Indonesian army continued, based on an initiative from Gatot Mangkupraja, assisted by Haji Agus Salim and Oto Iskandardinata. This was named Pembela Tanah Air (Defenders of the Fatherland), abbreviated to Peta, and among its members were Singodimejo, many *kiyayi* (Muslim religious leaders) and *pemuda* (youths from the nationalist movements). Generally speaking, the older leaders from Muhammadiyah became battalion commanders, while the younger men became company commanders. It has been said that those of us who entered Peta became servants of the Japanese or that we helped the Japanese, but that is not true. From the very beginning we had intended to organize an armed force, and then we were given this opportunity.

If there had been no Peta, I simply can't envisage how in 1945 we could have organized a new army from scratch. What we learned from the Japanese in Peta was how to form an army from the ground up, and it was this that impressed us most of all. In September, those of us who had been in the Surakarta Battalion of Peta received a telegram from Urip Sumoharjo, who had been appointed chief of staff. Mulyadi Joyo Martono, a Muhammadiya supporter who had been our battalion commander of Peta, was ordered to take control of the regional government from the Japanese. The commander of Company IV, an ex-member of the board of Parindra, was appointed to form the Badan Keamanan Rakyat (People's Security Force, BKR).

At that time we faced two problems. First, we had to defend the proclamation and the nation, the Republic of Indonesia. For that, we needed an official army. The other matter was how to chase out the colonialists. For that we used the irregular rebel troops, which in 1947 were finally formed into a single body, named the Tentara Nasional Indonesia (TNI) or Indonesian National Army.

But an army needs a leader who is respected and a government needs a defense minister who understands military matters. Since this army had never fought a war, how was one to know whom to appoint? As unusual but ingenious solution was found to this problem.

In 1945 Sudirman became our first commander in chief through a poll that we organized. When the poll began there were seven candidates. After the first ballot, five were left; and after the second ballot, three remained: His Excellency Sultan Hamengku Buwono, Sudirman, and Urip Sumoharjo. A consensus was reached that Sultan Hamengku Buwono would become minister of defense; Sudirman would become commander in chief, bearing in mind that a large proportion of TNI troops were former Peta members; and Urip Sumoharjo would be chief of staff of the KNIL element.

15

*

The Japanese Occupation

WILLIAM H. FREDERICK

When the Japanese arrived in Indonesia in 1942, they found there a colonial regime incapable of defending itself effectively and weakened in
a number of other respects. The decade-long threat of a Pacific war,
followed by the fall of Holland to the Nazis in 1940, left the Dutch colonial community isolated and deeply divided, relations between the
colonial government and Indonesian nationalists more difficult than
ever, and much of the colonial order in a state of suspension or disarray.
In the month before the Japanese landed on Java, the Dutch pursued a
terrifying scorched earth policy, and a widespread lawlessness over-
took the countryside in many areas as colonial authority began to dis-
solve. This signaled a dramatic end to the Netherlands East Indies
before most Indonesians had laid eyes on a single Japanese soldier.

The Japanese intention of destroying the mystique of white supremacy in Indonesia, which was accomplished swiftly, required considerably less effort than their primary purpose, which was to replace
European rule with something more appropriate to the changing
times. In Japanese eyes and the long view, this meant not an independent Indonesia but a program of "Meiji-fication"—guided modernization on the Japanese pattern—that was termed the "New Order."
Initial energies were therefore devoted to restoring peace and quiet,
stabilizing prices and social restlessness, and making critical repairs.
Nationalism was discouraged, though mass mobilization movements

were launched in order to pull together support for the Greater East Asian War. Understandably, the Japanese had no desire to promote social ferment or to revolutionize Indonesian life, though they frequently expressed the hope of supplanting its "colonial mentality" with a more vigorous and confident indigenous outlook. Nor did the Japanese seriously entertain notions of "Nipponizing" Indonesians and their culture, though they made limited and thoroughly pragmatic efforts to teach the rudiments of their language and to proselytize some of the values of their civilization. Beyond a successful conclusion to the war, what Japan desired from the occupied regions of Indonesia was that they become model clients, self-confident but at best semi-autonomous, within a Greater East Asia Co-Prosperity Sphere centered on Tokyo. This could be achieved, the occupying forces believed, by applying Asian wisdom and experience to Asian problems—in general, translating Japanese successes into Indonesian ones—and by tutoring or prodding Indonesians into fruitful cooperation.

In this broad effort the Japanese were for the most part disappointed. They were neither well informed about nor especially comfortable in their new Indonesian environment, and they discovered before long how spurious were the implications behind their "Asia for the Asians" slogan. Urban administration and attempts to mobilize city dwellers were never entirely satisfactory, for example, and occupation authorities exercised at best a tenuous control over the countryside. The new style of colonial rule, which to Indonesians appeared unpredictable, arrogant, and brutal in entirely unfamiliar ways, engendered widespread fear. Economic policies, aimed at improving the former system at the same time as dealing with the exigencies of war, failed in these objectives and earned a bitter response from all classes of Indonesians. Heavy-handed promotion of Japanese rice-growing methods was deeply resented by local officials and farmers alike; insistence on regional self-sufficiency brought dislocation and, in some areas, deprivation; coercive recruitment of labor and collection of rice were hated and avoided whenever and however possible; and these difficulties contributed to the rise of corruption in all corners of public and private life. With the luxury of retrospection, it is possible to see that these circumstances were often far more complex than meets the eye: total rice production may actually have increased in many areas, for example, but gone unrecorded and poorly distributed. The general conditions thus provoked, however, contributed substantially to the contemporary In-

A frame from a Japanese propaganda film shot in Indonesia in the last weeks of the second World War. The film of a marching crowd was accompanied by voices singing "Indonesia Raya", the national anthem of Indonesia whose words appeared on the screen. In this frame are the opening words: "Indonesia my homeland, land where my blood is shed". The banner bears the slogan: "Indonesia-Japan, One life, One death".

Courtesy of Stichting film en Wetenschap, Utrecht, Holland.

donesian view of the occupation as a dramatic change from the "normal times" preceding it, as a period of fear and suffering that ended—with a certain justice—in a revolution during which the Japanese became public targets quite as much as the returning Dutch.

In many important respects, however, the occupation was, rather than a cataclysmic experience, a transitional one for Indonesia, though not precisely of the sort the Japanese had intended. That such was the case may in part be accounted for by recalling that, after mid-1943, the Japanese military position in the Pacific grew weaker and occupation authorities felt compelled to be increasingly responsive to Indonesian nationalist pressures in exchange for promises of cooperation in the war effort. Two additional factors, often forgotten despite their significance, were also at work. One is that the occupation period was one of comparative tranquillity, not the physical turbulence generally associated with wartime. Indonesia passed the war far from the lines of battle, and Japanese with experience elsewhere portrayed the archipelago as a haven in which sugared coffee could be sipped at leisure and the native population was thoroughly domesticated. Though this view was limited and naive, it nevertheless reflected with a certain accuracy the surface calm of occupied Indonesia, in particular the absence of open violence there.

The second factor is the high degree of confluence between some Japanese reform policies on the one hand and a number of long-standing ideas of modernist-nationalist Indonesians on the other. The occupation government, for example, eliminated separate forms of government, administration, and law for Indonesian and European communities, as well as for rural and urban areas; created a single line of administrative responsibility where previously Dutch and indigenous civil servants' responsibilities had overlapped; similarly consolidated the educational system by removing discrepancies between "European" and "Native" schooling tracks; and showed an aversion to the "feudal mentality" of the colonial *pangreh praja* (indigenous civil service), promoting a more modern, engaged style of pumping new blood into the civil service system. These policies and attitudes closely echoed those espoused by progressive Indonesians under Dutch rule, and they found it logical, whatever else they may have thought of the Japanese regime, to take advantage of this correspondence.

These conditions favored the rise to real, if still rather circumscribed, power of a varied class of educated and politically interested Indonesians who had been associated with the prewar independence movement, the *pergerakan*. These intellectuals had attempted to combat Dutch rule by building their own modernizing Indonesian state within the colonial one, in preparation for the day when European imperial initiative failed against indigenous pressures. They believed themselves to represent the best hope for an Indonesia of the future, the rightful leaders of Indonesian society as a whole in the modern age. In short, they unapologetically sought to replace not only Europeans (whose rule they considered immoral and unprogressive) but traditional elites (whose power they thought feudalistic and backward-looking) in positions of authority, and to answer the needs of the masses by creating a forward-looking, reformed Indonesian society. While different groups had different political ideas about how all this might best be accomplished, they were broadly united in their national, modernist outlook and in their self-identification as leaders.

In the 1930s these intellectuals had expressed an obvious interest in Japan, mostly as an example of an Asian nation that had successfully answered the Western challenge, though exceptionally few became "pro-Japanese." During the occupation, they were confused and often fearful of the Japanese, and yet could not help but admire them for their victory over the Dutch. Their eventual position during the occupation was even more severely pragmatic than that adopted earlier: they cautiously utilized every opportunity to acquire authority in their own society, finding wherever possible a niche in Japan's new order of things. There was a reasonably large number of such positions available, not only because Japan's internment of the Dutch left openings in the administration, but also because occupation authorities were by temperament and circumstances disposed to favor modernist intellectuals as leaders. Since the Japanese were also well aware of this group's anti-colonialist bent, the relationship was never entirely trusting, but it was the best the Japanese could hope for and, on the whole, the most familiar and workable that Indonesian intellectuals could find. In this way the occupation was shaped, for a significant group of Indonesians, as much by continuities as by changes inherent in Japanese rule.

Something similar may be said about a younger generation of Indonesians, the celebrated *pemuda* who seemed to emerge suddenly in 1945 as a new and dynamic social force. Although the Japanese, unlike the Dutch, did pay special attention to youth—largely urban and schooled in modern systems—they did so to control rather than to radicalize them, to harness rather than unleash their energies. The occupation government refused to arm youth or to permit more than a few even to train with arms; most youth organizations during the occupation required instead heavy doses of drilling, manual labor, and lectures on politics, economics, and patriotic behavior. The style of much of this may have been somewhat unfamiliar, but the content was far from new. Most of the youth concerned had social and intellectual roots in the pre war *pergerakan* and had been cultivated by a plethora of youth organizations. During the occupation period they discovered that their principal mentors continued to be *pergerakan* intellectuals, on whom the Japanese were forced to rely, and to whom Japanese goals of discipline, self-confidence, idealism, and patriotic thinking were quite acceptable, for precisely these attributes had been emphasized in prewar programs for youth.

The *pemuda* were therefore figuratively—and very often literally— the children of the *pergerakan* and its leadership, a circumstance the Japanese occupation did not much alter. At the end of the period, when independence seemed imminent, differences did open up between youth and their elders with established positions in the new order. The *pemuda*, for example, turned on the Japanese, attempted to mobilize the general population, and pressed leaders for a bolder stance against both Japanese and Dutch. The quarrel, however, was essentially one over methods rather than direction. It was caused primarily by the changed role of intellectuals, who now acted to safeguard the state which they stood on the verge of inheriting, rather than Japanese effects on youth. *Pemuda* had a vested interest only in the nation as an idea, and were naturally inclined to be less cautious than their elders in reaction to crisis and in their invocation of the popular will. For the most part, however, they belonged squarely in the same intellectual world as their mentors, whose social views they came to share and whom they eventually joined, imitated, or replaced. This expansion of a new elite represented the most important continuity which the Japanese occupation furthered rather than diverted, and the one which perhaps has been of greatest relevance to Indonesia since.

16

*

The Story of a Japanese

AN INTERVIEW WITH

SHIGETADA NISHIJIMA

I'll be completely honest: before the war I knew absolutely nothing about Indonesia; in fact, I studied sociology in Japan. At that time, Japan was fascist, and I joined in revolts against the government of the day. Soon after I entered high school, which was in 1930, I was arrested by the police, because in those days even studying Marxism was banned and whoever did so was branded as a communist. I was arrested and detained for about two or three weeks, and then released; of course the school punished me too. Then in 1931 I was arrested again by the police, and in 1932 was expelled from school and immediately went underground. I worked underground trying to stir up the people against the government, and so on. But really, you know, I was too young. A year later, I was again arrested by the police. This time I was tortured in all sorts of ways, and put into prison. You see, I had ideals, or you might say a "direction," and I suppose it was leftish for those days.

Later on, I was picked up again and forced to join the army, where I ended up for one and a half years. In those days the situation in Japan was critical, because by then the Japanese army had already entered Manchuria and China. I was worried that if I stayed in Tokyo, or even Japan, I would be sent away as a soldier to join in the invasion of those places. So I looked for a way of leaving the country. It was pointed out to me that some people had gone to Manchuria, or to the Philippines,

Shigetada Nishijima, long-time friend of Indonesia and rebel against Japanese "fascism" in the 1930's, photographed in his home in Tokyo in 1984.

Courtesy of the BBC.

but I was actually seeking somewhere even further away from Japan. Just after that, by chance I managed to get a job in the Chiyoda Store, or Warenhuis Chiyoda as it was known in Dutch, which had branches in Bandung, Jakarta, and Malang, with its headquarters in Surabaya. Now, after I arrived in the Netherlands East Indies, I began to see differences between the Dutch and the Indonesians, very great differences. The Dutch were, you could say, incredibly rich, but as for most Indonesians. . . . their lives were full of suffering. My sympathy for those who were being trampled on was already there, so, don't you see, that is how my respect for, or rather my interest in Indonesians began.

Many foreigners suspected that all the Japanese who were there before the war were spies or something; that's not true at all. As an employee of a store, I was very interested in Indonesia. Of course I also wanted to serve, to give moral support to the Indonesian people, because I was also learning a lot there by watching the situation.

Just as the war was about to begin, most of the Japanese in the Netherlands East Indies were evacuated to Japan. But several friends from work and I were forced to stay behind to look after the interests of the store. At the time, I had a wife and two children who had already gone back to Japan. In December 1941 we were all arrested and sent straight to Australia. We were there for approximately eight months, after which there was an exchange of prisoners. Many of the Japanese held there were allowed to return to Japan, in exchange for American or English people held in Japan. So I left for home, but only got as far as Singapore. From Singapore most of the others went on to Japan, but I purposely turned south and headed straight for Indonesia.

By this time Indonesia was occupied by Japanese forces. Was there not danger for a Japanese who sympathized with the Indonesians?

No, not at all. And anyway, I made a point of not telling my friends, especially the Japanese ones, that I sympathized with the Indonesians.

At any rate, I returned to Indonesia in October 1942, and in that same month the chief naval liaison officer, Rear Admiral Maeda, opened his office. Even though I didn't know Maeda himself, I did know a certain Sato Nobohide, who had been in Jakarta before the war. He was Maeda's chief assistant on political affairs. To make a long story short, I got a job dealing with Indonesian affairs. We all had become involved in managing Indonesian affairs, so I got to know all the leaders at that time: Sukarno, Hatta, and the others. They always opened their hearts to me and my other friends, and told us that they believed Indonesia had to become independent. That will, that desire, made a great impact on me. Besides, Japan, the Japanese government itself, had promised, as it was about to invade Indonesia, that Indonesia would be given its independence. The "Indonesia Raya" and the red and white flag were all to be permitted. The radio constantly broadcast this propaganda. As it turned out, after the Japanese landed these things were forbidden. The flag was not allowed to be flown, the national anthem was not allowed to be sung, and political organizations were completely banned. They wanted to run everything just like the Japanese nation. So of course all the Indonesians were muttering about this: Wasn't this different from the propaganda of the Japanese? Everywhere complaints were heard, and those who did try to work towards independence were arrested, branded as communists, labelled as being anti-Japanese, and so on. When anyone was arrested, many people would run to me or to other friends like Sato, to try to get them released. It was the military police, known then as the *kenpeitai*, who arrested them all. So when they were arrested, we would rush over to the *kenpeitai* headquarters, and say, "These are our friends," and so on, and they would be released. That's how it was.

In 1943 it was announced in Japan that Burma and the Philippines would be granted independence. The former Netherlands East Indies would be granted the right of mere political participation, termed "joining in politics." This is what made people like Mohammad Hatta furious. "Why has Burma been given independence, the Philippines been given independence, while we are only allowed to 'join in politics'? It would have been better not to announce it at all."

By that time the tides of war had begun to turn a little and it was retreat, retreat, retreat. The will of the people, not just their leaders, had really begun to awaken, so Japan had to change its attitude. But even if the Japanese forces in Java had sympathized with the people, they couldn't have done anything; they had to wait for directions from Japan, from the central command. The central command didn't understand the situation in Indonesia, however. They thought, "Well, the people there aren't too strong-willed, there are raw materials, and there is oil, there's this and that, so it would be much better not to give them independence now. If we grant them independence, then they probably won't go along with the Japanese government anymore." So in September 1944, Prime Minister Koisho promised that the Japanese government would grant independence to Indonesia "at some time in the future." While of course Indonesia thanked him, Indonesians were also very annoyed. Why "at some time in the future"?! Java was then under the 16th Army, Sumatra was under the 25th Army and the other areas were under the Navy, so consequently they were zig-zagging all over the place trying to settle on a single course of action. As time dragged on, the view became even more strongly felt: "What do the Japanese think they're doing?!"

But certain Japanese were, by now, beginning to realize that Indonesian nationalism was a powerful sentiment. One of them was Rear Admiral Maeda, who often met Sukarno, Hatta, Subarjo, and others, listening to their wishes and desires. Although he couldn't speak their language, I was one of his interpreters, along with the late Ogura Suzumi and several others. This is how their wishes were conveyed to him. So Maeda began to think, "Ah, something must be done about this."

In February or March of 1945, there was a naval meeting in Surabaya led by the late Admiral Shibata. The three of us—Maeda, Suzumi, and myself—all went along, as did various other people from the area under the jurisdiction of the Navy. There, decisions were made on when independence should be granted. What should Indonesia consist of? Certainly Java, but what about Sumatra, and how about the other areas? All this was decided. At that time, leaders like Shibata, Maeda, and others, were already sure that the Indonesian nationalist movement was like the current of a river, a river which flows. No matter what we did, we couldn't stop it. That thought was already there. Thus it was the will and desires of the nationalist leaders which made such an impact on and influenced the Japanese like Maeda and me. If they hadn't revealed their longings, and had just kept their feelings to themselves, how could we have given them anything? So of course I acknowledge that at that time the Indonesian will was so strong that we were influenced by it.

17

*

The Point of No Return

BENEDICT R. O'G. ANDERSON

In the world of the 1980s, in which old-style colonies have largely disappeared, while over 160 nation-states are represented at the United Nations, the independence of Indonesia seems unremarkable, even natural. Under what conceivable circumstances could the country still be a colony today, one might ask. Forty years ago, however, when Indonesia became the first colony in postwar Asia to proclaim its independence, nothing seemed less natural or inevitable. For in the 1930s the Dutch had easily dominated the colony's 80,000,000 inhabitants with less than 40,000 poorly-trained troops. In 1942, the Japanese had seized the colony in a matter of weeks, and had no trouble with the natives for the next three years. What in 1945 seemed natural and inevitable was that the prewar colonial order would be restored as soon as Japan had been defeated. Precisely for this reason, Indonesians were eventually forced to join that minority of colonized peoples who have fought bloody wars to defend their freedom. But that they were given the chance to do so at all was the result of a chain of circumstances unforeseeable by anyone at the time.

In May 1945, the immediate future of the colony seemed crystal-clear. Nazi Germany's collapse had made Japan's defeat a mere matter of time. General Douglas MacArthur, who had retaken Manila in February, had been assigned by the Allies the task of reconquering the former Netherlands East Indies. Although tiny Holland had herself only just been liberated from Nazi occupation, her colonial officials, long attached to MacArthur, believed that America's overwhelming military power would quickly restore their former colony to them. But when Truman, Stalin, and Attlee met at Potsdam on July 16, they decided, for reasons having nothing to do with Indonesia, that the task of reconquering it would be transferred, as of August 15, to Lord Mountbatten's South East Asia Command, which had only just retaken Rangoon. Dutch leaders were appalled by the change. The British were quite unprepared for their new assignment: they were logistically overextended; their military strength was incomparably weaker than America's; and their eyes were fixed, first and foremost, on Malaya and Singapore, not on the Netherlands East Indies.

Tokyo, meanwhile, having now lost Burma and the Philippines, and aware of its weakness in the archipelago, decided to offer the Indonesians the sorts of dubious independence it had conferred on the Burmese and Filipinos in 1943, hoping thereby to win more active support from indigenous political leaders and their popular followings. But scarcely had this decision been made when Tokyo learned that the Soviet Union was about to end its neutrality in the Pacific war and invade Manchuria. Accordingly, on July 29, the Japanese government instructed its proconsul in Southeast Asia, Field Marshal Terauchi, at his headquarters in Saigon, to arrange the announcement of a Committee to Prepare Indonesian Independence the minute the Russians moved.

Thus on August 7, just hours before the Soviet Union declared war, Terauchi made his announcement, completely unaware that the whole Pacific war would be over within the week. The day before, August 6, an American atomic bomb had obliterated Hiroshima, and no one in Japan paid the slightest attention to the Indies thereafter. But far away in the tropics Terauchi proceeded according to his obsolete instructions. On the morning of August 9, as Nagasaki was incinerated, Indonesia's two best-known nationalist politicians, Sukarno and Hatta, were flown to Saigon. On August 11, Terauchi formally installed them as chairman and vice-chairman of the Preparatory Committee in a ceremony at his elegant villa in the highland resort of Dalat, French Vietnam's equivalent of Darjeeling. With the same unreal sedateness the two leaders were then flown home, stopping overnight in Singapore to pick up three Sumatran members for their Preparatory Committee. Thus they landed in Jakarta on the very same day that the Japanese government agreed to surrender unconditionally to the Allies, August 14.

A frame from a newsreel film of Sukarno with his first cabinet in August 1945, guarded by Indonesian soldiers still wearing Japanese uniforms. Back row (left to right): (second from left) Ali Sastroamidjojo; Sukardjo Wirjopranoto. Middle row (left to right): Sartono; A.G. Pringodigdo; Prof. Supomo; A.A. Maramis. Front row (left to right): (second from left in dark jacket) Amir Sjarifuddin; Ahmad Subardjo; Sukarno; Hatta; Wiranatakusuma.

Courtesy of EMI/Pathé.

So unimaginably fast had the surrender come that Mountbatten, the scheduled liberator of the Indies, was still thousands of miles away. Furthermore, he was under orders not to accept any Japanese local surrenders in Southeast Asia until MacArthur had done so in Tokyo itself, which did not occur until September 2. However, concerned that in the interim desperate and vengeful Japanese commanders in Southeast Asia might attempt to create political *faits accomplis*, Mountbatten radioed them strict orders to freeze the political status quo everywhere, on pain of severe punishment for any violations.

In Jakarta, the speed of Tokyo's surrender came as a traumatic shock to the Japanese officers. As one of them later put it, one felt like a passenger in an express train brought to an instant dead stop. But decisions had to be made on how to respond to Mountbatten's commands. To those officers with direct governmental responsibilities, it appeared only prudent to obey: their own lives, and the future of their emperor and their country, seemed at stake. Others, however, in less exposed positions and sympathetic to Indonesian national aspirations, felt that Japan would be eternally dishonored if the independence she had promised Indonesia was now opportunistically cancelled. Of these the most important was shrewd, liberal-minded Rear Admiral Maeda, head of the Japanese Navy's liaison office in Jakarta, who had wide informal contacts in Indonesian nationalist circles.

By August 15, the news of Japan's unconditional surrender was generally known, not merely among the established nationalist leaders, but also among the *pemuda*. These youthful militants, who for months had listened to radio broadcasts of Japanese military "victories" ever nearer to Tokyo, and thus had become increasingly impatient with their elders' passive acceptance of Japanese policies, now decided to act. That night a *pemuda* delegation came to Sukarno's house to demand that he and Hatta declare national independence at once, and without any involvement by the defeated Japanese. Fearful of a violent Japanese crackdown, the two leaders refused, arguing instead that they should work through Terauchi's committee. Angry and frustrated, the delegates marched off to rejoin their comrades.

A few hours later Sukarno and Hatta were awakened from their beds, pushed into waiting cars, and driven to Rengasdengklok, a small township northeast of Jakarta. Their *pemuda* abductors again tried to force them to proclaim independence, but again they refused. Meanwhile the dreaded *kenpeitai* had begun a manhunt for the missing leaders.

It was at this point, the morning of August 16, that Maeda made his decisive intervention. Using his private contacts, he reached the group in Rengasdengklok and negotiated the return of Sukarno and Hatta by promising a real declaration of independence and guaranteeing the physical safety of the abductors. Hinting that if they were inflexible there might be savage rioting, Maeda talked the military authorities into permitting a declaration of independence, provided it could be worded so as not to contravene Mountbatten's orders directly. The final language, worked out at Maeda's house that night, ran as follows: "We, the Indonesian people, hereby declare Indonesia's independence. Matters concerning the transfer of power and other matters will be executed in an orderly manner and in the shortest possible time." To the Japanese in positions of responsibility, these undramatic words said, "Go ahead, but with no mention of any transfer of sovereignty, and no rioting!" At 10:00 A.M. on August 17, in the small yard of his home, Sukarno read out this odd proclamation of independence, as the red and white Indonesian national flag was hoisted at his side. Within hours activist youths had sent the word out over radio transmitters and the telegraph system. The next day the members of the Preparatory Committee, now calling itself the Indonesian National Committee, elected Sukarno and Hatta president and vice-president of the newborn Republic of Indonesia.

Six weeks were to pass before Mountbatten's so-called liberation forces arrived. Meantime, thanks to *pemuda* bravado, Maeda's mediation, and the prudence of Sukarno and Hatta, a real if gradual transfer of power into Indonesian hands took place. In an extraordinary, largely spontaneous upheaval, independence was locally proclaimed in town after town, village after village, no longer in the ambiguous phrases of August 17, but in the passionate language of national revolution: *merdeka atau mati*, freedom or death! Japanese-trained military units, forcibly disbanded after August 18 at Allied demand, rapidly reformed on an independent and local basis. Everywhere demoralized or sympathetic Japanese handed their weapons over to militant *pemuda*. So it was that when the British—meaning English officers and Indian and Gurkha troops—finally appeared at the end of September, together with a few Dutch officials, they found to their astonishment an armed revolutionary resistance confronting them. It cost three weeks of brutal combat and the life of an English general to gain control of Surabaya. After that Mountbatten, in any case preoccupied with Burma and Malaya, lost any heart for reimposing Dutch colonialism by British arms.

The Dutch, however, faced with the permanent loss of the second most populous and profitable colony in the world, remained determined to hang on. It took four years of intermittent fighting finally to change their minds. Indonesians have never forgotten that their independence was dearly paid for in blood, even if they do not always recognize how fortunate they were that the price was not even higher. That is why the cautious, unheroic words spoken by Sukarno on 17 August 1945 can still bring tears to their eyes.

18

*

The Writing of the Proclamation

AN INTERVIEW WITH

THREE PARTICIPANTS

Adam Malik: I worked in the Domei news agency, where all the telegrams arriving from Tokyo were translated into English and then
broadcast. We dealt with news not only from this office but also news
taken from the Allies. Of course, that from the Allies was not allowed
to be broadcast; it was top secret and was only given to the Japanese
leaders. So for those of us in Domei, much of the news we read was
objective. But the news bulletins Domei then published were quite the
opposite! When the Japanese were defeated at Guadalcanal, they
merely said there had been heavy fighting in Guadalcanal and men-
tioned nothing about their defeat. Still, we knew that they had been
defeated! And when Hiroshima was bombed, they didn't say it was an
atom bomb. That's the way it was.

As we were making preparations towards the end of the Japanese
period, two conflicting lines of thought emerged among the leaders.
Bung Karno and his friends were summoned to Saigon by the Japanese. When they returned from Saigon, they were very pleased because
Field Marshal Terauchi had promised that Indonesia's independence
would be proclaimed in no more than three months' time, and since it
was then July [actually, 14 August] that meant in September [October].
My friends and I, who had been following the progress of the war, had
known ever since May that the Japanese were retreating, retreating, retreating, on all fronts. The climax came when we heard of the bomb-

Rear Admiral Tadashi Maeda (1898–1977) who had some sympathy with the aims of the republicans, photographed in May 1945. The writing on the photograph says: "Jakarta—Maeda".

ings in Japan, on Hiroshima and Nagasaki. That was around the beginning of August, I think. We urged Bung Karno and Bung Hatta to proclaim independence immediately, irrespective of Japanese wishes. But they said, "No, we can't, Japan can't possibly lose; we ought to wait for instructions from Tokyo before we make the announcement. We can make preparations, but we can't announce it." We opposed this. We wanted independence to be announced because, in our opinion, if it were left to the Japanese the announcement would conflict with the responsibilities they had been given by the Allies and it was therefore unlikely that they would allow it. If we announced independence now, ourselves, the world would know that we were not independent simply because of instructions from Tokyo. That was the argument. But Bung Karno and Bung Hatta still didn't want to announce independence, so we made up our minds—it was now the evening of the 12th or the 13th—that if by the following day Bung Karno still hesitated, and Bung Hatta were also still in doubt, then we should just carry them off. We got everything ready in Rengasdengklok, and we took them there. Actually we wanted to proclaim independence right away on August 15. When we brought them to Rengasdengklok, Sukarno was very angry at being coerced like this and so was Hatta. But it was only then that Bung Karno began to realize that he might have got it wrong, so he said: "If it really is true that the Allies have defeated Japan, and if it is true that Japan has surrendered, then I will make the announcement, but who can convince me?" We agreed to call the most senior-ranking Japanese. At that time, Bung Karno asked for the chief of general affairs (sōmubuchō), a certain Colonel Nakayama [actually, Major General Nishimura.] Of course there was no hope of getting him, because he was in the army. So we chose Rear Admiral Maeda. He was in the navy, and our relationship with the navy was much closer because Subarjo, who had come out to see us in Rengasdengklok, worked for the Navy. Eventually, we returned from Rengasdengklok to Maeda's house bringing Bung Karno, and there Maeda explained to Bung Karno and Hatta: "It's quite true, we have lost. So you see, now I can't do anything, the Japanese can't do anything, it's up to the *pemuda* and the people of Indonesia if they want to proclaim (independence)." But Bung Karno still wasn't prepared to do so that night. He asked to meet the *gunseikan* [the Japanese head of the military administration, who at that time was General Yamamoto] or the *sōmubuchō*, as they were the two most senior officials. Eventually, the person who did receive him from the First Army said, "Yes, we have to obey the Allies, so we can't give the Indonesians permission to proclaim independence." You see how their tune had changed from the promises that they had made in Saigon; it was all very different now. So we forced Bung Karno: "Tomorrow morning the proclamation must be made," meaning the morning of August 17. The night before, we prepared the text of the proclamation at Rear Admiral Maeda's house; it was very simple. In the morning, it was read out in Bung Karno's house in Pegangsaan in Jakarta.

Shigetada Nishijima: On August 15, the emperor himself announced the capitulation. At that time, psychologically, most of the Japanese people in Jakarta and other parts of Indonesia were in a state of total collapse; everyone had almost completely lost hope, and some people committed suicide, and so on. Then the Allies ordered that the status quo had to be maintained, which meant that we could not do anything. The Army was too busy sorting itself out to receive Sukarno and Hatta. So the three of us—I was asked to come along as an interpreter —went to see Rear Admiral Maeda. Then they questioned Maeda, and the question asked by Sukarno was: "Is this news true or not?"

The next day, the 16th, I was summoned by Maeda in the morning. You see, Subarjo had been to Maeda's house and told him that Sukarno and Hatta had disappeared, most likely arrested by the army to "safeguard the peace." So Maeda ordered me: "Quickly now, you must find out where those two people are. Because the situation is so critical, while the leaders aren't here, there could be trouble between the Indonesians and the Japanese." Now I knew that many *pemuda* had often said, "We don't want to receive our independence as a gift from the Japanese." Many of them had said that, including Chairul Saleh, Sukarni, Adam Malik, B.M.Diah, Wikana, and others. So I went straight in search of Wikana and said, "I've known you for a long time, and I've always wanted to be a bridge between our two peoples, why don't you trust me? Just don't do anything foolish." So after that, they went to Rengasdengklok, where Sukarno and Hatta had been kidnapped by the *pemuda*. I didn't go there with them, but eventually Sukarno, Mohammed Hatta, and Subarjo (who had gone out to Rengasdengklok in pursuit of the two leaders) were brought to Maeda's house, escorted by Chairul Saleh and Sukarni.

So we began to talk. Subarjo said to me, "I promised that the proclamation would definitely be announced tonight. If it isn't, my throat

will be cut." Then Maeda said, "Do calm down, you *pemuda*, we understand what you want, but don't do anything rash," and so on. He
went on and on trying to appease them, but they still didn't want to
take any notice. It was nearly midnight when Sukarno said to Sukarni,
"Now don't start a rebellion." Then Sukarni stood up and I followed
him, Trimurti came with me, and we three went out to make sure that
everything was still calm and prepared, but by the time we got to the
radio station the *kenpeitai* were already there guarding it. We were all
nearly arrested, but were released after I had telephoned Rear Admiral
Maeda. And when we returned, they still hadn't finished talking. Then
Maeda telephoned Major General Yamamoto, and told him to come
over, but he refused; then he called Saito,who was once ambassador to
Indonesia, but he also refused; finally Maeda was told to go to Major
General Nishimura's house, and he went there with Sukarno and
Hatta. But Nishimura took the attitude that the Japanese could no
longer do anything because of the status quo order. So everyone returned to Maeda's house and we held a round table conference. There
was talking, and more talking, for a very long time but without reaching any agreement, and finally the proclamation was drawn up. Try
and picture the scene in Maeda's house: in the dining room, there was a
round table, and around this sat Maeda, Sukarno, Hatta, Subarjo, myself, and Yoshizumi from the army, and we discussed what the text of
the proclamation should be.

The *pemuda* were waiting outside—Sukarni, Chairul Saleh, and the
others. They had asked for a very tough-sounding text, something
sensational. They wanted to seize power from the Japanese. Now I myself was a Japanese, and what's more, I knew a bit about international
law, and knew that if the Japanese admitted that they had agreed to a
text like that, the Allies would be very angry with us. So the words had
to be juggled around and there had to be changes. One of these
changes involved the word *penyerahan* or "surrender," which implies
that something is given, surrendered, and we weren't having this. Nor
would we accept *perebutan,* meaning "seizure." So in the end we agreed
on *pemindahan kekuasaan* or "transfer of power." Now they also wrote
diusahakan at first, meaning "will be attempted." This word was soft,
too soft, and it was Sukarno himself who wrote instead *diselenggarakan,*
meaning "will be carried out."

To tell you the truth, the Indonesians didn't want to admit the Japanese involvement. I could understand this point of view, because I was

arrested again by the Dutch and interrogated over this matter. Neither Maeda nor I myself admitted that we had participated in this affair, because at that time the Dutch wanted to brand the proclamation as a Japanese creation, because the date read '05 (2605). Now 2605 was the Japanese year, and they had written it that way rather than '45 (1945). I felt strongly about this matter, but I could also understand how the Indonesians felt that this proclamation was a truly historic event and did not want to admit the Japanese involvement.

Wangsa Wijaya: I worked in Putera, and then I worked in the Hokokai [both Japanese-sponsored organizations] but I also assisted Mohammad Hatta. And because of that, I witnessed the events in Rear Admiral Maeda's house the night before the proclamation. All the *pemuda* were gathered there; I was also a *pemuda* then. That night, I saw Bung Karno and Bung Hatta sign the proclamation. Before this, Bung Hatta had requested all those present to sign the proclamation, but no one dared to, no one wanted to sign it. Then one of my friends, Sukarni, asked that the proclamation be signed only by Bung Karno and Bung Hatta. So just those two signed it. After that, Bung Karno requested us all to meet at ten o'clock the following morning, a Friday, at his house at No. 56 Pegangsaan Timur. By nine o'clock in the morning we had all gathered, and at ten minutes to ten o'clock, Bung Hatta arrived. Then at ten o'clock, after making a short speech, Bung Karno announced the proclamation. The atmosphere was of course rather tense because at any moment the Japanese could have attacked, but we were all prepared to face any eventualities. There were about thirty people gathered inside the building; outside were *pelopor* (young pioneers) led by Sudiro. And by eleven o'clock, we had dispersed. Yes, we really were very tense indeed, but we were all prepared to sacrifice ourselves if necessary.

19

*

Sukarno the Politician

JOHN D. LEGGE

The Japanese occupation of the Indies was a period of opportunity for the leaders who had shaped the pre-war nationalist movement. The Japanese not only destroyed the myth of Dutch omnipotence, they also provided a political framework within which nationalist leaders were able to consolidate their position and prepare for the situation which would follow Japan's ultimate surrender. For Sukarno, one of the members of that elite, it created very special opportunities, for it was peculiarly suited to the exercise of his own political skills.

In the late 1920s Sukarno had made a spectacular beginning as a nationalist leader. As chairman of the PNI he discovered his great gifts of oratory, and his speeches dwelt upon the injustices and humiliations of colonial rule. He was the prophet of Indonesian unity. The Indonesian islands, spread along the equator and containing a large number of distinct ethnic and linguistic groups, were not natural candidates for united nationhood. Dutch rule had helped to shape them into a unity and later the revolutionary struggle was to confirm the nation's sense of identity. But it was Sukarno more than any other who created among the diverse peoples of the archipelago a vision of themselves as one nation. For that he suffered arrest, imprisonment, and exile. Later, his sparkling mercurial style, his personal magnetism, his superb political resourcefulness and his apparent self-assurance were to make him one of the most vivid leaders of the post-war world. It is possible that

Sukarno exhibits his charismatic powers at the great public rally at the Lapangan Ikada on 19th September 1945, when a potentially disastrous confrontation with Japanese peace-keeping forces was averted by Sukarno persuading the crowd, estimated to be up to 100,000 strong, to disperse peacefully.

Courtesy of Frans Mendur IPPHOS, Indonesia.

he was less self-assured than he appeared, that behind the surface appearance lay uncertainty and vulnerability. But outwardly he was poised and confident.

Nevertheless, in 1942, when he returned from his eight years of exile, that future destiny was far from clear. There were other leaders who might have a claim to share the spotlight with him and it was by no means certain at that time that Sukarno would emerge as the dominant figure. That he did so was in large part due to his role during the Japanese occupation, which we may divide into two important tasks: dealing with the Japanese and dealing with nationalist colleagues.

In order to make their rule acceptable, the Japanese were anxious to reach a swift understanding with prewar nationalist leaders and it was for this reason that Sukarno was appointed as an adviser to the new regime. Early in 1943 he became chairman of the Pusat Tenaga Rakyat, or Putera, a widely representative political organization, and later of a Central Advisory Council established in Jakarta. In due course Putera was replaced by the Jawa Hokokai, an organization more tightly under the control of the authorities but with Sukarno, again, as its chief Indonesian leader.

His appointment to these positions was a reflection of the reputation he had already achieved, but in occupying them his standing was confirmed and extended. In part this was due to his ease of access to the population at large. The Japanese had introduced wirelesses into villages to enable their wishes to be made known to the rural population; but these also made known the voice and ideas of Sukarno. No prewar nationalist leader had had such a channel of communication to the masses of Indonesia and by 1945 he was known more widely and more directly than any other person.

Such a public position had its dangers, and Sukarno had to walk a dangerous tightrope during the years of occupation. On the one hand he had to avoid offending the authorities. On the other he had to keep the brightness of his popular image and avoid appearing as a servile tool of the Japanese. For all their gestures of consultation with Indonesian leaders, and their later promises of independence, the Japanese were oppressive rulers. They banned independent political activity and forbade even the flying of the *merah-putih*, the red-and-white, or the singing of "Indonesia Raya." They commandeered food and labor. And Sukarno's job, in Japanese eyes, was to mobilize Indonesian support for the regime and its war effort. But that made him useful and gave him some bargaining power.

Some of the tasks he had to perform were unpleasant and indeed degrading. He had, for example, to support the notorious *romusha* program, in which perhaps more than 250,000 Indonesians were conscripted for forced labor in Java and overseas. It was a cruel program and the majority of those conscripted never returned to their homes. Other responsibilities carried less shame but were distasteful nevertheless. In his speeches Sukarno could not depart too far from Japanese requirements. He attacked the West—the best-remembered slogan was *Amerika kita setrika. Inggeris kita linggis* (We'll flatten the Americans, crush the English)—and was able to do so wholeheartedly. But he was also obliged to praise Japan for providing a new leadership for Asia. As occupation rule became harsher, such praise must have been difficult to give.

For all his apparent support of Japan, however, Sukarno later claimed that his speeches were really pure nationalism; and it is true that he did refer repeatedly to the idea of an Indonesian nation. Again and again his remarks about standing on the same side as Japan were followed by a call to his listeners to prepare themselves for a difficult future struggle. On occasion he was able to manipulate the Japanese into making concessions to nationalist feeling as when, by a premature announcement of the formation of Putera, he tricked them into accepting such an organization.

In his dealings with the conquerors, then, Sukarno steered a skillful middle course, giving the required degree of support to the Japanese but advancing nationalist ideas in his speeches and turning occupation policies to nationalist ends where it was possible to do so. And in presiding over the participation of Indonesians in the formal structures of government, he contributed to Indonesian readiness to take control of the state when Japanese power was withdrawn. A question must be asked nevertheless about his consistency at this time. Before the war he had followed the path of noncooperation with the Dutch. During the occupation he cooperated with the Japanese. Why the change?

We know now that, in 1934, Sukarno had feared exile and had been willing to promise to abstain from political activity in the future. In 1942 he was faced with a difficult choice: to accept a position under the Japanese and to use that position as best he might to serve the nationalist cause, or to refuse and turn to the dangers and impotence of underground activity. He made the choice, it seems without real hesitation. Certainly he found it congenial, after his exile, to hold public office and to have access again to the masses of Indonesia. He moved into his new role with fewer pangs of conscience than did his colleague Hatta, who preferred the Dutch to the Japanese fascists, and for whom cooperation seemed like a betrayal of principle. However, that is not to say that Sukarno's choice was made for purely selfish reasons. For him the great enemy was Western imperialism. He had long predicted that a war in the Pacific would bring Western domination to an end, and the Japanese invasion of the Indies appeared to fulfill his prophecy. Certainly it presented an opportunity to advance the nationalist cause, and unlike Dutch rule it was likely to be short lived. It was natural that Sukarno should quickly commit himself to the path of temporary cooperation with the conquerors.

His second task—that of dealing with his nationalist colleagues—also showed him to be a skillful persuader and conciliator. His aim within Putera and the Hokokai and in other bodies was always to smooth over differences and to emphasize harmony. In June 1945 his Pancasila speech was designed to provide a series of principles which all could accept, and for the time being he succeeded even in allaying the suspicions of Muslim leaders.

His skills as a unifier of the different streams of nationalist opinion were indeed formidable. Years later, as his presidency drew to a close, Sukarno became a controversial figure. He was accused of extravagance. He was seen as wasting the nation's resources in policies of national aggrandizement at home and dangerous adventure abroad, and as presiding over economic decline and runaway inflation. His critics at that time tended to forget his earlier contribution to the vision of Indonesian unity, and later his ability to conciliate and balance the opposing forces that might have torn the country apart in the 1950s and 1960s. These were, of course, precisely the skills which he displayed to such advantage between 1942 and 1945. He had then to protect his people as well as he could, while persuading his Japanese masters that he was serving their interests. And he had to persuade other sections of the nationalist movement of the need for unity.

These years show Sukarno at his most resourceful and successful. They confirmed his central position in the public eye and made him the indispensable leader in 1945. The same qualities were important in the years that followed. The struggle for independence was not always to be a united movement. There were deep divisions and rivalries—ideological divisions and differences about strategy—during the struggle against the Dutch. It was Sukarno's great contribution, in the midst of those conflicts, that he could serve as a potent symbol of unity during the years of revolution.

20

*

Sukarno the Man

AN INTERVIEW WITH

SURASTRI KARMA TRIMURTI

I first joined a political party in 1933. At that time I was in Bandung, and I studied under Bung Karno, learning about politics from him.

In the same year I committed an offence known at that time as *spreekdelict* (speech offence). However, I wasn't tried because the Dutch felt I was too young, and anyway, they assumed it was all due to Sukarno's influence. So I was considered not to be acting of my own free will, and was freed. Towards the end of the Dutch colonial period, after the Japanese entered the war against the Allies, I was put in an internment camp. At that time I was carrying my second child. When the Japanese came, I was freed from the internment camp, and I gave birth straight away. But not long afterwards, my husband was arrested by the Japanese, and a few weeks later I was also arrested, even though I had a tiny baby. The Japanese accused me of forming an anti-fascist, anti-Japanese movement. And they were quite right! You see, before the Japanese arrived we were already members of an illegal organization, which was anti-fascist in the sense that we supported democracy —that's what they were referring to. Somehow, the Japanese must have found out about that underground organization. But at that time I was not too heavily implicated—I mean that the accusations against me did not carry that much weight—because I had been interned since the start of the Pacific war. So the Japanese knew that I couldn't have been

Surastri Karma Trimurti as she is today. In 1933 she was a student of Sukarno's at the Bandung Institute of Technology.

Courtesy of S.K. Trimurti.

up to much during the fighting since I had been in a camp the whole time; that's how it was.

For the duration of the Japanese occupation, my husband was under arrest; he was in jail for three whole years. I was also detained, but I was placed under house arrest as the Japanese knew I had a tiny baby—perhaps they were a little sorry for me—and I remained so throughout 1942. Then in 1943 I was able to move to Jakarta with a guarantee from Bung Karno, who had asked the *kenpeitai* to release me. That's not to say I was completely free, for I was officially under Bung Karno's supervision.

When I arrived in Jakarta, to begin with I worked for Putera, which like all organizations at that time was a Japanese creation. After that I moved to the Jawa Hokokai, just to give me some kind of alibi since otherwise the Japanese would have suspected that I was up to some kind of mischief. It was only just before the proclamation in 1945 that we were able to organize activities, without Japanese knowledge, in order to prepare for independence.

After the Japanese capitulation, we got together with all the veteran independence fighters, although we still had no official organization because, as long as the Japanese were still around, no such organizations were allowed to be set up. So we just gathered to discuss our plans, and then carried them out immediately; that's how we worked. Hence we were able to move swiftly in our preparations for independence. After the proclamation, we searched for funds and other things, to do this and that. Some of us became fund-raisers, others had other tasks; the division of labor was quite spontaneous.

After the proclamation, I became a member of the Komite Nasional Indonesia (Indonesian National Committee or KNI). This body was set up to assist the president before there was a parliament or any other body, because by that time only the president and vice-president had been chosen. Individual national committees also sprang up spontaneously in the regions, but in Jakarta we had the Central National Committee and I took part in its various affairs.

The tasks of the Central National Committee were very similar to those of a parliament, and it established its own executive board, which held sittings to discuss politics, the budget, and other matters. I didn't sit on the executive board because although I had been elected I nominated someone else to take my place. I preferred to work in my political party, with the people.

In 1946, we set up a party. It was called the Partai Buruh Indonesia (Indonesian Labor Party, PBI), with its headquarters in Yogyakarta, and I was a member of its central committee. Some people might ask why I chose the Indonesian Labor Party. This is the reason: at that time I saw that our immediate priority was to take over the reins of power, to take control of the factories, offices, agriculture, and industries. All these things which used to belong to the enemy now had to become the property of the Republic of Indonesia. So the most important groups for me to contact were the workers, because workers were found everywhere, in farms, in factories, and in all kinds of circles including the communications network. Thus if we succeeded in mobilizing the workers, the takeover of power would be achieved more swiftly. And everything that we took control of we would write down as belonging to the Republic of Indonesia; it would not be the property of individuals, but of the republic.

During the course of this takeover of power, it was clear that lives might be lost. Now no one will willingly sacrifice his life unless he has a deeply philosophical outlook. Unless a person believes in the immortality of the soul, he will, of course begrudge the loss of his life. But in those days, people didn't regret giving up their lives because most of us were brought up in some sort of religion, and we all believed in the immortality of the soul. We believed that life carries on, it is only the flesh, the body, which changes.

Throughout the years 1933 to 1945 you were close to Sukarno. What sort of man was he? How well did you know him in those early years?

I really was very close to Bung Karno in those days, because I was one of his pupils. In Bandung in 1933 I lived in a hostel with other female cadres, right next door to his house. Thus we met very frequently, not just officially but also when we mixed socially with the family. Bung Karno's wife regarded me as one of her own children, and often asked me to run small errands for her. They often gave me guidance, as if I were one of the family.

What was my impression of Bung Karno at that time? He lived a very simple life. You see, his wife at that time was older than he was, and every time he wanted to go to his office or leave the house to do something for the struggle, he was given money, like a little boy being handed pocket money. I can't remember how much he got, whether it was 10 cents or 25, but each time she gave him money it was like a mother giving money to her child, just enough for his fares and a few other things, because he didn't even smoke in those days. So he was still completely unspoilt; yes, he was only thinking about the struggle. You see, when he was still young, he married an older woman, and this woman knew how to make a living, and she also willingly sacrificed everything she had for the good of the party and the revolution; that's my opinion of her. But later on, Bung Karno married several times, perhaps because in the past. . . let's say, a really hungry man will sometimes eat from more than one plate. Yes, we can excuse this, as long as not everyone copies him. There is certainly good in everyone, people have positive points and negative points. But in some people the positive points are very pronounced and in others the negative points are very pronounced; in some people the positive points can be very minor, as can be their negative points. That goes for everyone, whether they are gods, or spirits, or priests, or people who are considered to be of high rank. Everyone has faults, however small. On the other hand, however bad a person is, there must surely be a ray of goodness in him, only this hasn't been nurtured. That's why I have learned to respect people, whatever their outward characteristics. The older I grow, the more I understand that if only we could see within a criminal, for instance, we would find seeds of goodness, however small. The opposite is true too, and however righteous a person may appear to be, within him will be blemishes, you see. Thus there is no point in being too intolerant about people.

I regard Sukarno as my teacher, my friend, and my older brother. Because of this, I feel I am the person who probably dared most to criticize him honestly, but just face to face. I would not criticize him publicly.

21

*

The First Crises

AN INTERVIEW WITH

ADAM MALIK

When we made the proclamation on August 17, the Japanese govern-ment and the Japanese army had in fact not yet been affected. Not a single organized movement existed. When we began to announce the proclamation of independence, various small conflicts with the Japa-nese broke out. We distributed pamphlets throughout Jakarta, and all through Java. We sent the news through messengers, by telephone, and also by radio. That's why the proclamation was only heard in Sumatra on August 19—it was only broadcast then. In other places it was heard on August 21, so it didn't all happen simultaneously. But that didn't worry us, since what was important was to get on with things after we had made the proclamation. And we did many things. For example, we forcibly occupied several offices, the railways, and government build-ings. So you see, that's when these minor conflicts with the Japanese took place. But the Japanese still didn't want to move out yet.

On September 19 we called a mass meeting at Ikada Square, and this proved to be the decisive event. After we had gathered so many people together, the Japanese wanted to open fire and shoot a lot of people, in order to disperse them. However, seeing how excited the people were, they ordered them to disperse peacefully. The people agreed to go . . . as long as Sukarno came to speak to them. So that's why I fetched Bung Karno from the government offices, and took him to the square. It was in Ikada Square that he was first convinced that the Indo-

A still from the newsreel film of revolutionary youth riding on a railway engine near Jakarta shows the ferment of public enthusiasm for the new Republic during the weeks between the surrender of the Japanese Imperial Forces and the arrival in Java of British troops in late 1945.

Courtesy of EMI/Pathé.

nesian people really did want independence immediately. But he was worried because all Japanese soldiers were at their posts, guns ready. So he just spoke for about three minutes: "Brothers and sisters, I can understand your excitement after the proclamation, and because of that, let's guard this proclamation of independence of ours carefully and let's return home quietly." The people were disappointed, really disappointed. We *pemuda*, after seeing the people's disappointment, began that very night to take control and occupy the Japanese offices. We really wanted to raise our flag; of course there were incidents, but we didn't care.

The people's spirit had really flared up, and could no longer be restrained. Anyone who was alive at that time will certainly remember seeing how in every village, everything was ready and waiting, and if anyone went into those villages, they would definitely be searched. There was a genuine revolutionary atmosphere; no one was not for us. Psychologically, that was the right time to act, so we did, and it was these actions which caused the conflicts. For example, we took over the railway stations at Kota and Manggarai in Jakarta, and then occupied the Japanese offices. If anyone resisted, we arrested them. So, there we were, Japanese morale was declining because our people were rising, full of spirit, and it was this which ultimately hastened the Japanese defeat. And they were afraid to shoot, because there was an extraordinarily large number of people; so psychologically the Japanese had begun to...how would you say?...go downhill, and although we had known the Japanese as being very courageous, at that time they were no longer respected. Many of them were killed if they went into the villages. So the Japanese called upon us, called upon President Sukarno, to try and stop this. He got us together, and he said the people could not be disciplined. As long as the Japanese held out, and stayed put in their offices, there were bound to be incidents. Hence it would be better if the Japanese retreated. If possible, their weapons should be surrendered, leaving us to keep the peace. The Japanese didn't want to do this, except for a few individuals, and some of the navy leaders, several of whom gave us arms.

Ten days after the Ikada Square mass rally the first British troops set foot in Jakarta under Lt-Gen. Sir Philip Christison. Less than seven weeks had passed since the proclamation. But with the Allies (British and British-Indian troops) came Dutchmen, whose presence once again inflamed passions, particularly among the pemuda.

At that time, I was one of the heads of the Central National Committee, and also a member of the executive board. The Allies had just started arriving. They requested that there be no clashes with their troops. It was Christison who first issued an appeal: "Let's not have any clashes, we've just come to fetch out the internees." That was the start of the negotiations between us and them. Then the Dutch smuggled themselves in too. The English who were in command let all the internees out, but the Dutch internees were taken off by Dutch officials, who provided them with weapons. These were the ones who kept picking fights with us. That's why we were so angry with the Allies at that time. There were clashes in Sukabumi, Bandung, and other places because of that. If the English had taken out all the prisoners of war carefully, and hadn't allowed them to be armed, there would have been no incidents. Because we kept coming across so many armed Dutch, there were continuous shootings, and we were forced to retreat from Jakarta to Yogyakarta.

The republican government took refuge from the increasing violence in Jakarta and moved to Yogyakarta in January 1946. But, meanwhile, what had been happening in other parts of Indonesia?

It depended on the attitude of the Japanese forces in Medan, in Aceh, and elsewhere, on whether they handed over their offices without incident and gave us the opportunity to take control. We knew there was no point in fighting the Japanese any more. But because they were soldiers, there were several places where they didn't want to surrender; they didn't give up their offices, hand over their keys, or allow the Indonesian flag to be flown. They said, "We are meant to be carrying out the Allied orders, and the Allied Command has ordered us not to do anything except maintain the status quo." Maintaining the status quo between the Japanese and the Allies was fine, but we Indonesians had already made our proclamation, so there could be no status quo. It was up to us to make decisions. So inevitably there were more incidents.

There were outbreaks of violence wherever the tide of nationalist feelings was frustrated or opposed. But by far the bloodiest clash took place in Surabaya in October and November 1945.

After the Allies landed, if I'm not mistaken at Priok, under Lieutenant General Christison, we were obliged to negotiate. The first negotiations concerned the disarming and imprisonment of the Japanese forces. There were some Japanese who were pro-Indonesian and gave us weapons. Of course the Allies were very angry, because those weapons did not belong to us, and the Japanese were supposed to obey the rules and surrender their weapons to the Allies. But the Japanese didn't want to, and so we got most of the weapons; there were incidents about this too. After we had gotten these weapons, the Dutch then rearmed some of these Japanese prisoners, turning them against us. This was the root of all the trouble. The truth is, the Allies—the English—shouldn't have brought the Dutch along. After they began operations against us, we fought continuously, and we no longer trusted them. So when the Allies landed and set off for Bandung, we fought in Sukabumi and Cianjur, and attacked them on the road. So there were incidents all the time. The climax of this crisis was in Surabaya. In fact, there was no need for this incident in Surabaya to have happened, but as I explained earlier, every Allied force always contained Dutch soldiers. We saw the presence of these Dutch as a provocation. Brigadier General Mallaby was also acting provocatively when he landed at Surabaya looking for the Dutch who had been released from the Japanese internment camps. He also looked for Chinese regarded as being pro-Dutch, and they were given arms too; at that time they were known as the Poh Antui force. Of course violence could now no longer be prevented, and shooting broke out. The English, as the Allied leaders, ordered us to retreat several kilometers outside of Surabaya. Of course the people of Surabaya didn't want to go. That's how it all built up until the incident happened and Mallaby was killed. Only then did government leaders from Jakarta fly in and arrange a ceasefire. Otherwise, it would have carried on. Yes, of course there were many victims. The Allies had more arms. The Indonesians had more people and their spirits were high, but they didn't have enough arms. That's the truth of it.

22

*

The British Are Coming

CHRISTOPHER THORNE

At the end of October 1945, a fierce battle took place at Surabaya between troops of Britain's 23rd Indian Division and the local inhabitants, whom they had tried to disarm. The British force only just managed to avoid being destroyed altogether. Its commander, Brigadier General A.W.S. Mallaby was killed. Only after three weeks of bitter fighting were new troops of the 5th Indian Division able to take control of the area.

Indonesian nationalists were now seeing Britain as their enemy, alongside the Dutch. Yet at the same time, many of the Dutch on the spot were themselves critical of the British. They believed that Britain was not doing as much as it could and should do to ensure that Dutch rule was re-established in the Indies. And to this day there are some people in the Netherlands who blame Britain for the loss of their prize colony.

The fact is that the Indonesian issue presented the British Labour Government with a totally unexpected and unwelcome dilemma. During the war, British opinion generally had come to accept that imperial territories should move much more quickly, through what was termed "partnership" with the colonial power in question, to self-government or independence. The government in London was itself already embarked on the course that was to lead to independence for India and Pakistan in 1947, and for Burma and Ceylon in 1948. Even before the

Brigadier General A.W.S. Mallaby, Commander of the British forces in Surabaya, who was killed in the confusion of street fighting in that city in October 1945.
Courtesy of Imperial War Museum, London, U.K.

Brigadier Mallaby's grave in Menteng Pulo, the Commonwealth Cemetary in Jakarta.

Courtesy of Kieron Cooke.

Japanese surrendered, the Allied supreme commander in Southeast Asia, Lord Louis Mountbatten, had made contact with the Burmese nationalist leader Aung San, and arranged to cooperate with his forces, despite the fact that Aung San had previously collaborated with the Japanese.

Mountbatten's argument was that British policy must recognize the increased strength and long-term importance of nationalisms in Asia. But at the some time, there were others on the British side—including men like Ernest Bevin, the foreign secretary, who, though basically sympathetic to Asian nationalisms, believed that any transfer of power by imperial states should not be rushed; that those in occupied colonial territories who had collaborated with the Japanese should at least not be given advantage over those who had refused to do so; and that the sovereign rights of states like Britain, France, and the Netherlands must not be taken away without their consent.

It is also important to remember that at the end of the war Britain was facing enormous problems on a much wider scale, involving the welfare of her entire society at home and her international position as a whole. One quarter of her national wealth had gone as a result of the war. Without massive financial help from America, her currency and economy looked likely to collapse. She was desperately short of manpower and vital raw materials. Her exports, like many of her cities, urgently needed rebuilding. Her people were weary after six years of war.

How had Britain become involved in this delicate and emotional struggle? When Mountbatten's South East Asia Command had been set up in 1943, only Sumatra of all the Indies was included in its area. But in 1945, as General MacArthur prepared to attack Japan's home islands, it was agreed between London and Washington that the remainder of the Indies would be taken away from MacArthur's command, and be added to Mountbatten's. This proposal did *not* come from London. It came from the American Joint Chiefs of Staff, and it was only reluctantly that London agreed to add this huge new area to the difficult tasks already facing Britain's forces in the region. Even then, there was a delay before those forces could arrive in Java. That territory came below Singapore, Indochina, and Thailand in the list of priorities once Japan had surrendered. And in any case MacArthur insisted that everything must wait until after the main surrender ceremony in Tokyo Bay.

So the main body of British troops didn't begin to arrive in Java until 29 September 1945. Mountbatten's instructions were to disarm the Japanese, to rescue Allied prisoners, and to prepare for the eventual transfer of administration to the Dutch, whose civil affairs officers came in with the British forces. But those instructions had been drawn up when there was no awareness at all in Allied political and military circles of the strength of Indonesian nationalist feelings and the swift moves to establish an independent republic. Mountbatten, like those in London and Washington who gave him his orders, assumed that there would be an easy and tranquil return to Dutch rule. So they suddenly found themselves in an extremely difficult and totally unexpected situation in Indonesia.

Affairs in Southeast Asia were given only a low priority at such a time. With inadequate forces, and dependent on the Americans for such things as shipping, Mountbatten found himself responsible for 1,500,000 square miles of territory and nearly 130,000,000 people, with large numbers of Japanese troops to be disarmed and with misery and the threat of starvation widespread. In fact, the British forces had to be spread out so thinly across the area that even in one of Britain's own territories, Burma, the civil governor was privately warned that if the local nationalists under Aung San staged an open revolt, he must not expect to get any substantial military help to put down such a rising.

There was yet another complication besides sheer shortage of men. A large proportion of Mountbatten's troops were Indian, and in India during that autumn of 1945, nationalist fervor was mounting, accompanied by the demand that Indians must not be used by Britain to suppress the freedom struggles of fellow Asians. Out of the 30 battalions that Mountbatten eventually had in Indonesia, 26 were Indian, and among the Indian soldiers there was strong sympathy for the Indonesians in their determination to throw off colonial rule. Moreover, Mountbatten was getting urgent warnings from the viceroy of India that the more he used those troops against the Republic of Indonesia, the more explosive the situation in India itself would become.

These were facts that could not be wished away. But what about attitudes among the British themselves regarding the Indonesian situation? The short answer is that they were very mixed, but that as time went on, feelings became more and more uncomfortable over what was happening, and outright support for the simple restoration of Dutch rule grew weaker.

At the beginning, in the summer of 1945, there was a great deal of sympathy and support for the Dutch in London itself. The British chiefs of staff wanted to see more Dutch troops sent out to the Far East, ready to reoccupy the Indies. They were unable to get this done only because the Americans would not make available the shipping that was needed. In the British Foreign Office, the Dutch were regarded as important allies; Britain must keep in close touch with them in terms of both the defence and recovery of Western Europe and the stability of the colonial areas of Southeast Asia. Moreover, both the new British prime minister, the Labour Party's Clement Attlee, and his foreign secretary, Ernest Bevin, were basically pro-Dutch in their attitude, even when the difficulties in Indonesia began to grow between September and November 1945. Bevin wrote privately in October, "No recognition should be given to any authorities not approved by the Netherlands government." And Attlee wrote to the Australian prime minister early in November, "We have need for good relations with our neighbor in Europe and we should indeed be most reluctant to do anything to suggest that sovereignty is a factor that can be lightly set aside." There was also a good deal of anger when nationalists resorted to force, especially when Mallaby was killed. The Foreign Office's political adviser in the Indies wrote at the end of November, "The fact is that the Indonesian leaders are incapable of exerting their authority."

But from the start there were other views among the British that pointed in a different direction. Mountbatten himself quickly realized that in Indonesia the nationalist movement was already so strong by September that even if he had wished to do so, he simply did not have enough troops to impose a military solution. In his view, therefore, it was vital and urgent that the Dutch government's representatives should negotiate with Sukarno and that they should announce their intention to grant some form of independence. Both Mountbatten and his local military commander, Lieutenant General Christison, became increasingly critical of what they saw as inflexible attitudes and a desire on the part of the Dutch to try to settle things on the spot by force. They were also concerned about having to use Indian troops, and about the declining morale of even the British troops under their command.

At the same time, the government in London was coming under pressure from other directions. The Australian government, like its chief observer in the Indies, was also very critical of Dutch attitudes. More importantly, disapproval of the Dutch approach was growing in the United States, and soon Mountbatten was told that he could not use American ships to move more troops to Java. Within Britain itself, the left wing of the ruling Labour Party were increasingly demanding that the government should support, not help to suppress, nationalist movements in Asia. In the press the view was increasingly expressed that this was not Britain's affair, and that Britain had troubles enough without adding to them in the Indies. Above all, British opinion generally did not support imperialist causes.

Not surprisingly, then, the British government began in November and December 1945 privately to urge the Dutch government to adopt a more flexible attitude towards the Indonesian republic. But of course, neither London nor Mountbatten could control the decisions of The Hague or Dutch officials in the Indies. For Britain, the issue continued to pose an uncomfortable dilemma until her forces were finally with-drawn. At the end of 1945, those forces established control of Batavia. And in 1946, the British diplomat Lord Killearn worked to bring about the Linggajati Agreement between the republic and the Dutch. It was not until late in that same year that Mountbatten's South East Asia Command was dissolved and responsibility for Java and Sumatra handed over to the Dutch. By that time, another outsider was becom-ing more deeply involved in the dispute in Britain's place; it was now the turn of the United States.

23

*

The Story of a Soldier

AN INTERVIEW WITH

GENERAL ABDUL HARIS NASUTION

When the Japanese invaded Indonesia I was a cadet in the Dutch army, posted to the 3rd Battalion in Surabaya. But the war didn't last long, and my battalion had retreated to Jember when the capitulation came. Since I didn't feel Dutch, I evaded internment and made my way back to Bandung again on a bicycle. The Japanese had occupied the towns, and on my journey back the roads were largely deserted, since most of the people had stayed evacuated for fear of the fighting. I had quite an adventure, as you can imagine, returning to West Java alone on a bicycle. But as soon as I arrived back in West Java, many people said to me —even those in the house that I went to—"Don't come near us, because if the Japanese find out, they will take measures against us and punish us." So I went into hiding in Sukabumi for three months. Then the Japanese government announced that it would only continue to detain soldiers of Dutch nationality; the Indonesians would be released. So after three months I was free, in the sense that I now dared to reappear on the scene. Then I had a marvelous opportunity, because before long the Japanese in Bandung, by way of consolidating their power, organized a commemoration of the first anniversary of the Pacific war, and all the youth organizations were asked to join in a big parade. I happened to be chosen leader of all those who joined in the march. From that time on I was well known in Bandung, because of the time I led all the *pemuda*.

General Abdul Haris Nasution in 1945 when, at the age of 27, he was Commander of the Siliwangi Division of the Republican army in Bandung.

Courtesy of H.A.H. Nasution.

A one-time school master, the young Nasution was a thinking soldier. The years of Japanese occupation ended abruptly in August 1945, leaving an Indonesia with its independence proclaimed but no organized national army to defend it. There was a kind of armed force of disparate bands of pemuda *willing to fight alongside a formal army. He urged the political leaders to create a national army at once.*

In fact, as a military man, I had frequently asked the political leaders in Bandung why we hadn't made the proclamation when the Japanese arrived. We should have proclaimed a national government and formed a national army, however small, so at least we could do something. Now during the Japanese period, my fellow *pemuda* and I had been making preparations, so that if the war reached Java, we would be ready to raise the national flag in various places and declare a national government with its national army, even though it would not be fully complete. These preparations proved to be highly successful, since the fighting hadn't reached Java yet and since Japan capitulated even sooner than expected because of the dropping of the atom bomb. After the proclamation, we rose up more easily than if the war had reached Java. Around that time we in Bandung sent a delegation to Sukarno and Hatta in Jakarta, to have Peta—that is, the army of Indonesians formed by the Japanese to help Japan—proclaimed the national army immediately. But due to political considerations, Sukarno and Hatta didn't do this. Diplomacy was their priority.

The day after the proclamation, in my capacity as a leader of the *pemuda*, I went from Bandung to Cimahi to visit our battalion commander, Haruji, and said to him, "Declare this the national army, and we *pemuda* are behind you." But he said it was unnecessary, because the Japanese also supported our proclamation, and he even told us that the Japanese had promised to start giving them heavy arms that very day. So I left the battalion commander's house, but before I had even got back to Bandung, he had returned to his battalion only to find all the arms had been collected and the place surrounded by Japanese troops. So throughout Java all our units were completely disarmed that same day. I really regretted that. Because of this event, we no longer had any official standing in the situation.

In the meantime, the Dutch soldiers in the internment camps had had firm contact with the Dutch army officers in Australia. Several intelligence agents were dropped into each town, and they organized the

Dutch units within the camps, so that they emerged as troops, and in general, they faced us with clear feelings of enmity. Wherever they saw the Red-and-White flying among other flags, they took it down, and they tore up all the publications of the republican government, and incidents began to happen in Bandung, in Jakarta, in every single town. That is how the fighting between us and the Dutch started. I think there was a misunderstanding; the Dutch colonial government in Australia probably thought that all they had to do was enter the country, they didn't know there was now an Indonesian government, and they thought the situation was just the same as before. We also took it for granted that the Dutch wanted to return to power, so we confronted them. Now it was clearly a great shame that due to that lack of understanding there were a great many victims.

What I see as a very important factor in Indonesia's history is this: the emergence of the dualism between our military and political leaders, right from the moment of the proclamation. Because there was time—in fact, roughly several days after the proclamation—to declare officially that the Japanese-created army called Peta (Pembela Tanah Air, Defenders of the Fatherland) was henceforth the national army, but this was not done, and in the end it was disbanded by the Japanese. But we were forced into conflict with the NICA (Netherlands Indies Civil Administration) the Dutch-created forces. So with whatever weapons we could find—police arms, any arms at all—and by disbanding the Japanese here and there, we began to fight without any leadership. And this only ended when the British marines landed in Jakarta at the end of September, if I'm not mistaken, arriving in Bandung by the middle of October. So over two months of good time was wasted. We had already been fighting with arms, just in gangs, all over the place; and only on October 5 did the government officially institute the Tentara Keamanan Rakyat (People's Security Army or TKR), with General Urip Sumoharjo as the chief of staff. General Urip then announced that the government could not pay the cost of weapons and equipment; everyone had to forage for himself. So right from the start we had to work autonomously. But what was more difficult, of course, was to think through one's own political position, independently, in any given situation. This state of affairs carried on right through the revolution, until the Dutch left. And because I happened to be senior commander throughout, I experienced this problem even more strongly, not only when I was division commander in Bandung and ordered the city to be burned, but also later in Yogyakarta when I had become commander for Java. The problem was that were always conscious of a kind of dualism.

You have seen this dualism as a disadvantage in general terms. But did it not have a certain virtue at the time?

Yes. At that time, it had not been officially decided to form a national army, so a People's Security Army (TKR) was formed. This was probably because it was safer diplomatically for the government not to have its own army, but to have a people's army. Now this gave us soldiers, especially the late General Sudirman, the impression that we were primarily an army of the people. Later on, this was taken to mean that what we considered to be in the interests of the people was not always the same as the government's interests; at times, they clashed. So this gave rise to a certain process. The TNI (Tentara Nasional Indonesia or Indonesian National Army) often regarded itself directly as the people's army, and only secondly as the government's army. But little by little, the government obviously tried to turn it into an army that was obedient to the government. That remained a problem until the period in Yogyakarta ended.

As a young man who grew up in Bandung, who thought of that city as home, you found yourself in 1946 having to defend it against what most people believed to be a superior military machine: the combined British forces. Wasn't this a very difficult situation for you, requiring difficult decisions?

Yes. In early 1946, when I happened to be the commander in Bandung, things had gotten to the point where we could no longer avoid conflict. To tell the truth, as a military man I had difficulty in seeing how the British could spare enough logistical equipment to move their 23rd Division to Bandung from Jakarta, via Puncak. But this was apparently what they planned to do, and we felt that this was our chance to intercept them. But in actual fact, the British had decided to take the alternate route, fetching the Japanese from camps around Sukabumi first, and then proceeding to the camps in Lembang, north of Bandung. So just as we were preparing to intercept them, they were already entering our territory from an unexpected direction. Fighting broke out, and at one stage there were many British-Indian casualties in Sukabumi. In Bandung I attacked the positions of the British troops with mortars, but of course we were new to the game and not yet very skilled in combat, so many of our shots missed their targets. Since not all our shells hit, we didn't manage to drive the British back. Consequently, the British commander in chief, Lieutenant General Christison, issued an ultimatum ordering the Indonesian troops to leave Bandung, if I'm not mistaken, within forty-eight hours. Prime Minister Syahrir sent an envoy, Syafruddin Prawiranegara, to Bandung to convey that order, because the government had already agreed with the British that Bandung would be evacuated. The leaders in Bandung and I shared the view that the people would never obey the order just like that. So with the help of General Hawthorn, the British division commander, I flew to Jakarta to meet Syahrir. I put forward this problem, but the prime minister replied—and I acknowledge the truth of his words—"You are too small to oppose the British, who are so strong." So we weren't allowed to disobey the order. "We are working diplomatically," Syahrir said, "and this diplomacy will succeed and the towns that are now occupied will be surrendered to the republic, so it can be done diplomatically. If you oppose them now, you will be destroyed. But later on, we will get that city back, and since you won't have been destroyed, we will have an army." But in those days, and in those conditions, of course the *pemuda* would find this very difficult to understand. So when I arrived back in Bandung, we conferred with the *pemuda* leaders and other revolutionaries. We decided: "Let's burn Bandung rather than simply evacuate the city, and that's what we'll hand over to the British." So that's how it happened.

Of course, these are my own personal views, but I believed that if what I suggested earlier had been taken seriously—if the Peta army had been decreed the national army before it was disbanded by the Japanese —that would have ensured that we needn't have confronted the Dutch, because we would have been strong. I also believe that, even after this first initiative failed, the Allies were not yet strong, because they had such a limited number of troops and a great many commitments stretching from Libya to Indonesia, and they simply couldn't cope. My military opinion is that by working diplomatically we gave the British time to occupy everything, and to hand it over to the Dutch in good condition; but if we had instead carried out coordinated attacks on all the occupied towns, the British would have been unable to do this. Of course these were only my views in those days, when I was still a young commander. But in later years, I read the same analysis from the British point of view, and once, when I was an official guest in London, I did have an opportunity to talk to Mountbatten, who had been the supreme commander during that period. And in fact it was true: even the British had thought that they didn't have enough troops then. They had wanted to occupy only West Java, not Surabaya and the other cities. So what I had felt as a young commander about our position vis-a-vis the British after the proclamation, I know now was in fact true.

24

*

Meanwhile in Bukittinggi

AN INTERVIEW WITH

MARA KARMA

There was no ceremony for the proclamation in Bukittinggi. Nothing. Everything that happened in Bukittinggi after the proclamation was in the form of *pemuda* activities, up until November 10. In that month, the government—that is, Vice-President Hatta—announced that political parties should be set up. One day, roughly a week after August 17, a friend came to me and said that independence had already been proclaimed in Java. This was certain; he had heard it from a friend who worked for the Japanese government. I was persuaded to go along that night to attend a meeting at the MIT school (Makhamah Islam Tinggi), which was an Islamic educational institute founded in West Sumatra and well known in that region. So I attended this meeting, and there I saw about fifteen *pemuda*, some of whom had come specially from Padang. A large proportion of them were politically experienced cadres; I was one of the juniors. So I listened to what had happened. The gist of that meeting was that we all agreed that something had to be done, because everyone believed that the leaders didn't really know what needed to be done next. That was the decision that night, and it was proposed that we in Bukittinggi should act promptly to form an organization to get on with it. So the next day after this meeting at the MIT, I summoned all my friends and we formed a *pemuda* organization for Bukittinggi. I was chosen assistant leader, the leader was Nuzirwan. In addition, my seniors seemed to think it necessary to form a *pemuda* organization for the whole of Sumatra. They formed the PRI Sumatra, which stood for the Pemuda Republik Indonesia Sumatra or Sumatran Youths of the Republic of Indonesia, and Nuzirwan involved himself more and more in this pan-Sumatran organization.

One of the activities the PRI Sumatra carried out was the distribution of publications everywhere, even as far as Aceh, since at that time Bukittinggi was the administrative center of the Japanese occupation government, and the center of activities for the Indonesian movements. I was put in charge of things in Bukittinggi, and from that moment on we engaged in all sorts of activities. The first thing we did was to try and get all the people to fly the red and white flag from their houses. This was not an easy thing to do, because at that time Bukittinggi was still occupied by the Japanese military government. But because everyone joined in to make it a combined effort, the Japanese couldn't do anything about it. We carried this out in an orderly fashion. At that time, graffiti were also being written on walls. Communications with Java started up, especially with Bandung. Our fellow *pemuda* in the PTT (Post, Telephone, and Telegraph office) frequently contacted Bandung. Little by little, we learned about developments in Java. Now one day, as I was so well known to the Japanese, I was called to the *kenpeitai* headquarters, where I was asked—not threatened, but asked—what the *pemuda's* plans were. I answered that there were no plans; whatever struck us as being necessary we would do. That is, as I remember, how we worked. That was the first thing. Second, we tried to take over the government buildings one by one. This also included taking over vehicles, ammunition, all sorts of things. Here, small struggles broke out and all sorts of incidents arose until sometimes we compromised, sometimes we coerced, and sometimes we played along with the Japanese, because the Japanese themselves were not really doing very much any more. In practice, the government was no longer active, and even the police themselves asked for our help. So in practice, it can be said that it was the *pemuda* who controlled the situation in Bukittinggi, and events were mainly concentrated in the area of Agam Tua. I travelled to several towns to help spread the news of the proclamation. The reception from the people was excellent. Everywhere there were minor outbreaks of fighting, because some of these *pemuda* were rather impatient and wanted to take control quickly. Japanese control of the whole of Sumatra, and Singapore and all sorts of other places, was centered in Bukittinggi, because of the way that the Japanese war administration had split up the area. So politically and militarily Bukittinggi was the second most important town after Jakarta. What happened in Bukittinggi was a kind of barometer for all the other towns in Sumatra.

One day in the third week after the proclamation, we *pemuda* held an informal meeting. I was urged by the leaders of *pemuda* group branches throughout Bukittinggi to take more aggressive measures immediately, one of which was to raise the flag on the top of what is called the Jam Gadang or Clock Tower because, symbolically, whenever a flag is raised there it means that whoever owns the flag is in control. When the Japanese arrived, the first thing they did was replace the Dutch flag on the Clock Tower with the Japanese flag, so it was a very symbolic action with enormous political meaning. I said that the Japanese would not allow this—of course it wasn't allowed—but all the *pemuda* carried on pressing me to do it by force, until I was called a coward; "If that's the case, then you, the leader, are a coward, and you ought to resign your position." I was furious, and I said that it wasn't that I wasn't brave, but I—we—had to use our brains being brave: "I promise you all that I will raise the flag on the Jam Gadang. If I don't succeed. . . well then, when I'm dead you can go and raise it yourselves. But I'm going to try first." So, after the meeting, I was really in a state, I was also mortified at having been called a coward, so much so that I couldn't sleep that night. At about one o'clock in the morning I went out and roamed around with some friends, wondering how to raise that flag on the Clock Tower. We had three alternatives. Beneath the clock was a police post. The first alternative was to reach an agreement with that police post. Secondly, the police post could be ambushed, and the police tied up. Or we could secretly break down the door of the Clock Tower and raise the flag by ourselves. But these last two choices were no good, because the next day the flag would certainly be taken down by the Japanese. What we wanted was to fly a flag which the Japanese could not, would not, take down any more. And we wanted it to be raised officially. By coincidence, approximately after midnight, Dahlan Jambek, who used to be in the Giyugun (a volunteer brigade which occasionally joined in Japanese army exercises) apparently couldn't sleep either, so we worked out a compromise. We decided then that, starting in the morning, we would secretly announce to all the people that at 9 A.M. the following day we would raise the flag on the Jam Gadang. That was the initiative that emerged in the middle of the night. In the morning, we went around everywhere. We sent children around to try to make sure that all the people were ready to set out by 7 A.M., and this succeeded, to the extent that hundreds of thousands of people gathered there.

By January 1946 Allied troops had moved into Bukittinggi.

In the last week of October, 1945, I accompanied a delegation of youths from West Sumatra to attend a congress which was held in Yogyakarta from November 10-12. We set off, and I did not return to Bukittinggi until the beginning of January, because the journey took so long. When I arrived back in Bukittinggi I saw that the town was occupied by Allied troops, under a British commander. I had in fact heard about this while still on my way home, but when I arrived in Bukittinggi I saw that it was true; I saw their uniforms, and the Indian soldiers, and so on. I became active again as a leader. One day a jeep came to our office and ordered us to present ourselves at 9 A.M. the next day at the British commander's office, which was over at the military barracks. So I went there the following day, and I met Dr. Rivai, head of the KNI and Dahlan Jambek, representing the BKR. We three faced the commander of the British forces. We were asked first to order the people to take down their flags, especially those flags flying from government offices. Second, we were asked to try to get rid of the various slogans which were scribbled on the walls and everywhere else. We said in reply that the people had not raised flags because we had ordered them to, but because they themselves had wanted to; and that we didn't know anything about the graffiti, since we hadn't ordered them either. But he said, "You are the leaders, you give commands, and you are responsible. If you give orders, obviously the people will obey." We replied, "If we order the people to take down their flags, we will no longer be seen as leaders, we will in fact be regarded as traitors. Similarly, if we order the slogans erased from the walls, we will be treated as enemies." "I'm not concerned about that. The point is that we are ordering you three to take the flags down, and wipe all those slogans off. Don't try to oppose this." Then he continued, "We are the soldiers who won the war, we won World War II," he said, "We know how to fight, so don't disobey our orders." At that time, we were using an interpreter, so we bluffed, "Very well, we'll try, but we can't promise anything." We were given 48 hours in which to do this. We went home, and one by one we discussed how to carry this out, but you see, it really was quite impossible. In fact, giving an order like that carried a very high risk for each of us, whether for Dr. Rivai, or Dahlan Jambek, or me. So we didn't pay any attention to the order. We even spread it around that we were each going to start living away from home, to avoid anything happening, as the whole of Bukittinggi was under surveillance. Furthermore, we had witnessed how the NICA soldiers who had infiltrated the British forces in Bukittinggi increased in number as time went on, causing frequent incidents.

Then, after about 24 hours, a jeep came to my headquarters, at about 6 A.M. In it were two men dressed in Allied clothing. They ordered the placards outside the building to be taken down. We just listened to them. They spoke English, but it so happened that a friend of mine knew by the accent of their English that they weren't English, but Dutch. So my friend asked them directly in English, "Are you English or Dutch?" and when they heard this, they didn't reply, but got straight back into their vehicle, and drove off. About an hour after that, our headquarters was completely surrounded and dynamited, and the whole thing was completely destroyed. From that moment onwards, the first fire flared. . . that Friday, as I was saying my prayers, the situation in Bukittinggi became increasingly critical.

25

*

Running the Blockade

AN INTERVIEW WITH

PARAMITA ABDURRAHMAN AND MARA KARMA

Paramita Abdurrahman: My generation grew up during the Japanese occupation. This was the time we started to take an active role in the
struggle for independence. So when the revolution was announced, we
plunged straight into it, and I became secretary to the minister of foreign affairs. Before this I had worked with Mohammad Hatta, but then
the *romusha* office was closed. When I started work in the Department
of Foreign Affairs, I was asked to help set up the Red Cross, but my
role was really as a courier, carrying letters and other things. Then,
when Jakarta began to be threatened with attacks from outside, from
the Dutch and the British, the government felt that Jakarta could no
longer be defended as the capital, and the cabinet had to move to
Yogyakarta. In order to set up or organize a new capital there, of course
we had to get permission from Sultan Hamengku Buwono, and I became the courier to bring the letter of request from that first cabinet.
Travelling incognito as a member of the Red Cross, I went to Yogyakarta. By pure coincidence, I found that I had acquaintances within
the palace confines, and through them I managed to convey the message to the sultan. So that mission was completed successfully; in it I
only acted as a courier, and after that I was no longer active.

Later on, when the first women's congress was held in Madiun, I
was chosen to be, or rather confirmed as, the representative from West
Java, and I had to convey the conclusions of that women's congress to

Jakarta. After that, of course, if there were matters to be discussed with Jakarta, I was often asked to carry letters to Jakarta for Dr. Leimena, who was there at that time. I wasn't the only courier, there were many of us, so basically it just depended on having the opportunity, and of course the people in Yogyakarta knew who could be trusted to carry messages.

Once, I remember, I was bringing a letter to Dr. Johannes Leimena with my friend Miss Kurnianingrat, who later became the wife of Ali Sastroamijoyo. On that occasion in Jakarta, I met an old school friend, a Dutchman who, unknown to me, had become chief of intelligence, and he said, "The Dutch are searching for you, you'd better go back." So we returned with a safeguard from the Dutch, but what they didn't know was that at that time we were carrying replies from Leimena to Hatta. In the end, we memorized these messages, and while crossing a river we threw the letters away. But this was only a small part of the courier work that went on. Of course, with the first and second Dutch Police Actions, the number of couriers increased dramatically, and the conditions for courier work became even more dangerous.

Naturally, the couriers were not only carrying messages within Java, which was dangerous enough, but right from the start we, the republic, had been sending couriers to Bali, for instance, and to Sulawesi, Sumatra, South Kalimantan, and Maluku, but only the cabinet knew about it. In fact, we were only part of one very small circle; we knew exactly who our own contact persons were, but we didn't know, for example, who was trusted to carry messages abroad. But of course if we look at the history of the revolution, those outside contacts were very important, I mean not just outside Java, but in foreign countries too. And in fact it's this aspect that we often forget, that clearly these couriers were—how would you put it?—not a symbol, really, but they showed that Indonesia too had educated, even sophisticated people, who could carry an image, a picture of Indonesia to these other countries. Thus we had unofficial representatives in Singapore, in Thailand, in India. And these high-level couriers travelled by plane, from Burma, from India, so that when the first Inter-Asian Conference was held in New Delhi, in 1947 if I'm not mistaken, Indonesia was already able to send a very large delegation.

But messages were not all that was carried through enemy lines, other necessities were also smuggled through, weren't they?

Yes. Blockade running is something that we usually depict purely as a means of procuring arms, but besides these weapons, we also obtained foodstuffs and medicine. We Indonesians didn't just ask for these commodities, we always paid for them. We paid with whatever we could get hold of, gold, diamonds, vanilla pods, or cloves. I remember clearly that we didn't want to become *musafir*, or travellers just relying on other people's hospitality. So if people abroad really did want to help us, then we would accept, but we could also buy things ourselves. It was like that. This system had been pioneered in the earliest days. And later Indonesia also sent students to India. Actually this was because education had been able to continue uninterrupted throughout the revolution, with the opening of Gadjah Madah University, enabling us to send students abroad, in technical fields, to become engineers. Now they are all active in high government and military posts.

When Paramita Abdurrahman was working inside Indonesia, Mara Karma, a leader of the pemuda *in Bukittinggi, found himself going overseas to help the republic from outside.*

Mara Karma: I left for Singapore for a particular reason, namely that when I returned to Bukittinggi earlier, Medan had been occupied by the Dutch. So hordes of *pemuda* and leaders from Medan moved—or rather, were evacuated—to Bukittinggi, which continued to be an important town politically. They came down to Bukittinggi in their different groups, each with its own ideology. Not long after they arrived in Bukittinggi, I saw the strength of the communists; the number of communist youths, especially Pesindo (Pemuda Sosialis Indonesia, Indonesian Socialist Youth), became greater and greater. They infiltrated my organization, which as time passed became smaller and smaller. Before, all the *pemuda* had been in my organization, but after the setting up of political parties in November, many *pemuda* aligned themselves with those political parties, establishing their own youth wings. PRI was infiltrated by Pesindo until Pesindo was able to take over control of the leadership of my organization. I was anti-communist at that time, and couldn't bear to see this situation. I had to choose my path. I couldn't just swing in the wind in Bukittinggi; I had to play an important role. So I decided to go abroad to increase my knowledge, while doing whatever I could for the republic. That's why, after consulting my teacher, I went to Singapore.

In Singapore, it turned out that my activities had given me a reputation as a youth pioneer. I found myself making lots of speeches. I was invited to speak to workers' parties and all sorts of other groups. I played a part in setting up the Indonesia-Malaysia Association, and was chosen to become its secretary. As a consequence of this I also participated in founding the API—Melayu organization in the Geylang area. The name was an abbreviation of Angkatan Pemuda Insaf, or Generation of Conscious Youths. So I got to know many people. I was often asked to carry out tasks, one of which was to take barter trade ships from Singapore to Pekanbaru, carrying a mixture of goods and ammunition. These jobs took up so much of my time that the university preparation course I was attending in Singapore was often interrupted because of these "sidelines."

I once took a ship, and I didn't even know what its contents were. Then the ship was apprehended in Tanjung Uban. I was arrested in Tanjung Uban, but I managed to stuff all my letters into a pipe on the ship. These letters declared that I was in charge [of an operation], and I had been meant to deliver them to the republican resident in Pekanbaru, Dr. Utoyo. Now this made it difficult for me, because in my passport it said that I was a student, and the real documents were gone. So I was arrested and held for two days in Tanjung Uban, and released after a week. Then I set off for Pekanbaru. I reported this incident to Governor Tengku Hassan in Bukittinggi, but I did not have much proof, because my ship had fallen into the hands of the Dutch, whose blockade was very strong. In the end the British found out about my political activities in Singapore. In 1949 I was arrested in an early morning raid, and then I was immediately deported to Jakarta.

I did know about other blockade runners; I had many friends who all had their own assignments. There were some from Cirebon, and others from Palembang, whose job it was to bring agricultural produce and other goods to Singapore, and to return from Singapore bringing consumer items. . . . and hidden beneath them, weapons. Some of my friends from that time are now ministers and ambassadors, and some have already retired. But these are reminiscences for all of us, those events of the late 1940s.

26

*

An Englishman Joins the Struggle

AN INTERVIEW WITH

JOHN COAST

The Siam-to-Burma railway was finished in October 1943 and after that, in the new year of 1944, the Japanese brought us down to the big base camps and wondered what to do with the prisoners. During that period, about six months, we had a camp theatre. Half the Malayan Civil Service were prisoners and among prisoners from the Netherlands East Indies were numbers of Eurasians and Indonesians, as well as Dutch people. And after learning some Malay, I got fascinated by stories about the dances in Central Java and the arts of Java in general. We formed our own *keroncong* band—*keroncong* is a vaguely Hawaiian, popular singing style, vogue-ish in the 1930s—in prison camp and, though it seems stupid to say so, I've never heard a better band of keroncong players than we had on the River Kwai. I also formed a theatrical company, which presented so-called Javanese dances on stage; these productions couldn't have been less authentic. We used the wrong music and the costumes were made from stolen Japanese mosquito netting.

But it made me extremely interested in the arts of Indonesia. From one of my teachers I heard about President Sukarno, and how there was an independence movement in Indonesia, although we heard nothing about this from our Dutch friends. I was absolutely fascinated by stories I heard of the *serimpi* court dancers in Central Java and things like that. I got the ambition, after the war, to come back to Southeast

136

John Coast in 1986.   Courtesy of John Coast.

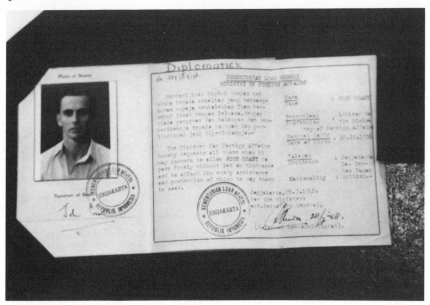

Coast's 1948 Republican Government pass.   Courtesy of John Coast.

Asia and somehow or other see these dancers and put together a company and tour them round the world. This was a sort of crazy prison
camp dream I had.

When the war was over I came back to London. The first thing I
wanted to do was meet Indonesians. At that time—November 1945—
there were, I think, two Indonesians in the whole of London, and these
were advisers to the Dutch delegation at the United Nations in San
Francisco. Both of them later became very prominent in Indonesia.
One of them was Sumitro Joyohadikusumo, who later became minister of economic affairs. The other one was Dr. Zain, who went out
later to Singapore, where I knew him during the revolution, and who
became an ambassador in various parts of Europe after independence.
My interest had been in Indonesian art, but these people persuaded me
that, for the time being, if I was going to be able to see anything of the
arts of Indonesia, I had to get interested in the politics of Indonesia and
the independence of Indonesia. I thought this was, in a way, logical,
and being young and impressionable, I became an absolutely fanatical
Indonesian nationalist. I also had to earn a living, and thought, how
the hell do I get back to Southeast Asia with no money? I applied to the
Colonial Office and the Foreign Office, and I was accepted by both.
But the Foreign Office job was with the Far East Information Department, which said, "Well, Coast, you're a bit of a nutcase, but if we ever
open up an office in Yogyakarta, in a free Indonesia, you would be a
wonderful cultural liaison officer for us." So I said, "Okay, I'll join the
Foreign Office," and in September 1946, I did. By April 1947, I was no
nearer Indonesia, and things were going badly for the Republic of Indonesia. The Foreign Office said to me, "Might you not learn a little
bit about Southeast Asians and the way they work, if we send you out
to Bangkok instead? We've got a chance for you to go out there as second secretary for information at the embassy. We think it would be interesting for you anyhow to see what Thailand's like, not working on
the River Kwai, but as a diplomat." I was tempted by this and I agreed
to go. By this time I had translated *Perjuangan Kita*, the Syahrir pamphlet, helped by Suripno, who had arrived in London from Holland.
(He later became very left-wing and was killed after the Madiun Affair
in 1948.) Dr. Sumitro and Dr. Zain were also there in London. So I was
working with three pretty high-ranking Indonesians. Because I had
known them, my office in Bangkok at the British Embassy became a
sort of center of Indonesian information, much to the indignation of

Mr. Polderman, who was the Dutch consul general. He could see that an official of the British Embassy was acting as a sort of unofficial contact for every Indonesian republican who came to Bangkok. I was very flattered by this and greatly enjoyed it. I think my ambassador again probably thought I was a strange character.

After I'd been nearly one year in Bangkok, I told the ambassador I had been approached by Sudarsono, a representative of the Indonesian Socialist Party (Partai Sosialis Indonesia, PSI), who asked me if I really was serious and wanted to join the revolution and go down and work for the republic. I had said I was serious, and wanted to go. So I said to my ambassador: "I want to leave at the end of the first year." I put it that way because if I stayed in Bangkok for one year I wouldn't have to refund any of my passage out from London. At the end of my year, to everybody's astonishment, I left the British Embassy, made contact with my Indonesian friends, and joined them. That was in April 1948, and a few weeks later I flew down to Yogyakarta.

So in fact you joined the British Foreign Service as a way of getting to Indonesia.

Exactly; and that's what they did for me, too, they got me out to Bangkok. In Bangkok I made close contacts and started going down to Yogyakarta.

Was your enthusiasm for the Indonesian Revolution in any way frowned upon or thought improper for a British diplomat?

Yes, obviously. The senior members of the embassy thought that I was an unstable young man. The Dutch thought I was an adventurer and issued a lot of propaganda against me. I was undoubtedly a rather fanatical person at that time, because when I said "we" over the next two years I meant "we Indonesians." I became completely identified with the Indonesian Revolution. Anyway, having joined, I was to go to Yogyakarta and meet Syahrir, who was technically my employer. Syahrir at that time had his office in the Istana in Jogja. He was no longer Prime Minister. I'm speaking of May or June of 1948.

The first job that the Indonesian Government gave this diplomat— or ex-diplomat—to do, was to break the Dutch blockade. When in Bangkok, I'd had an entrée with Field Marshal Pibul Songgram. I had given him English lessons before he became prime minister. So, having had this contact with Pibul, the Indonesians thought I might use it to get some sort of landing rights in southern Thailand and with them run the blockade from Bangkok.

At that time, the head of the Indonesia office in Bangkok was a young man called Izak Mahdi, with whom I became very friendly. We did a survey of all the airlines in Bangkok to see which was the most suitable for our purposes, and we found one called Pacific Overseas Airlines, which would take a plane out of its Hong Kong schedule every week and fly down to republican Java and Sumatra. The first flight we organized was a bit chaotic. But one day in May, 1948, we eventually got through Singapore, landed in Bukittinggi, and then flew to Java, landing safely in Yogyakarta at Maguwo airport. (On that first flight we had Sudarpo and Sujatmoko, who were the Indonesian representatives at the United Nations. So we felt we were operating at a good and useful level.) Later on we flew regularly from Songkla in Southern Thailand, with Pibul Songgram turning a blind eye to our activities.

In Yogyakarta I went to Syahrir's office, which was at the back of Sukarno's office in the Istana. Syahrir said, "Well, I'll give you a contract for three months," and I replied, "What, for three months? I intend to work for you for the rest of my life." He said, "Well, you'd better see if you like us or not first." So he introduced me to the minister of information, Mohamad Natsir, whose secretary general was Ruslan Abdulgani, and I started to work for them.

Was there no thought in the back of their minds that you might have been a British government plant?

Of course there was. Later on I came to know Haji Agus Salim, the deputy foreign minister, who was at that time staying up in the mountains in Kaliurang, recovering from some illness. He said to me, "I sent for you. I wanted to meet you, I wanted to see who this *mata-mata* (spy) is that the British have sent to Central Java." That's exactly what they thought. But the thing was, at that time I was so obviously and openly and fanatically and dementedly pro-republican that they could see that I was rather naive, but also very useful. There I was, imbued with all this revolutionary fervor. I saw how badly off everybody was and how poor they were and how they were dressed, so I went around in shorts and an open-necked shirt and sandals. No one gave me any useful work to do at all. Then one day a friend came up to me and said, "You know, you're very young and look even younger, and if you run around in shorts and an open-necked shirt no one will think you're of any significance at all. And also you walk to places or go in a *dokar* (pony cart). That's no way to do things." So I changed the pattern of my life a little and smartened up.

Before long I found that Haji Agus Salim was living only two doors away from me, on Jalan Terban Taman. Very soon after that I really began to do useful work: minuting things, translating things, and doing really what you might call public relations work with Haji Agus Salim. This became extremely interesting; what they really wanted from me, however, was not my rather naive enthusiasm but the continuation of the breaking of the blockade. Air Commander Suryadarma, who was head of the Indonesian airforce, had this office on Terban Taman also, and I made a very necessary contact there, as we took our orders and received our payment through him. So we flew back and forth through the blockade. I didn't go on every flight, frequently staying in Yogyakarta to work. The flights were paid for from the small residue of funds in foreign exchange which the republic had, at that time. These were never easy to find, and I think we did a bit of bartering as well as paying in cash, because really the republic at that time was absolutely broke.

Part of the blockade-running activity was fund raising, wasn't it? That is, exporting the few things the republic had—spices for example—in order to be able to import arms and medicine? Some stories even say that a certain amount of drugs changed hands.

It wasn't exactly a matter of drug peddling. What happened was this. In the old days all the colonial powers, Dutch as well as British, had opium monopolies and, therefore, they had government-owned opium supplies. In 1948 the assets of the republic were so small that they decided for security reasons to move this opium supply from East Java to Sumatra. And at the time a well-known figure was the American flier, Bob Freeberg, a Texan with an independent Dakota labelled RI001. Once I wanted to get back to Bangkok and Bob's plane was going part of the way, so I got in the cockpit with him and said, "What are we carrying today?" He answered, "Can't you smell it?" And I could smell something pretty strange, but I didn't know what it was. He added, "It's a ton and a half of opium." I'm glad we weren't caught on that flight. We successfully transferred it to Bukittinggi, where it was held in reserve in lieu of currency, I suppose. I don't know why it should be any more scandalous for the republic to use the proceeds from opium sales than for the Dutch colonial government to support itself that way. After all, it was the Indonesians' opium.

Anyway, after this had been going on for some months, Haji Agus Salim said to me, "John, I want you to operate from Bangkok, not from Yogyakarta. You can make yourself chief of public relations for the republic in Southeast Asia. You've got such good contacts in Bangkok, you can keep the blockade running going with Izak Mahdi; I think it's better that you go back there." So I went back to Bangkok. My task now was to keep this blockade running operating smoothly, and so we instituted the idea of inviting prominent journalists to go down to the republic on these planes and leaking the news out beforehand so the Dutch would know that if they intercepted us, they'd think, Oh my God, we're getting into trouble, we've shot down the Associated Press man, or we've shot down the member of parliament from such-and-such a place. Among others, we took down Stan Swinton, from the Associated Press, and Kukrit Pramoj, who later became prime minister of Thailand. It was pretty dangerous. On one extraordinary occasion, we were flying through Sumatra and landed at Jambi. Now in Jambi in those days it was dangerous to go on the airport strip at night because there were so many tigers. What greeted us, however, was not tigers but Dutch Mitchell Bombers. After we had landed, these bombers circled above us, preventing us from taking off in daylight. At nightfall the Dutch planes left and we thought, "God, what do we do now? Tomorrow morning they're probably going to come over and bomb us." We had an emergency conference and worked out the exact flying time from Jambi to the southern tip of Sumatra, out to sea along the south coast of Java and then inland opposite Yogyakarta. Then the Indonesians got coconut shell halves, filled them with oil and a wick, and gave us enough light to take off. And we flew in absolutely stygian darkness, no lights and no radio, because any radio transmission would have been intercepted by the Dutch. Normally, when I'd been acting as sort of navigator, I'd have a school atlas in my lap, and I'd say to our pilot, Dave Fowler, "Over to the right a bit, you can't go there," or, "This is Dutch-held," and so on. You feel so exposed when you're up 9,000 feet in a Dakota in the middle of a revolution. You think everybody below must see you going over, but of course they don't, or they think it's one of theirs. But this particular bit of flying by Dave Fowler and his Siamese crew was brilliant, for we landed just as dawn was breaking over Maguwo airport. The Dutch must have gone back to Jambi at about the same time to look for our plane, and to their astonishment we had disappeared. It was a very exciting life.

I stayed in Bangkok until independence, working with Izak Mahdi. We were sent all over the place. I think I made about 25 trips down to Singapore. The worst was in connection with the opium, because Dr. Hatta, who was a pillar of respectability and reliability, had sent me from Yogyakarta to Singapore to explain that the Indonesian government was not selling opium on the Singapore market. Dear Bung Hatta, he didn't know that his own state bank officials in Bukittinggi were doing precisely that. Anyway, I called a press conference in the Indonesia office in Raffles Place. About an hour before the press conference was due to start, Nigel Morris, who was head of Singapore intelligence, asked me to stop by his office. There he told me, "I've got an item of news for you, before the press conference I gather you're giving shortly. We've just caught Cobley." I said, "What exactly do you mean?" He replied, "Your friend Cobley, who is flying an amphibian for the republic. We've just caught him in the Riau archipelago, with half a ton of opium on board. Good luck with your press conference!" That was quite a press conference. I had to do quite a bit of wriggling there, but I upheld Bung Hatta's statement that it wasn't an Indonesia government policy to sell opium, and indeed it wasn't. It was happening absolutely without his knowledge.

What was the actual importance of your activity? What do you think was your main contribution to the revolution?

The main contributions were two. First, keeping the blockade-running going, and second, doing public relations. To have someone who would write articles, give press interviews, and be familiar with the leaders of the Indonesian Revolution was at that time of some value.

At least for Southeast Asia, I think you could say that I was the main contact with the world media, for although the republic had an office in Singapore, it went unrecognized. Some governments gave the republic de facto recognition and, for example, Muhammand Yunus was a consul sent by Nehru to Yogyakarta, the first person to have an official consulate there during the blockade.

But my activities in publicity and blockade-running were very important nevertheless. I suppose another connected function was that I used to broadcast regularly from Yogyakarta, and this gave me the feeling that I was doing something useful. Certainly it brought the republican viewpoint to the English-speaking people in Southeast Asia.

After Haji Agus Salim told me to leave, I just managed to get out before the final police action in 1948, when the Dutch struck and took Yogyakarta, capturing Sukarno and the government. I was incredibly lucky at that time. A four-engined plane (a first for Yogyakarta) was lifting out the last of the republic's bullion reserves to Manila. Wanting to get out, I sneaked onto this plane and flew to Manila. When we arrived, we heard that Yogyakarta had already fallen. We had as narrow an escape as that!

From Manila I found my way back to Bangkok and was then sent by Haji Agus Salim to London, to lobby the British government to do whatever else I could. Unfortunately I made a lasting enmity while carrying out my duties. The would-be ambassador in London at that time (he was later ambassador, and a good one, for several years), Dr. Subandrio, did not like me being sent in over his head. This only happened because Subandrio was not officially recognized by London. But I was an Englishman and could go anywhere. I saw Stafford-Cripps at the Treasury; I saw John Strachey; I talked to leaders in the House of Commons; I did all sorts of extremely active things, not realizing all the while that I was deeply offending Subandrio, who was unable to do any of this because of his status as the official representative of an unrecognized state. He could only talk unofficially. I quite understand that it was very irritating for him to have an Englishman sent in, who could talk to all these people whom he could not speak officially. It was no great consolation that Subandrio had considerable sympathy in Britain, especially from left-wing socialists, who gave us unexpected support.

Then I returned to Bangkok, and after that to the Round Table Conference in the Hague, where Indonesia received its independence. I had an assistant this time, a young American. We worked on public relations for the republican delegation, and were frequently snubbed by the Dutch delegates and the Dutch people in general. It was perfectly understandable. By that time I felt my job was coming to an end, because Indonesia was obviously going to be independent and I didn't know how long I would continue to have a useful function for the republic. So I went back to my house in Bangkok and celebrated Indonesian independence there. Soon I would be able to visit an independent Indonesia and pursue my interest in its dancing and music.

27

*

The Military and Diplomatic Roles in the Struggle

HAROLD CROUCH

The final stage of Indonesia's struggle for independence began with the Japanese surrender in August 1945 and lasted until the transfer of sovereignty from the Netherlands in December 1949. The struggle was conducted on two levels, the diplomatic and the military. Negotiations between the Indonesian leaders and the Dutch were held several times during the four years of the *zaman revolusi*, the revolutionary era. The early negotiations, however, were not encouraging for the nationalists. It was only when negotiations were resumed in 1949 after an extended period of guerilla warfare that diplomacy brought success for Indonesia. Although Indonesia's military forces never actually defeated the Dutch on the battlefield, it was the inability of the Dutch to defeat the Indonesians that paved the way to the negotiations that resulted in the end of colonial rule at the close of 1949.

The proclamation of independence by Sukarno and Hatta on 17 August 1945 was enthusiastically supported by the people of Indonesia, but it was not recognized by the world community. As allies of the Netherlands during World War II, the major world powers continued to recognize Dutch sovereignty in Indonesia and British forces soon landed in Indonesia to disarm the Japanese and prepare the way for the restoration of Dutch government. Although the Indonesian leaders protested against the return of the Dutch administrators and soldiers, they lacked the military power to prevent it.

General Sudirman (with raised hand) about 1946, Commander in chief of the Republican armed forces, with on his right General Tahi Bonar Simatupang (see chapter 36), on his left General Abdulkadir and behind his left shoulder Anwar Cokroaminoto. Courtesy of ANP-Foto, Amsterdam, Holland.

On 5 October 1945, six weeks after the proclamation, the new republican government established what later became known as the Indonesian National Army (TNI). This new army was composed of local units spread throughout the archipelago, formed in most cases spontaneously after hearing news of the Japanese defeat, and often armed by seizing weapons from the Japanese. The backbone of the new army was made up of youths who had joined the Japanese-sponsored Pembela Tanah Air *(Peta)* which had been set up during the occupation to provide Indonesian military support for Japan in the event of an Allied invasion. The *Peta* officers had been given training appropriate to their intended role as battalion commanders acting under overall Japanese command. In addition to the *Peta* officers, who numbered around 1,600, the new army also attracted about 30 young officers who had been recruited into the Dutch army in the Indies just before the war and had received training in Dutch military academies at a much more sophisticated level than the *Peta* officers. Later other youths formed their own guerilla units, often with the backing of particular political groups, and many of these were also eventually absorbed into the TNI.

The Indonesian armed forces were of course no match for the British, and later the Dutch, forces in conventional warfare. The arrival of British troops in late 1945 had been met with fierce resistance in several places, most notably in Surabaya, but in the end the British and then the returning Dutch forces were able to establish themselves in the main cities. The Dutch military forces were officered by highly trained and experienced professionals who commanded disciplined troops equipped with modern armaments and equipment. The Indonesian forces, on the other hand, were little more than local bands of youths with limited training, virtually no fighting experience, and few armaments.

The Indonesian forces were also far from united. One of the former *Peta* officers, General Sudirman, was elected as commander in chief by his fellow commanders, but he had no way of imposing his authority on local unit commanders, whose strength was derived from the personal loyalty of their troops and who enjoyed, therefore, a considerable degree of autonomy. Moreover, many of the military officers had their own political sympathies, some being close to particular political parties or particular civilian politicians. Discipline was weak and it was not uncommon for troops to depose unpopular commanders and replace them with leaders of their own choice.

In these circumstances the leaders of the government had little alternative but to seek a negotiated settlement with the Dutch. They attempted to win international sympathy for their struggle through the United Nations and hoped that the Netherlands' allies, the United States and Britain, would apply pressure on the Dutch to recognize Indonesia's independence as the Americans had done in the case of the Philippines and Britain in India. But the policy of seeking independence through diplomacy was opposed by many of the nationalist forces both among the political parties and in the army. These groups regarded negotiations with the Dutch as a "sell-out" and demanded "100% independence." Tension between advocates of diplomacy and supporters of all-out armed struggle culminated in mid-1946 when a dissident group headed by Sukarno's rival, Tan Malaka, and including a young radical named Adam Malik, kidnapped Sukarno's prime minister, Sutan Syahrir. The dissidents had the sympathy of the army commander in chief, General Sudirman, but the prime minister was soon rescued by troops loyal to the government.

The republican government, which had been forced by the return of the Dutch to move its capital from Jakarta to Yogyakarta in the hinterland of Java, persisted in its efforts to negotiate. The result was the Linggajati Agreement in November 1946, according to which the authority of the republic in Java and Sumatra would be recognized but only as one state in an Indonesian federation united with the Netherlands under the Dutch crown. The agreement was denounced by many nationalist leaders as a betrayal of the struggle, but the government, conscious of its military weakness, felt that it had no choice. Meanwhile, Dutch distrust of the republic grew and eventually, in July 1947, they launched what was called a Police Action, which succeeded in bringing most of Java and the main economic regions of Sumatra under direct Dutch control. The Dutch action was criticized by the United States and Britain, which both believed that the Netherlands should concentrate on Europe, where the Soviet Union was looming as a threat, rather than dissipate her energies in the Far East. Pressed by her allies, the Dutch agreed to reopen negotiations with the republic. Reflecting the new balance of military power, the Renville Agreement was reached in January 1948 recognizing Dutch control of areas captured in the Dutch Police Action. Again the Indonesian government's willingness to accept such an agreement was greeted with strong opposition from within the nationalist camp with the result that the prime minister was forced to resign. But his successor, Vice-President Hatta, could see no alternative to continued reliance on diplomacy.

It was in this context that further upheaval took place in the nationalist camp. The Hatta government had embarked on a plan to "rationalize" the military by creating a smaller, well-armed, well-trained, and more disciplined force. But this plan involved the demobilization of militarily less effective troops. Among the units to be disbanded were some with leftist political affiliations. When some of these units rebelled in Madiun in September 1948 they were supported by the Communist party, which proclaimed the formation of a "National Front" government. However President Sukarno quickly rallied support for his government and the revolt was crushed, many of its leaders being executed.

A few months later, in December 1948, the Dutch launched what they called the second Police Action and what Indonesians called the second Dutch Aggression. The republican capital, Yogyakarta, was occupied and the leaders of the government, including Sukarno and Hatta, captured. As a result the leadership of the struggle moved in effect from the hands of the civilian politicians to the military which, under the command of the ailing General Sudirman, launched guerilla warfare throughout Java and Sumatra as well as in the eastern islands. While the Dutch continued to occupy the main towns they found it impossible to control the countryside and to protect their supply lines. Although the Indonesian forces were deficient in arms and equipment, they enjoyed overwhelming popular support. Eventually the Dutch realized that they were engaged in a war that was not only costly but unwinnable. In the middle of 1949 the republic's leaders were released and a new round of negotiations commenced which resulted in the final transfer of sovereignty from the Netherlands to Indonesia.

The Indonesian struggle thus ended in victory. Although the Indonesian military forces were weak by conventional standards, they had mass support and were able to make Dutch victory impossible, so that in the end the Dutch were forced to withdraw. But the period of guerilla warfare was brief and the Dutch did not suffer total defeat. In the final negotiations the Dutch were able to obtain important concessions. They insisted on a federal constitution for Indonesia (under which, they hoped, pro-Dutch elements in the outer islands would be influential), a symbolic Netherlands-Indonesian Union under the Dutch crown, guarantees for Dutch businessmen and their investments in Indonesia, and postponement of the settlement of the status of West Irian. It was only in later years that these remnants of Dutch rule were gradually removed. The federal constitution was abandoned in 1950, the Union was dissolved in 1956, Dutch investments were taken over in 1957 and nationalized in 1958, and West Irian was finally transferred to Indonesia in 1963.

28

*

Revolutionary Youth

ANTON LUCAS

Forward
For you, Oh Country
Prepare the fire

Maju
Bagimu Negeri
Menyediakan api

(Chairil Anwar)

Long before 1945—that is, ever since the Sumpah Pemuda or Youth Oath of 1928—*pemuda* had been "preparing the fire," namely the fire of Indonesian independence. Activities during the Japanese period were in fact a continuation of the nationalist movement which had started in the 1920s. It was during the Japanese occupation that many *pemuda*, particularly in the main towns, had an opportunity to be active. For the *pemuda*, it was not ideas but experiences which inspired action. And the experiences they had during the three and a half years of Japanese rule were very important, not only for those who had been leaders but also for the ordinary members of the para military groups and other associations formed by the Japanese.

One episode in Jakarta on 6 July 1945, on the eve of the Japanese defeat, clearly illustrates the great differences between the views and atti-

The scorched earth policy of the revolutionary youth (Pemuda)—Japanese aircraft destroyed on the airfield in Bandung to prevent their being used against the revolutionaries by the Dutch or Allied Forces.

Courtesy of H.G. van Maurik.

tudes of the *pemuda* and those of the older generation of leaders. For the first time, *pemuda* like Chairul Saleh, Wikana, B.M. Diah, Adam Malik, Bung Tomo, S.K. Trimurti, and Asmara Hadi were included among the leaders of a new organization to be called the Gerakan Rakyat Baru (New People's Movement, or GRB). In the meeting to decide the statutes of the GRB, the *pemuda* wanted to insert the words "Republic of Indonesia" in each clause, but this was rejected by the older generation, namely Sukarno, Hatta, Subarjo, Mohammad Yamin, and Abikusno, who said their demand was out of the question. A Japanese who was present at that time reminded them that it was only the Emperor of Japan who could determine whether or not Indonesia would become a republic. So the *pemuda* were outvoted and they left the meeting, protesting that they were not going to participate in the GRB any more. The revolutionary fire had already begun to flare up.

> *Come on! Bung Karno, give me your hand, let's*
> *make a pact*
> *I've had enough of your speeches, of being roasted*
> *by your fire, of being salted by your sea*
> *Ever since the 17th of August 1945*
> *I strode to the front and am right by your side*
> *I am now the fire I am now the sea.*
>
> *(Chairil Anwar)*

After the proclamation, it was the *pemuda* who kept fanning the flames lit by the proclamation, keeping up the fire of battle against the Japanese and the British, the fire of social revolution, the fire which demanded "100% independence," without negotiation, without diplomacy, "independence or death," the fire of personal freedom.

On one side were the Jakarta *pemuda*, spurred into action by the principle of "we don't want our independence as a present from the Japanese," while on the other side were the leaders of the older generation, Sukarno and Hatta, ever cautious and always waiting for reactions from Japanese military government. On 15 August 1945, Sukarno and Hatta were kidnapped by *pemuda* and borne off to Rengasdengklok, near Jakarta.

The kidnapping of the leaders set an example for *pemuda* movements in towns throughout Java. In the rural areas, the older generation were usually represented by former *pangreh praja* whose hesitant reaction to the proclamation reflected their own very cautious attitudes. Some of them awaited the Allied arrival and some of them waited for their "old bosses," the Dutch, to return. There were even some who waited for the official announcement from the Japanese authorities that Japan had formally surrendered to the Allies, although this announcement never came. This group was still fearful of Japanese recrimination when they were forced to lower the "Rising Sun" flag. It was the *pemuda* who forced the flying of the Red-and-White, and often it was they who took down the Japanese flag, so that in the end only the red and white flag flew without the Japanese flag by its side.

> *We who now lie between Krawang and Bekasi*
> *can no longer cry "Independence!" or take up arms*
> *once more*
>
> . . . .
>
> *Remember, remember us*
> *all that is left of us are bones covered with dust*
> *Thousands of us lie between Krawang and Bekasi*
>
> *(Chairil Anwar)*

Thousands of *pemuda* and ordinary people lay not just between Krawang and Bekasi, but also in Pekalongan, Semarang, Magelang, Yogyakarta, Bandung, Surabaya, Medan, Aceh, and South Sulawesi. Fighting started with attacks on those Japanese garrisons still left in regency and residency towns, in order to seize the Japanese weapons. Although these battles were usually successful, they claimed many victims; in Pekalongan the first battle on 3 October 1945 cost 32 *pemuda* lives, in Yogyakarta 18, and in Semarang, where 300 Japanese were killed with bamboo spears, the Japanese retaliated by taking 2000 Indonesian lives. Although Bandung became well known as a "sea of fire," to the *pemuda* of East Java this was no shining victory, and they sent lipstick to the *pemuda* of West Java as an insult. It was really the Battle of Surabaya that became a symbol of heroism, sacrifice, and the spirit of the revolutionary *pemuda*. Early in the morning of 10 November 1945, Surabaya was attacked by British mortars, bombs, and tanks. For three weeks, the *pemuda* and people fought back with just knives and krisses in their hands.

Far away from Surabaya, East Sumatra, and Aceh were also experiencing the upheavals of revolution, and here *pemuda* troops played a very big role. As in Java, the *pemuda* really only held sway in the towns. In Medan, capital of the then province of Sumatra, troops of *pemuda* coordinated by Xarim M.S., a leader of the older generation well known and influential in east Sumatra, suddenly had to prepare to face the infamous "Turk" Westerling. Only in January 1946 were the revolutionary movements able to reassemble and to tackle the governments of the Malay, and both the Simalungan and Karo Batak sultanates. Since the sultans had by now realized how weak the Dutch were, and also because of the fate of the *hulubalang* (district chiefs) in Aceh, they finally agreed to the demands of the Governor of Sumatra, Teuku Mohammad Hassan, that the governments of those sultanates be brought into line with the republic. Basically, the *pemuda* were demanding that the salute "Hail to thee, my lord!" be replaced by "Hail to the people!" But suspicions about the sultans' attitudes still lingered. What finally drove the *pemuda* into action was the Persatuan Perjuangan (Struggle Union) set up by Tan Malaka. Tan Malaka was in fact better known in eastern Sumatra than other central government leaders. The slogan of the Persatuan Perjuangan, "100% independence," and the *pemuda* slogan, "We'd rather bathe in blood than be colonized again," suited and inspired the *pemuda* struggle in east Sumatra and led to the overthrow of the rajas, who were still regarded as being the creatures of the Dutch. On the night of 3 March 1946, most of the royal families were murdered and their entire wealth seized.

In Aceh, the *pemuda* who had been influenced by events in Medan joined forces with the *ulama* or Muslim scholars in the organization called PUSA (Persatuan Ulama Seluruh Aceh or All-Aceh Ulama Union) under the leadership of Daud Beureu'eh, and drove away 107 Acehnese aristocrats who had held the position of *hulubalang*. Especially in the Pidie area, *hulubalang* led by Teuku Daud Cumbok tried to defend their authority by pouring scorn on the republic and the *pemuda*, but their efforts were in vain and in January most of them were murdered in the Cumbok War, which lasted two weeks.

> *Destroy again everything you have done,*
> *Vanish without inheritance, without kin,*
> *Asking no forgiveness for your sins,*
> *Bidding farewell to no one.*
>
> (Chairil Anwar)

But who in fact were these *pemuda*? The *pemuda* tradition was part of a tradition of social protest in Indonesia, especially in Java and Sumatra.

This tradition also thrived in *pesantren* (Islamic training centers), where *pemuda* would come to study with a *kiyayi* who was reknowned as a *silat* (martial arts) expert, or who possessed esoteric knowledge known as *nglemu* in Javanese, which was often called *ilmu kanuragan* or the "secret arts." The *jago* (local champions and toughs) and village school teachers were also associated with a tradition of social protest against the Dutch and the *pangreh praja*.

By the 1930s, the *pemuda* movements were already visible. Before the war there were already such *pemuda* movements as Indonesia Muda (Young Indonesia); Perpri (Persatuan Pemuda Republic Indonesia or Union of Youths of the Republic of Indonesia) which was the *pemuda* mass organization of Partindo and was based in Solo; and SPI (Suluh Pemuda Indonesia or Torch of Indonesian Youth) which was the *pemuda* mass organization of PNI Baru. Although Indonesia Muda was sometimes regarded as a "movement for picnics and playing ball games" by its more revolutionary comrades, nonetheless in 1945 it emerged in the big towns and played a role at the national level. These *pemuda* were often called "school *pemuda*" because they were Western educated. It was not uncommon to find them as leaders of the regional revolutionary bodies such as API (Angkatan Pemuda Indonesia or Generation of Indonesian Youths), centered in Jakarta; AMRI (Angkatan Muda Republik Indonesia or Younger Generation of the Republic of Indonesia) with its base in Semarang; and PRI (Pemuda Republik Indonesia or Youth of the Indonesian Republic) in Surabaya. In fact, it would be more correct to call these youth organizations "groups," with many different varieties. Some groups were well organized, but others were held together very loosely, and there were even some without names. There was often no communication between them, membership was not strictly defined, and people might in fact be members of several groups simultaneously. Their tasks were to join in the neighborhood night guard, or to guard the roads and offices; they knew what they had to do and where they had to be without orders. Members of the *pemuda* revolutionary bodies were often known as *pemuda rakyat* or "youths of the people." This should not be confused with the PKI mass organization of the same name of 1965; the *pemuda rakyat* in 1945 were non elite, poor youths from rural areas and villages on the outskirts of towns.

A *pemuda* was above all someone with revolutionary spirit. "A person with a revolutionary consciousness is someone who no longer just thinks about his plough or his buffalo," as someone who was involved with the struggle put it. *Pemuda* could not be judged by their age, education, or marital status, though it is true that most of them were young, and rarely possessed a Western education. Also, the majority of them were in fact still single; we must not forget that before the war, for example, only unmarried people could become members of Indonesia Muda.

The following scene from the revolution illustrates how even an older person could have a *pemuda* spirit. A village teacher, a head of a local KNI who had been appointed district chief in October 1945, was on a duty tour of the villages. As he passed a guard post, a middle-aged man stood up straight and shouted "Merdeka!" ("Independence!"). The head of the KNI stopped and asked, "Who are you?" "I am *pemuda* Marto," replied the man. Now this Marto was a *jago* well known in Dutch days for his ability to enter people's houses by prying open windows with an iron bar. So here was a known robber, aged at least fifty, nonetheless stating with pride that he was a *pemuda*. This was pure *pemuda* spirit. He joined in with the other *pemuda*, taking his turn at keeping watch.

Of course the meaning of "revolutionary spirit" has to be seen in the context of Indonesian culture. For example, one of the revolutionary values of the *pemuda* at that time was the rejection of hierarchy in everyday social mixing, reflected chiefly in their use of language. As a rule in Java, the *pemuda* rejected the use of high (*kromo*) Javanese, which is essentially a language for paying respect. They preferred to use the so-called "low" Javanese, or *ngoko*, in their general meetings, because it was regarded as a firmer language, more straightforward and daring. Apart from that, in parts of Java where a "social revolution" was taking place, such as along the north coast in the residency of Pekalongan, the *pemuda* and the people were constantly urged not to use titles such as *abdi* (your slave), *ndoro* (sir or madam) and others; these were to be replaced with *bung* (brother) and *saudara* (brother or sister). As greetings, *Merdeka!* (Independence!), *Darah!* (Blood!) and *Bebas!* (Free!) were used, courageous expressions brimming with hope and comradeship. *Semangat* (spirit) provided the basis for everything carried out by the *pemuda* at that time. If someone had no spirit, he was not regarded as a *pemuda*. He was just "playing at being a *pemuda*." In return for their duties of keeping watch in the regency towns in Java, the *pemuda* received a portion of *nasi ponggol* (rice wrapped in a banana leaf) cooked in a communal kitchen. Some *pemuda* were nicknamed *pemuda ponggol* by a leader, because they were reluctant to take over from their friends on guard duty if the *ponggol* rice had not yet arrived.

A more democratic use of language reflected the egalitarian values prevalent among the *pemuda* at that time. This was a *sama rata sama rasa* or "same share, same feelings" ideology, very important to the whole nationalist movement, not just the *pemuda*. *Rasa* is a Javanese word rich in meaning, one of which is "spiritual feeling." *Sama rasa* meant spiritual affinity between the *pemuda* and the ordinary people who fought together. For Pesindo or the Partai Sosialis Indonesia (Indonesian Socialist Party, PSI) this slogan stood for communal happiness, prosperity, and freedom. *Sama rata* meant that the apportioning of textiles or rice left over from the Japanese occupation had to be equal for everyone, irrespective of their different needs. Indeed, at that time, there was an important difference between *merdeka* or independence and *bebas* or freedom. Many of the *pemuda rakyat*, to quote a Muslim *pemuda* leader at that time, "desire personal freedom, but don't yet understand the meaning of independence." Very often, the greeting "Merdeka!" brought the reply "Bebas!" accompanied by a raised fist.

Still, *merdeka*—from the old Malay word *mahardiker*, meaning a free person (not a slave)—remained the key one used by *pemuda*. An Australian war correspondent who accompanied President Sukarno's entourage on a trip to East Java in early December 1945 reported that all along the train journey they were constantly greeted with ear-splitting shouts of "Merdeka!" Of course there were different interpretations of *merdeka*. For a fifty-year-old with the spirit of a *pemuda* who joined in guarding road blocks, *merdeka* had an ideological as well as a personal sense. Meaning in particular "The Dutch must go" (or rather, "they must not be allowed back in"), the greeting "Merdeka!" implied that the greeter was someone full of spirit, and quite unafraid of death; when such *pemuda* heard the news of the proclamation, their blood seethed and they became determined to defend that independence. The cries "Out!" and "Independence!" were battle cries, aimed at stopping the enemy: the Dutch civil administrators who had returned to Indonesia hidden among the ranks of the English troops.

The *pemuda* spirit did not generate the response many had hoped for. In the end, the *pemuda* were disappointed with both Tan Malaka's struggle and Syahrir's diplomacy, and with the results of the Round Table Conference in The Hague and the terms of the transfer of sovereignty in 1949. As Chairil Anwar wrote:

> *Have our souls flown away for independence,*
> *victory and hope*
> *or for nothing at all*

Nonetheless, *pemuda* hopes for a society based on the principle of *sama rata sama rasa* continue burning in many hearts down to the present day.

29

*

The Radio War

COLIN WILD

Radio started in Indonesia as a hobby for relatively prosperous people. "In large towns in Java in the 1920s and 1930s radio clubs (*radiovereni-gingen*) sprang up, whose members shared the cost of the technical equipment and facilities needed to make and transmit programs. The first of these clubs was the Bataviase Radiovereniging, whose members were predominantly Dutch. But by 1934 groups of Indonesians had established radio clubs in Batavia, Surakarta, and Yogyakarta. The colonial authorities tolerated the growth of small stations, but felt that a professional nationwide broadcasting network was needed. In 1934 the Nederlands-Indische Radio Omroep Maatschappij (NIROM) was established, broadcasting in both Dutch and Indonesian and soon audible throughout most of the archipelago." The response of Indonesian *radioverenigingen* was to form a union in 1937 called the Perikatan Perkumpulan Radio Ketimuran, and by the end of 1940 the PPRK had won the right to broadcast on social and cultural matters only, while NIROM remained the official news station.

But no sooner had this compromise been reached between Indonesian broadcasters and the colonial authorities than it was all swept away, for on 8 March 1942 the Dutch surrendered unconditionally to the Japanese. Not only did the Japanese immediately establish a tight control over broadcasting, they provided village radio sets and even took over all radio repair workshops. Radios were doctored so that

Raden Maladi, the first Director General of Radio Republic Indonesia, photographed in Jakarta in 1984.

Courtesy of the BBC.

none but Japanese stations could be tuned to. Listening to foreign stations became illegal.

Japanese monopolization of broadcasting was not entirely a negative factor, however. They reduced the number of studios and subordinated broadcasting to the purposes of government, creating a compact and disciplined organization. Since the Japanese could not run the stations without help, their Indonesian employees gained managerial experience the Dutch had previously denied them. Moreover, Sukarno was permitted to broadcast over the Japanese network on formal occasions. By the skillful use of allusions which the Japanese did not understand, Sukarno was able to bypass to some extent the official censorship and make himself and his ideas known to wider audiences, at least in Java, than he had reached before. As the war went on and the Allies began to get the upper hand, the Japanese increasingly needed the support of the conquered people. By early 1945 the Japanese-controlled radio stations were whipping up Indonesian nationalist sentiment.

Among the first Indonesians to know that Japan had capitulated to the Allies were the employees of the radio station in Jakarta (Hoso Kanri Kyoku), who had professional access to the bulletins of the Japanese news agency, Domei. The Japanese did not want their defeat to be made known, but the Indonesian broadcasting staff went on strike on 15 August 1945, rather than broadcast lies about the state of the war. Two days later the staff of the radio station on Medan Merdeka Barat in Jakarta smuggled the proclamation of independence into the studio and read it on the air. The Japanese, in retaliation, closed the radio station. But the staff of the studios were prepared; they continued broadcasting from another building using a mobile transmitter. This alternative studio with its illegal transmitters continued broadcasting under the name of Radio Indonesia Merdeka, or Radio Free Indonesia.

The radio initiative had now passed to the revolution. The political leaders of the revolution, however, perhaps because of their many other preoccupations at the time, did not give a high priority to broadcasting. On September 11, delegates from the eight former Japanese radio stations on Java met in Jakarta and formed themselves into an organization called Radio Republik Indonesia (RRI). They then went to meet Sukarno, who was too busy to see them. To another government official they explained their intention of acting as the government radio network; the official was astonished at the idea and would make no decision. Thus, although the leaders of the revolution, with all the cares of government now on their shoulders, showed little interest at this time in gaining control over broadcasting, the government found itself supported by a self-appointed radio system. Although Sukarno used radio to broadcast messages of national importance, it was not until 1 April 1946 that RRI was formally recognized as a government organization. This was not the last example of the professional broadcasters taking the initiative into their own hands.

After August 1945 radio performed a vital role in maintaining coherence among the fragmented elements of the revolution. As early as August 23, Sukarno was on the air promoting the idea of a political party to unite all republican factions—a (new) Partai Nasional Indonesia—and urging all former members of Peta and Heiho armed forces to unite under the banner of a new organization to be called the Badan Keamanan Rakyat (BKR).

The Allies were soon preparing to land in Indonesia. They had a delicate task, and needed to explain their intentions to the people. Radio was the best means of achieving this. On September 29, the newly appointed British commander of Allied forces in the Netherlands East Indies, Lieutenant General Sir Philip Christison, tried to allay the fears of the inhabitants of Indonesia as British troops began to land there by giving a press conference, which was broadcast from Singapore. Christison said the British were coming only to evacuate internees and Allied prisoners of war, to repatriate the Japanese and to maintain law and order. He added, "The British have no intention of meddling in Indonesian internal affairs." Lieutenant-Governor Van Mook considered that by allowing this to be broadcast Christison had virtually told the republican masses that he recognized the new republic.

Meanwhile in Surabaya the absence of central control over broadcasting was contributing to the growing tensions. On October 12, there arrived in Surabaya from Jakarta a young man called Sutomo, who knew how to use radio as a means of rallying public feeling. Bung Tomo, as he was known to his listeners, established Radio Pemberontakan (Rebellion Radio), which was soon on the air every night telling the rest of the country about Allied bombing raids on the city. He even had the vision to engage an English woman, who had adopted American nationality and later the Balinese name K'tut Tantri, to tell the world over the air in English about the struggle in Surabaya.

Bung Tomo was one of the few revolutionary orators worthy of comparison with Sukarno. His fiery, passionate broadcasts contributed to the emotional atmosphere which led to the uprising in Surabaya and the bloody battle between the British and the *pemuda*. In spite of two broadcasts by Sukarno to the people of Surabaya calling on them not to waste ammunition and discredit the revolution by fighting the Allies, it was broadcasts by Bung Tomo and by the governor of East Java, R.M.T.A. Suryo, which were the more effective. Suryo told the people that Surabaya would not submit to the Allied ultimatum to hand over their arms and the people who had killed the local British commander, Brigadier General A.W.S. Mallaby. Bung Tomo exhorted the people to fight.

Radio is a voice which can unite individuals or groups who share a basic aim but who might otherwise act independently and without co-ordination. It can sometimes transform beliefs into actions. It reinforces reality and the truth, and can reinforce strongly held views even if they are mistaken. But it cannot deflect whole populations from a deep conviction. Bung Tomo's messages were the messages the local *pemuda* and others wanted to hear. These were the messages they acted upon.

When similar trouble was brewing in other parts of Java in November 1945, Sutan Syahrir, the prime minister, and other leaders also frequently broadcast appeals for calm. But they too, had little effect. In the face of the spontaneous outburst of patriotic fervor which gripped Indonesia immediately following the Japanese collapse, when it looked as if the Allies were about to snatch away the newly acquired freedom, even Sukarno could not quell public emotions. But on many subsequent occasions radio was the medium by which Sukarno made known the government's will and it was often his oratory over the air which determined the direction in which matters would go. For example, on 26 June 1946 Sutan Syahrir was kidnapped by people opposed to his government. At first the facts were kept from the public. But on June 28 Sukarno assumed full governing powers and two days later went on the air to accuse those who disrupted the legal government of playing into the hands of the Dutch. Syahrir was immediately released.

Two years later, on September 19, 1948, Sukarno denounced the communist rebels in Madiun over the radio. The rebel leader, Musso, replied, also over the radio, with a bitter attack on Sukarno himself, declaring that he would fight to the finish. The adversaries having made their positions and mutual hostility clear so publicly, no further compromise was possible. Communist groups in other parts of the country as far away as Banten and Sumatra disassociated themselves from Musso; by September 31 Musso had been killed, and Aidit and Lukman had fled to communist havens abroad.

Meanwhile radio was also playing its part at the international diplomatic level. The broadcasts of the proclamation of independence on August 17 had already been heard by listeners in Australia and by this means had become headline news world wide.

On October 8, 1945, Sukarno broadcast an invitation to Nehru of India, Chiang Kai-shek of China and Carlos Romulo of the Philippines to come to Indonesia to see the situation for themselves. The radio was also used as a means of passing diplomatic messages to the outside world, like the messages of gratitude to the Australian trades union movement and to the leader of the Indian Congress Party, Jawaharlul Nehru, broadcast by Radio Indonesia Merdeka in October 1945.

The world was even given, in English, the Indonesian government's attitude to Dutch attempts to reoccupy Indonesia. Radio Indonesia Merdeka, in a reproachful commentary on the political situation, said: "The Dutch who have just been liberated from oppression are about to do to us [what the Japanese and Germans did to them]."

Back on the domestic front, radio was developing, but the government, though it made good use of it, showed anxiety about it. In January 1946, Raden Maladi, then director-general of RRI, formally inaugurated external broadcasting in English from Tawangmangu, a mountain resort near Solo. In April 1946, the same month that RRI was adopted by the government, Tan Malaka, the communist, was exiled by the government to Tawangmangu, and on May 1 a broadcast was made in English to celebrate Labor Day. The government began to be suspicious, thinking that the station in Tawangmangu was being put at Tan Malaka's disposal. Then, in early 1947, Siaran Nusantara was also started from Tawangmangu. RRI thought of this new station as a "second front" in case of political problems in Yogyakarta. The first Dutch Police Action in July 1947 seemed to justify this precaution. But after the Renville agreement on January 31, 1948 the English broadcasts were stopped by the government. Then, in October 1948, Siaran Nusantara from Tawangmangu also stopped. But, on 18 December 1948, a mere two months later, the Dutch attacked Yogyakarta in what is known as the second Police Action. As the troops approached the palace to arrest Sukarno, a broadcast was made from Radio Republik Indonesia conferring full power upon the minister of economic affairs,

Syafruddin Prawiranegara, who had flown to Sumatra a week before. The radio stations in Yogyakarta and Solo fell into Dutch hands, and because no preparations had been made in anticipation of this event, RRI went off the air. But the radio staff again showed their initiative. The essential parts of a transmitter and an electrical generator were loaded on to a truck and the director-general of RRI, Raden Maladi, and some of his staff, took to the road and managed about three weeks later to get the voice of the republic on the air again, though its studio, in a village in Central Java, was far from the emergency government in Sumatra.

Radio as a medium of communication was used effectively by the republican leadership but, as we have seen, there seems to have been some mistrust of the power that radio can wield. It was eight months before the republic gave RRI the official status it wanted, and even then the stations in Tawangmangu seem to have been perceived as a potential threat. Did Sukarno think others capable of subverting it to their own use, as he himself had during the Japanese period? Did he fear that it could be seized by others and used against him, as the communists had done in Madiun?

Whatever the case, the revolutionary leadership needed radio, particularly in times of crisis, and thanks to the foresight of the radio personnel, it was usually available to them when it mattered most.

30

*

The Press and the Radio

AN INTERVIEW WITH

BURHANUDDIN MOHAMAD DIAH

I became involved in the struggle against the Dutch through my education. My first school was a Taman Siswa school in Medan, and I continued my secondary education in the Douwes Dekker School, part of an institute in Bandung. I feel that I know a lot about the struggle of the Indonesian people because the leaders of that struggle were also the leaders of my schools, they were people like Ki Hajar Dewantara and Dr. Douwes Dekker, who had worked for the cause of Indonesian independence. So that was why I began to participate in the struggle for Indonesian independence, and I threw myself into the press because I saw this as the best field for reaching the public, the ordinary people.

I started off as an ordinary reporter, and then I went on to write editorials in which I developed my thoughts on Indonesian independence. In fact, I was following an existing pattern, namely conducting a struggle through the dissemination of information, through thoughts on how a nation had to be free. This involved studying the struggles of other nations, such as India, Burma, and China, and looking at how Japan, for instance, took on the strength of Western imperialism as part of its national development.

When the Japanese came to Indonesia, of course we *pemuda* were very happy at first, and we hoped that Japan would make us a present of our independence. But it soon became clear that imperialism is the same everywhere. Colonialism is always the same, whether the people are white and Western, or yellow and Asian. Imperialism and colonial-ism are the same thing. So we had to fight for our independence, be-cause the aim of the Japanese was just to oppress us to fulfill their desires for power.

So the whole struggle was automatically directed towards indepen-dence. When we talk of the struggle for independence during the Japa-nese period, it mustn't be forgotten that Japan controlled Indonesia 100%, because it was still at war with the Allies. And if Japan lost, of course the Dutch would step back in. So it was taken for granted that the struggle for independence was directed at two forces: the Dutch forces aided by the Allies, and the Japanese forces. Hence we were thinking not only about chasing out the Japanese but also about not al-lowing the Dutch back into Indonesia.

By the last half of 1945, there was open opposition towards the Japa-nese. I led a movement, the new generation of 1945, and we automati-cally directed our struggle against the Japanese forces, but we did this officially. At this time Japan was putting forward its policy on inde-pendence for Indonesia. So we naturally used this opportunity to put forward officially our concept of the Indonesian struggle for indepen-dence, not the Japanese concept. This is where the conflict lay: the Jap-anese still wanted to do it their own way, but we didn't want that. Also, the Japanese kept wanting to delay the date for the so-called "indepen-dence" which according to their plan would be given, but we, the *pe-muda*, didn't agree. We wanted to announce our independence by ourselves.

We saw that our struggle had to be supported by a newspaper, since at that time the only newspaper run by Indonesians, *Asia Raya,* was controlled by the Japanese through censorship and other methods. We believed that a nationalist newspaper had to be published. So on Octo-ber 1945, I established the paper *Merdeka* by force; this wasn't a take-over in the normal sense, as we simply seized control of the printing press where *Asia Raya* was printed, and used it to print *Merdeka.*

Of course the Dutch tried to suppress the publishing of *Merdeka,* but since representatives of all the Allied countries had come to Indonesia, the Dutch didn't have complete control. So we were able to use this opportunity to consolidate *Merdeka's* position as an independent news-paper, acting as the trumpet and voice of the Republic of Indonesia. I believe that it was here that the seeds were sown, right under the noses of the Dutch authorities, which later allowed *Merdeka* to continue ing published even when the Dutch had gained control. But I also think that the Dutch saw this as an opportunity to show the world how democratic they were by allowing *Merdeka* to be published.

Merdeka was the voice of the people of the Republic of Indonesia, which meant that this newspaper conveyed the voice of the Republic of Indonesia led by Sukarno and Hatta. Although subsequent governments were set up, this didn't mean that *Merdeka* supported whatever government that was in power at the time, in the sense of supporting their administration or methods of governing. But the independence of Indonesia, led by Sukarno and Hatta: that was what *Merdeka* supported wholeheartedly.

Merdeka was always published in Jakarta, but we also had contingency plans. In the event of *Merdeka* being closed down, we already had our own newspaper in Solo as well. So we were well prepared.

I feel that the role of an Indonesian newspaper in the Indonesian language, as opposed to the ones in Dutch, was very important. Since the early twentieth century, Indonesian newspapers had developed as a means of conveying messages from the leaders; it was the only means at their disposal. We didn't control any other means of communication, but we could publish newspapers. Because of that I feel it was the most important instrument of the struggle: the one and only tool we could use was a nationalist newspaper, so when we became independent we immediately published *Merdeka*. Thus the history of the Indonesian press is a history of assisting the whole Indonesian struggle for independence over the years. It was like this too in the Japanese period, for even though power was in the hands of the Japanese government, the dynamism and militancy of thoughts of independence were spread through articles by the leaders and by quoting speeches by the Indonesian leaders.

Radio was not used very much during the occupation, but because the Japanese themselves used it, it was a very good medium for leaders like Sukarno and Hatta in the period before the Dutch reoccupied Indonesia. Since they were legitimate and recognized by the Japanese, they managed to get the best possible use out of radio during the Japanese period. Things were certainly very different between 1945 and 1949, because Radio Republik Indonesia was broadcasting in the areas not occupied by the Dutch. Hence there was a radio war. We Indonesians who had proclaimed our independence had our own radio station in Yogyakarta, and until Yogyakarta was occupied by the Dutch, that radio was our means of reaching all Indonesians throughout Indonesia.

Because the spirit of independence was so strong, and had been completely instilled into the Indonesian people, the dissemination of messages through radio and newspapers automatically took on a great importance. I believe that it was really the leaders of the newspapers who were the bearers of the ideas of independence. This was especially important at a time when our leaders couldn't speak independently or freely about their ideals, or confront the colonizing nations with our problems.

When Indonesia was still occupied by the Dutch, *Merdeka* had quite a substantial circulation, approximately 45,000—50,000 copies a day, a quantity sufficient to enable us to carry on the struggle through newspapers. These were distributed either by smuggling or through the normal channels, because the restrictions on *Merdeka* were not too tight. So in this way, we were able to use newspapers to the best of their ability in the struggle for Indonesian independence.

31

*

Diplomacy in the Service of the Revolution

IDE ANAK AGUNG GDE AGUNG

Indonesia's success in defending its proclamation of independence
was due to the great sacrifices made by the people and the physical
struggle of the *pemuda* of Indonesia, who never yielded in their fight to
defend that independence. But this glorious success would have been
very difficult to achieve if, in the international arena, Indonesia had not
received very valuable help from friendly countries and the United
Nations. So from that point of view, the Indonesian government's diplomacy during the national revolution was a very substantial part of
the struggle of the Indonesian nation.

Tan Malaka, the left-wing leader, believed that there was no need to
negotiate with the Dutch or to approach friendly countries for help;
armed struggle with the colonizers was the most important way to
succeed in the revolution.

When Sutan Syahrir became prime minister of the Republic of Indonesia, he consciously set about making overtures to friendly countries,
especially Asian and Arab countries, to get help and diplomatic support for the Indonesian independence struggle. When the Inter-Asian
Conference was held in New Delhi, the Indonesian government was
invited to attend. Syahrir led a big delegation to the conference, where
he had the opportunity to make his first speech in front of an international conference. With great statesmanship, he described the Indonesian people's struggle for independence. Syahrir used this good

opportunity to describe the basis of Indonesia's foreign policy. He said that it was the responsibility of every newly-independent nation to distance itself from alignment with either block in the game of international politics. On the other hand, all nations should strive to get rid of differences between themselves and help create a world which desires lasting peace. After Syahrir's visit to New Delhi, relations between India and the Republic of Indonesia were stepped up. The Indian government appointed a political representative in Yogyakarta even though India already had a consul-general in Batavia.

Apart from establishing political and diplomatic relations with India, Prime Minister Syahrir also wanted to widen the Republic of Indonesia's diplomatic relations with other countries, for instance the Arab countries, with whom Indonesia was linked by the religious tie of Islam. On the 18 November 1946 the Arab League met in Cairo and the foreign ministers of the Arab countries decided that the Arab League would suggest to all the Arab countries that they should recognize the de facto and de jure authority of the Republic of Indonesia. The Arab League sent a special envoy to Yogyakarta to convey this decision to the government of the Republic of Indonesia. The Egyptian consul-general in Bombay, Mr. Mohammad Abdul Mun'im, arrived in Yogyakarta on a special flight from Singapore on 13 March 1947. He immediately had an audience with President Sukarno and held talks with Prime Minister Syahrir to inform him of the Arab League's decision and to discuss subsequent measures. It was agreed that the Republic of Indonesia would send a diplomatic delegation to the Arab countries.

A diplomatic delegation was formed, headed by Deputy Foreign Minister Haji Agus Salim, who was regarded as having wide political knowledge of Arab and Middle Eastern countries. The most important destination of this Indonesian diplomatic delegation was Cairo. After he had held talks with the Egyptian prime minister and foreign minister, it was decided that Egypt would acknowledge the de facto and de jure authority of the Republic of Indonesia. As a result, an agreement of friendship between Egypt and Indonesia was signed on 10 June 1947 by the Egyptian foreign minister, Mohammad Fahmi al Nokrasyi, and Haji Agus Salim. As a follow-up to this historic event, the government of the Republic of Indonesia opened its very first embassy in Egypt with H. Rasyidi as the chargé d'affaires.

Haji Agus Salim's diplomatic mission continued its visit to other

Arab countries. On June 29, Lebanon granted Indonesia de facto and de jure recognition, and was soon followed by other countries such as Saudi Arabia, Iraq, and Syria. This latest development showed that as a consequence of Syahrir's diplomacy, the Arab nations were the first group of countries to recognize the government of Indonesia. This historic development was a milestone in the history of our diplomacy and foreign relations.

Negotiations between the Dutch and Indonesian governments did not solve the problem of Indonesia. Under pressure from the British government, these negotiations were held under the supervision of a British mediator who worked very hard to help the two sides to reach an agreement. In March 1946, the negotiations between Lieutenant Governor-General van Mook and Sutan Syahrir, under the supervision of Sir Archibald Clark Kerr, succeeded in arriving at an agreement which then had to be annulled because the Dutch government would not accept it. This also happened with the Linggajati negotiations between Syahrir and a commission of Dutch generals, under the English mediator Lord Killearn, which succeeded in bringing forth an agreement. However, because the Dutch government then put forward so many one-sided interpretations of this agreement, this Linggajati agreement could not be implemented.

Finally, the Dutch launched their first Police Action to force their will on the Republican government. One result of this Police Action was that the Indonesian problem took on a new dimension with the involvement of the United Nations, who appointed a Three Nations Commission to help the two sides reach a negotiated settlement. From that moment on, the problem of Indonesia became an international problem under the jurisdiction of the United Nations. This was opposed by the Dutch, who had always taken the stand that the Indonesian problem was an internal problem which only involved Indonesia and Holland. Thus the decision of the United Nations to participate in the settling of the Indonesian problem was a diplomatic victory for the Indonesian side.

Further negotiations between Dutch and Indonesian delegates under the supervision of the Three Nations Commission were carried out on the deck of the American warship *Renville*, and on 17 January 1948 they succeeded in producing the Renville Agreement. However, this agreement did not in fact bring the two sides any closer, and tensions arose. An initiative from the members of the Three Nations Commission also failed because the Dutch were not prepared to accept these suggestions as a basis for negotiations. Mohammad Hatta, who replaced Amir Syarifuddin as prime minister, was very disturbed to see the tensions that were arising between the Dutch and the Indonesians because of the failure of these talks. Hatta believed that the Dutch would probably try to launch a second Police Action on the republic in an attempt to force its political will. To overcome this worry, Hatta worked hard to get the United States to sympathize with Indonesia's position, because he was convinced that as the strongest superpower at that time, and as a member of the Three Nations Commission, the United States was capable of giving Indonesia valuable help. This made Hatta revoke the consular agreement between the Republic of Indonesia and Russia which had been signed by the Indonesian political envoy in Prague, Soeripno, without the permission of the government of the Republic of Indonesia. Of course this action distanced and complicated relations between Russia and the Republic of Indonesia, but on the other hand it increased the American government's sympathy for the Republic of Indonesia's struggle for independence.

The American government's respect for the Indonesian government grew after Hatta's government succeeded in putting down the communist revolt in Madiun which broke out on 19 September 1948. The positive and unhesitating action of the Indonesian government in suppressing this communist uprising convinced the American government that the Indonesian government led by Hatta was a responsible government of moderate nationalist leaders whose only aim was to succeed in the struggle for independence for the Indonesian nation. Thus the United States government determined to help the Republic of Indonesia in the hope that this would result in the formation of an independent, sovereign Indonesian nation with a stable government, capable of contributing to the political stability of Southeast Asia.

The United States government's attitude manifested itself when the Dutch government launched its second Police Action on the Republic of Indonesia on 19 December 1948. The United States staunchly opposed this military action, and on their initiative the Security Council met to condemn the aggressive Dutch action. At the suggestion of the American representative, the Security Council passed a resolution on 28 January 1949 which ordered a ceasefire on both sides, and gave instructions for a detailed plan to be used as a basis for negotiations between the Dutch and Indonesian governments. Furthermore, the

Dutch government was ordered to release Sukarno, Hatta, and the other Republican leaders from their exile immediately and return them to Yogyakarta, so that authority could be restored to the Indonesian government.

Proof that the United States government really intended this Security Council resolution to be carried out came in the form of clarification from Washington that the United States would halt its Marshall Plan aid to the Netherlands unless the Dutch government negotiated on the basis of the Security Council resolution of 28 January 1949. With this development, the Dutch government's position became even more isolated, until they had no option but to reopen negotiations with the Indonesians.

So these negotiations started on April 14 in Jakarta under the supervision of the United Nations Commission for Indonesia. The Dutch delegation was led by Ambassador van Royen while the Indonesian delegation was led by Mohammad Roem. On 7 May 1949, these negotiations succeeded in bringing forth an agreement known historically as the Roem-van Royen Declaration. This agreement stated that Sukarno and Hatta agreed to the participation of the government of the Republic of Indonesia at a Round Table Conference to be held shortly in The Hague, where the transfer of sovereignty to an independent Republic of the United States of Indonesia would be discussed. It also stated that the Dutch government agreed to release Sukarno and Hatta and other leaders of the Republic of Indonesia and to return them to Yogyakarta, restoring authority to the government of the Republic of Indonesia.

This Roem-van Royen declaration opened up the path for the Round Table Conference in The Hague which was officially opened on 23 August 1949 and ended successfully on 2 November 1949. In a solemn ceremony in the Den Dam Palace in Amsterdam, Queen Juliana signed the Charter of the Transfer of Sovereignty in front of an Indonesian delegation led by Mohammad Hatta, which established as a reality the foundation of the independent and sovereign United States of Indonesia. In his reply at that historic ceremony, Prime Minister Hatta stated his regret that the Dutch government was not prepared to surrender the territory of West Irian (New Guinea) to Indonesia, and this matter subsequently became a thorn in the flesh of the Indonesian-Dutch relationship. The Dutch government's imprudent attitude poisoned Indonesian-Dutch relations for the next twelve years, and in 1956 forced Indonesia unilaterally to revoke the Indonesian-Dutch Union and all the agreements of the Round Table Conference.

For the Indonesian government, this transfer of sovereignty represented a big diplomatic victory which had been engineered by the wisdom and brilliance of Indonesian statesmen like Sutan Syahrir, Mohammad Hatta and Mohammad Roem. For the United Nations, this event was an important and historic milestone in its role as an international organization because it had succeeded in helping a nation in its struggle for independence. In this way it also created political stability in Asia, which had great significance in the context of its efforts to protect world peace, the most important function of the United Nations.

32

*

The Victory of the Republic

ANTHONY J.S. REID

The events which brought the Indonesian struggle for independence to fulfillment can be viewed in two lights. They constituted a struggle between European colonialism and Asian nationalism fought out on the battlefield, at the negotiating table, and in the hearts of men. But they also constituted the climax of a revolution, such as France had experienced after 1879, Russia after 1917, or Vietnam in step with Indonesia from 1945. Once a revolution breaks the domination of the past it tends to move steadily further to the left as it seeks a new source of legitimacy and legality in something mysteriously known as the sovereignty of the people (*kedaulatan rakyat*). Each setback suffered by the leadership tends to produce new leaders better in touch with the radical demands from below, until at last one group is able to suppress its rivals and establish a new equilibrium in the name of the people.

The Indonesian revolution is crucial in both respects. It showed for the first time that a determined European colonial power could be forced out of Asia by a mixture of military and diplomatic pressure. It also created, through revolution, a new political system. The definition of that system continued to move to the left until 1948, when it shifted sharply back to the center.

The Dutch attack of 20 July 1947 on the areas surrounding their seven urban enclaves in Java and Sumatra failed completely to overturn the republican government as Van Mook had hoped it would. All it did

Citizen soldiers go home—a group of T.N.I. (Indonesia National Army), returning to Republican controlled areas, pass a Dutch checkpoint on the "frontier" at Sidikalang in North Sumatra.

Courtesy of H.G. van Maurik.

was bite off the most lucrative parts of republican territory—the plantation areas of West Java and East Sumatra and the oil installations near
Palembang—as well as the areas adjacent to Surabaya, Semarang, and
Padang. Economically this strengthened the Dutch and weakened the
republic, but economic pressure seldom stops a revolution. If anything,
the growing hardship in the remaining republican-held areas of Java
and Sumatra, overcrowded with refugees, lacking resources, and
blockaded from external trade, increased radical demands for total
popular resistance against the Dutch. Moreover the outbreak of open
warfare between Dutch and Indonesians shocked a war-weary world,
which would henceforth insist through the newborn United Nations
that the conflict must not be resolved by force.

Every republican government was obliged to try to retain international sympathy by meeting the Dutch halfway in negotiations, even
though this compromised the popular demand for 100% *merdeka*. The
United Nations-inspired negotiations which led to the Renville Agreement of January 1948 were particularly painful, since the republic had
to acknowledge de facto the seizure of territory in the Dutch aggression of 1947. Even though the concession was essential, the prime
minister who made it had to pay the price for it in popularity, just as
Syahrir had had to for earlier concessions.

This prime minister was Amir Syarifuddin, who tried to be at once a
Marxist and a Christian, a democrat and a communist, a nationalist
and an internationalist. He led the most leftist government Indonesia
has ever had, with 10 of the 34 ministers, including Amir himself, later
declaring themselves to have been communists. Renville provided an
opportunity for PNI and Masyumi to withdraw their support for him
as premier, and for Sukarno then to name Hatta to form a "Presiden-
tial" Cabinet with no Marxist representatives, no longer responsible
like previous cabinets to the KNIP (Parliament) where the Sayap Kiri
(Left Wing) was dominant. The parties of the Sayap Kiri thereby lost
their leadership of the revolution, including the key ministries of defense and interior, which they had hitherto controlled. In this major
turning point it was Amir the Marxist who appeared the naive believer
in parliamentary legality, outmaneuvred by the realpolitik of Sukarno
and Hatta.

The Marxist parties, now calling themselves Front Demokrasi
Rakyat, or Peoples' Democratic Front (FDR), tried to make up in popular support what they had lost in power, by developing a more radical

economic and social program than the revolution had yet seen. They now opposed any compromise with the Dutch, encouraged strikes for better conditions, notably at Delanggu and Cepu, and pressed for nationalization of enterprises and distribution of land, especially *bengkok* (land assigned to village officials), to the landless. Meanwhile the army was also becoming polarized between supporters and opponents of the government's plans to demobilize unruly and poorly-armed units, especially those sympathetic to the opposition. Internal conflict between Left and Right, and between rival military units, was accentuated when the FDR leaders, demoralized by their loss of power, accepted the radical policy which Musso brought from Moscow in August 1948. The FDR parties merged into a larger and more aggressive PKI.

In Yogyakarta and Solo the powerful Siliwangi Division gave the government a stronger position, but in the Madiun area Pesindo forces of the Left were stronger. When the PKI acted first to strengthen its position in Madiun, local conflicts erupted into a savage civil war. In successfully crushing this so-called Madiun Rebellion of September 1948, the republican government achieved three important aims: it eliminated the rival leadership, ending the movement of the revolution to the left; it created the beginnings of unity in the army (TNI), at least in Java; and it demonstrated to the United States, the key force in the United Nations, that moderate nationalists (rather than colonialists) were the best guarantee against communism.

The reputation of the republican government in the United States was therefore highest when it was most needed: 19 December 1948, at the moment of the second Police Action. Dutch paratroops attacked all the remaining republican cities, capturing Sukarno, Hatta, and most of the cabinet in Yogyakarta. Once again, this Dutch aggression arose out of despair with other methods of defeating the republic, and ended up hurting the Dutch much more than the republic. The attack was a clear challenge to the authority of the United Nations. The United States immediately suspended Marshall Plan aid to Holland. Moreover Indonesians of various kinds—Left and Right, republicans and federalists, military and civilian—could unite against this outrage. The cabinets of Negara Indonesia Timur (NIT) and Pasundan, the two largest of the Dutch-created federal states, resigned in protest at the Dutch action.

The so-called *zaman gerilya* (guerrilla period) lasted until 6 July 1949, when the Dutch admitted the failure of their military venture by restoring the imprisoned republican leaders to power in Yogyakarta. In this period republican forces discovered that the Dutch superiority in weaponry and training was no longer effective, since guerrillas could attack them from rural bases almost anywhere. For the military this period also became a model for military–civilian relations. With the leading civilians in Dutch hands, the army led the popular resistance, receiving warm support from villagers in the form of food and hospitality.

Many guerrilla fighters did not find it easy to accept that after 6 July 1949 leadership passed back to civilians and the struggle moved to the conference table. To stop the revolution would be even harder than to start it. In many parts of Java, Sumatra, and Sulawesi guerrilla units refused to disarm, claiming that the cause for which they fought had not yet been realized. Calling themselves Darul Islam, some of them continued their struggle for another fifteen years.

Even if the revolution had not quite achieved unity by 1950, it had exalted the ideal of unity as a sacred goal. Paradoxically it was the Dutch, who had governed the Netherlands East Indies as a centralized state, who tried to use a very decentralized federal system as the basis for retaining influence in post war Indonesia. In each of the areas they controlled after the 1947 military action the Dutch fostered autonomous *negara* with their own cabinets and representative assemblies attempting to represent all ethnic interests. In practice, however, these structures were held together by the steel frame of the colonial army and bureaucracy. By contrast, what united the republic was not structures but ideals. Especially at the beginning of the revolution, Yogyakarta had hardly any means to control the spontaneous movements for *Indonesia merdeka* all over the archipelago. Yet even the unruly *pejuang* (fighters) of Sumatra, Sulawesi, Banten, or Surakarta agreed that the ideal of unity must be defended against the divisiveness of Dutch-inspired federalism.

The compromise negotiated at the Round Table Conference in The Hague between August and November 1949 was for the independent federal Indonesia (Republik Indonesia Serikat) already foreshadowed at Linggajati. But for many this was only acceptable as a stepping stone to the unitary republic proclaimed in 1945. Once sovereignty was transferred by the Dutch on 1 January 1950, the federal states one by one began to merge into the Yogyakarta republic.

On 17 August 1950 Indonesia became in fact the unitary independent republic which had been proclaimed five years earlier, and dreamed about for half a century. The sense of common identity forged in that revolutionary struggle had been extraordinary. If we compare the subsequent history of Indonesia with that of India or Indochina it becomes clear what a remarkable achievement in five short years that sense of unity was. The thousands of islands, dozens of ethnic groups and languages, several major religions and ideologies of Indonesia would henceforth be united in a bond that was sealed not only by words and institutions, but by common sacrifice. *Satu tanah air, satu bangsa, satu bahasa.*

33

*

Republic Under Seige

AN INTERVIEW WITH

SRI SULTAN HAMENGKU BUWONO IX

About six months before the second Police Action, Sukarno, Hatta, Sudirman, and I held a meeting to decide the central government's course of action in the event of a Dutch breakthrough into Yogyakarta. We decided that the central government would leave Yogya. Sudirman would also leave Yogyakarta, but it would be my task to stay behind to help our troops. And six months later, on 19 December 1948, the Dutch launched the Police Action against Yogyakarta and occupied the city for six months.

On that day I was actually ill, but when I heard an airplane overhead, I opened a window and saw a Dutch B-25 circling over Yogyakarta. I had a feeling that this meant that the Dutch were launching a second offensive. So I went straight to the airport and met Suryadarma, the chief of staff the Indonesian Air Force, and after that I met Bung Karno and asked him what the central government was going to do. Bung Karno was wondering whether to stick to the plan of leaving Yogyakarta. I told him that if the central government did actually intend to leave, the only way out was to the east. Then I told him that I would go to my office, the vice-regent's office (*kepatihan*) to instruct all the *pangreh praja* and soldiers to guard the central government on its journey eastwards. After leaving Bung Karno's room I met Syahrir, and we went to the *kepatihan* to give these instructions. After this, we continued our journey to Kaliurang, but on the way there we met Bung Hat-

Dutch soldiers during the second Police Action in 1948.

Courtesy of ANP-Foto.

ta's party returning to Yogyakarta. Since I was at the wheel I turned the car around, but then we saw a small plane dropping explosives from time to time, and we were forced to turn into the villages. We were only able to return to the state offices (*gedung negara*) between half past twelve and one o'clock. When we reached the state offices, I met General Sudirman, who told me that there had just been a cabinet meeting at which it had been decided that the government was not going to leave Yogyakarta. Immediately afterwards, I met Bung Karno again, and he told me the same thing. But then I received word from one of my brothers, who asked me to come back and calm down all the refugees who had sought shelter in the palace. So I returned immediately and tried to calm down the people who had gathered.

Afterwards, at about half past one, I set off again for the state offices, but on my way there I met some men from KRIS (Kebaktian Rakyat Indonesia Sulawesi, republican troops from Sulawesi) who said that the

Dutch troops had reached the post office, so I didn't try to get to the state offices but returned to the palace, and just waited there. At about five o'clock that afternoon, the Dutch commander, Colonel van Langen, came to see me and he gave me a map of Yogyakarta on which the palace was encircled in red ink. Van Langen told me that for reasons of my own security I should not go beyond the red boundary. So I didn't know exactly what had happened in that cabinet meeting held in the state offices.

From that moment on, our troops used guerilla tactics. Of course this affected the people, and around the end of January they really were in very low spirits. By chance, when I was secretly listening to the radio one day—the BBC, or Voice of America, or perhaps an Australian radio station—I heard that at the beginning of March a meeting of the Security Council would be held to discuss the Indonesian question. I grabbed hold of this and it gave me, first, a means of raising the spirits of the people again, and second, a motive for organizing something which would attract attention.

So that's why I sent a letter to General Sudirman at the beginning of February, asking him to consent to the launching of a general offensive—in the daytime—acknowledging, of course, all the risks that such an offensive would entail. Sudirman agreed with this plan, and he told me to contact directly the commander concerned, namely Colonel Suharto, who is our president today. We held a meeting on February 14 and fixed the date of this general offensive for February 28. Then somehow the date leaked out, so we rescheduled the offensive for March 1 at 6 A.M., to be signalled by the sound of a siren. So this general offensive was launched and it turned out to be very successful. We managed to reoccupy Yogyakarta until 3 P.M., because at 2 P.M. I had received information that the Dutch cavalry—that is, tanks—had set off from Magelang and were heading for Yogyakarta. So in order to avoid too many casualties, I suggested to Suharto that we retreat, and exactly at 3 P.M. the TNI retreated. I considered that this had been sufficient to attract the attention of the Security Council.

News of this incident was broadcast from our transmitters in Playan in the Gunung Kidul region to Bukittinggi, and from Bukittinggi it was relayed to India, and from India to the United Nations. And this news appeared to have a very great impact, resulting in the Security Council's decision that the republic must be restored. A consequence of this decision was the holding of the talks between Roem and Van

Royen. The Dutch troops left Yogyakarta on June 29. Bung Karno and Bung Hatta returned from Bangka on July 6, and thus the government was restored to Yogyakarta.

I have often been asked why I never contacted the emergency government. To me, this was a very important issue, because during the Dutch occupation of Yogyakarta I was very much aware of the efforts made by the Dutch to break up the relationship between me and the president. Thus I felt it was necessary to prove my loyalty to the president of the Republic of Indonesia, not to the emergency government.

Furthermore, communications with the emergency government were very difficult. That's why, when I was asked if I was willing to officiate in the restoration of the government to Yogyakarta, I laid down only one condition, namely that I had to have full powers from the president. So I went to Bangka (where Sukarno was being held); I was granted full powers and then returned to assemble all the ministers, departments, and other things. After that, the Dutch withdrawal went very smoothly; there were no incidents at all. And when Bung Karno returned on July 6, all the complications had been sorted out.

Later on, I was designated to receive back all the provinces from the Dutch troops, and then to receive the transfer of government from the Netherlands East Indies to the Republic of Indonesia. On that occasion, Bung Hatta went to the Round Table Conference to obtain Indonesia's independence, and I stayed in Jakarta to officiate at the transfer of government ceremonies.

34

*

A Personal View of the War

GEORGE McT. KAHIN

In August 1948 I drove my third-hand jeep from Dutch-held Purwo-kerto across the truce line at Gombong and on to the first major repub-lican town at Kebumen. Not wanting to be mistaken for a Dutch soldier, for jeeps were associated with them, my battered vehicle flew American flags. But I had not reckoned with the fact that Dutch flags had the same three colors. This was brought home to me soon after my escort, Lieutenant Sutrisno, and I were half way through lunch in a Ke-bumen restaurant. In the square adjacent, a crowd of nearly a thousand people soon gathered and were progressively noisier. Becoming in-creasingly worried, Sutrisno said, "They think you are a Dutchman. You've got to make a speech and explain to them about the flags and that you are an American." I was astonished how, despite my meager knowledge of Indonesian, under this stimulus a torrent of Indonesian gushed out of my mouth as I explained the difference in the flags and that I was an American and that we'd had our own anti-colonial revo-lution.

As the capital of the revolution, Yogyakarta was animated and throbbing with intensity. But it had its somber side because the thou-sands of refugees from Dutch-occupied areas and the undernourish-ment they and many other inhabitants showed because of the Dutch blockade. Living across from Dr. Yap's eye clinic, I daily saw the long lines of people going blind from vitamin deficiency that he could no

188

longer remedy because that blockade had closed off the supply of medicines as well as food.

As the only American in Yogyakarta, I initially encountered a great deal of suspicion, for this was a period when Indonesians thought that the United States was backing the Dutch. At first few people could believe I was merely an American graduate student collecting material for his dissertation, who in order to ensure greater freedom of movement had brought a press card with him. At first army intelligence concluded I was actually the same man as a prewar Dutch official of the East Java Steam Tramway Company. And the Communist party later charged that I was a secret United States government agent to whom the republic had turned over the conduct of its foreign policy. But despite such accusations I was finally accepted as a friend of the republic and came to know many of its leaders well.

The magnetism of Sukarno's personality impressed me immediately, and I witnessed how his speeches could raise the political consciousness of huge crowds of peasants or townspeople. He knew his people well and, to an extent unmatched by any other leader, understood how to appeal to them in language and imagery they could understand. He had an intellectual side that has often been underrated—a broad knowledge of Western and Eastern political thinkers, especially those concerned with nationalism. His understanding of Islam was also clearly deeper than generally assumed, and like Hatta and Syahrir he believed that religion—including Islam—and socialism could work harmoniously together. And for him, together with Hatta, and leaders of the progressive wing of the Masjumi such as Mohammad Natsir, Mohammad Roem, and Syafruddin Prawiranegara, the concept of Islamic socialism seemed a reasonable and possible objective. But Sukarno was the political eclectic par excellence, and unlike these other men believed strongly that there were precolonial traditional Indonesian values calling for social justice and a more egalitarian society which could be adapted to present needs, whether the result was called Indonesian socialism or something else. Like Hatta, Syahrir, and Amir Syarifuddin, Sukarno accepted only limited elements of Marxism, feeling that some of its key parts such as class analysis and the concepts of class struggle and dictatorship of the proletariat had no relevance for Indonesia. For Sukarno national unity was the top priority, taking clear precedence over the attainment of socialism, and on several occasions he emphasized to me that to work for that unity would be his major task, a goal that might take as long as a decade to achieve fully.

Mohammad Hatta was, I think, one of the most underestimated leaders of the republic. During the critical years 1948-1950 he was its central pivot, overseeing internal military, economic, and political affairs, as well as the struggle against the Dutch. He and Sukarno worked well together in those days, and complemented and reinforced each other's effectiveness. Hatta's grasp of Marxist theory was more profound than that of any other top leader, with the possible exception of Syahrir. I can vividly remember witnessing a critical meeting of the Central KNI's executive board during the Madiun rebellion, in which Hatta employed Marxist ideas effectively to demolish Musso's socio-economic analysis as well as his argument that the republic should abandon its neutralist stance and align with Moscow. Musso seemed not only to have a less sophisticated knowledge of Marxism, but he had been so long away from Indonesia that when, shortly before Madiun, I witnessed him address the Indonesian Student Union, his old-fashioned language brought many howls of laughter from the students, who also asked him embarrassing questions about Tito and the recent communist take-over in Czechoslovakia.

Hatta told me that one of his greatest hopes was that Islam would play a progressive socio-economic role in Indonesia. Repeatedly he said: "Social justice and the brotherhood of people are the pillars of Islam" and "the basis of Islamic thought is in the direction of socialism." He hoped that within his lifetime Indonesia would achieve a mixed economy with a limited capitalist sphere confined to small business co-existing with a substantial cooperative component and a large socialist sector.

The views of Syahrir, Hatta, and Sukarno were fairly close at that time, but Syahrir was the most deeply concerned over the possibility that totalitarian ideas might prevail and Indonesia ultimately become a fascist state. He believed that among many Indonesians Japanese indoctrination had strengthened surviving traditional authoritarian ideas that had already been reinforced by the nature of Dutch colonial rule. He was deeply worried that this would incline too much of the population to an unquestioning submission to authority, and that this would work against prospects for democratic government in Indonesia. Syahrir repeatedly told me that after independence had been achieved the greatest danger facing Indonesia would be the threat from men who pressed for a totalitarian state, and he saw that threat as coming from both the communists and the army.

One of the most interesting of the top leaders was Amir Syarifuddin, a man who was regarded as the republic's ablest orator after Sukarno, and whom Sukarno told me had been one of his chief political lieutenants on Java when he was in exile at Benkulen. Despite their criticism of Syarifuddin's role in the Madiun Rebellion, Hatta, Syahrir, and Sukarno all insisted that he had never previously been a communist. All three believed that it was Syarifuddin's bitter disillusionment with the United States over its refusal to honor a promise to make the Dutch live up to their part of the Renville Agreement, which he as prime minister had negotiated, that brought him to join with Musso. This accords with my own impression of Syarifuddin when I talked with him shortly before that event. His major interest in that discussion was when Indonesia could expect that the progressive anti-colonial forces that President Franklin Roosevelt had previously represented would return to power in the United States. When I answered that it would probably be at least another four years, he looked very grave and commented, "That will be too late."

The sudden Dutch attack on Yogyakarta of 19 December 1948, caught everyone by surprise. Exactly a week before, when I was breakfasting with Sukarno, he assured me that with the United Nations' Committee of Good Offices meeting in nearby Kaliurang, the Dutch would not dare attack. He was preparing to leave on the 19th on a plane Nehru was sending to fly him to India, where radio facilities were to be provided so that he could appeal to the world for support against the Netherlands. I was assigned a seat on that plane as far as Bukittinggi, where another republican leader was to be picked up. But the Dutch refused to let Nehru's plane through their blockade and instead, early on the morning it was due to arrive, they attacked Yogyakarta and other parts of the republic.

Most of the republic's army units stationed in the capital withdrew to the mountains according to plan, and the Dutch quickly encircled the city. The intensity of the Dutch bombing, rocketing, and strafing made it too dangerous for the republic's leaders to get to the radio station to broadcast appeals to the people. As the Dutch encircled the city and began to close in, Sukarno, Hatta, and Natsir wrote out speeches that were to be read over Radio Republik Indonesia, calling on the people to resist with all means. But before they could be broadcast, Dutch planes destroyed the radio station. Only the fiery speech of Syafruddin Prawiranegara, head of the republic's emergency government in Sumatra, was heard, it being broadcast over the radio from Bukittinggi.

Dutch marines spearheaded by the KNIL fought their way up Terban Taman street where I lived. Most of the windows and light fixtures in the house were shot out before they entered it. Haji Agus Salim was forced out of a neighboring house, and I had the honor of being captured together with him, Hamid Algadrie, Didi Jayadiningrat, and Imam Pamujo. Some of the Dutch planes and tanks still bore United States insignia, and I was later shocked to see one Dutch major who had been trained in the United States with "U.S. Marines" printed over his breast pocket. So it was easy to see why many Indonesians concluded that the United States backed the Dutch.

Because of my press credentials I was sent to Jakarta and released, and two weeks later was able to return to Dutch-occupied Yogyakarta. It was a city of noncooperators and the Dutch were having great difficulty. The republican underground was strong, and right under the noses of the Dutch I was able to see many old friends, including one of the government ministers, Dr. Leimena. Not surprisingly, after a few days the Dutch arrested me again and locked me up on the top floor of the Hotel Merdeka. That night the TNI counterattacked, penetrating almost to the hotel and mortaring a building directly across the street. The Dutch were clearly shaken by that experience, and it seemed clear they wouldn't be able to hold out long. The next morning, while I was once again on the way to the airport under custody of Dutch military police, two courageous girls of the republican underground, Jo Abdurrachman and Jo Kurianingrat, managed to slip me the undelivered speeches of Hatta, Natsir, and Sukarno, and I was able to deliver them later to Yusuf Ronodipuro of the republic's underground organization in Jakarta and to Tom Critchley of the United Nations' Committee of Good Offices. Yusuf must have run an efficient organization because within a few days Jakarta and West Java were flooded with copies of these speeches calling on Indonesians to resist.

35

*

Emergency Government

AN INTERVIEW WITH

SYAFRUDDIN PRAWIRANEGARA

During the Dutch period I was one of the group usually termed "co-operators." I believed then that the Dutch really did intend to educate us to a level which would enable us to become independent and handle our own affairs. So I didn't agree with the stand taken by people like Sukarno, Hatta, Syahrir, and Yamin, who wanted independence immediately, because in my opinion, Indonesians were not yet ready to run an independent country democratically. Because eventually, if we became independent, we would have to run the country democratically, and we would have to be capable of modernizing the country, and for this too many of our people were still ignorant and unskilled, and there were far too few graduates who could work in the economy and in industry.

I changed this stand after I saw how the Dutch gave in to the Japanese just like that. This was despite the fact that before Japan invaded, we had submitted a petition to the Dutch to try and get them to form an Indonesian militia so that we could help to defend our country, and the proposal was rejected out of hand by the Dutch, because they said that they were quite capable of defending Indonesia against the Japanese by themselves. But it became quite clear that they were totally unable to defend Indonesia against the Japanese, and the way I saw it, they surrendered without a fight. So I was very, very disappointed with the Dutch, and that was the moment I completely lost faith in their aims.

Sjafruddin Prawiranegara lands at Yogyakarta in July 1949 after leading the Emergency Government in Sumatra while Yogya was in Dutch hands. In the picture (from left to right) are: Agus Yaman, an official of the Department of Information; Dr. A Halim (one-time Minister of Defence); Sjafruddin Prawiranegara; Mohamad Natsir (one-time Prime Minister); Loekman Halim, Minister of Finance of the Emergency Government.

Courtesy of Sjafruddin Prawiranegara.

Then along came the Japanese, and it became very clear that they were even more cruel that the Dutch; I didn't believe that the Japanese could or would free us and give us our independence. Take Sukarno, for instance. People like him, including Oto Iskandardinata, believed that the Japanese would free us when the war ended, but I myself didn't believe this. So I felt that, whether or not we were ready for it, we had to become independent and manage our own affairs.

I agreed wholeheartedly with the proclamation of independence, and at that time I actively tried to persuade those of my friends who had initially hesitated, to join in and fight for and defend this independence. Take Mr. Maramis, for example. He was appointed minister of finance, but he didn't dare go into the Department of Finance for fear that the officials there would not recognize his authority! I myself was a financial official, one of the heads of the tax office in Bandung, so I took Mr. Maramis to the Department of Finance and introduced him to all the officials, and he was accepted by them as their minister. Initially, it was indeed difficult to convince them that this really was their minister.

After we were given the opportunity to form political parties in November 1945, I found it really difficult to decide whether to join the PSI or Masyumi. This was because it was Syahrir and Amir Syarifuddin who had brought me into the executive board of the KNI, so I owed them a personal debt and really should have joined the PSI. But at the same time, as a Muslim I felt this wasn't right, when I had the choice of Masyumi, an Islamic party. So in the end I chose to join Masyumi, but I retained a sympathy for the struggle and ideals of the socialists.

When the Dutch held their second Police Action and Sukarno and most of the ministers were detained, the Dutch had predicted that without Sukarno as president, and without Hatta too, the world would soon witness the collapse of the Indonesian opposition. This was the Dutch prediction. They simply hadn't noticed, hadn't realized, that this revolution wasn't an artificial Japanese creation, but really arose from the convictions of the people and their burning desire for independence. The time was now really ripe for independence, and even though it could be said that the people themselves weren't yet ripe, they were ripened by that time itself. So when Sukarno was detained, after I had been convinced that they had really been arrested, my friends and I who were in Sumatra proclaimed an emergency government to carry on the struggle. And it was because of this that we were able to carry on the struggle, and even though Sukarno, Hatta, and the other ministers who had been detained became Dutch prisoners, they were not cast loose, because they were still, morally speaking, linked with the emergency government. So the fact that they were able to hold talks with the Dutch was only made possible because behind them was the emergency government of the Republic of Indonesia (Pemerintah Darurat Republik Indonesia or PDRI), and behind this PDRI were the people of Indonesia, especially the people of Sumatra. Yes, the people of Sumatra, and the people were ours in Java too, because even though most of Java was occupied by the Dutch, the people still remained loyal to the Republic of Indonesia, with Sultan Hamengku Buwono leading the way. So even though Yogyakarta was occupied by the Dutch, in spirit it was still part of the Republic of Indonesia, under the leadership of the sultan. And in Sumatra, it was the PDRI who led the people; a large part of Aceh, for example, had never been occupied by the Dutch. So although the Dutch would talk insultingly about the PDRI—"a jungle government," they called it, "an orangutan government"—I retorted, "O.K., so we're orangutan, but at least our government is legal!"—because when they moved to London, according to their own constitution, the Dutch government had not been legal.

We were based in West Sumatra, but we moved from place to place. We started off in Bidar Alam, a village in the south of West Sumatra, then we moved northwards in stages until we arrived at Kota Tinggi. There we set ourselves up at the Padang Jepang, and were met by Natsir, Leimena, and Dr. Halim, who had come to bring us back to Yogyakarta, and they persuaded us to hand back the mandate to President Sukarno. When we did return the mandate to President Sukarno, the PDRI was nearly seven months old, having lasted from 21 December 1948 to 13 July 1949.

We led and coordinated the struggle in Sumatra and Java. In Java, for instance, we appointed the Central Government Board of Commissioners (Dewan Komisaris Pemerintah Pusat). We also forged links with other countries and gave them progress reports on the struggle within the country, so that they could fight for our cause at the United Nations and abroad; we had Mr. Maramis, who was the foreign minister of the emergency government. And the physical struggle, the military struggle, was conducted under the leadership of Commander in Chief Sudirman in Java, and in Sumatra was under the command of the territorial chief of Sumatra, Colonel Hidayat.

We had radio contact—both fixed and mobile, with mobile radio units and transmitters, for example—and then the PDRI also had a liaison officer or communications officer, Captain Diktamimi. In the meantime in Java, there was Raden Maladi, later minister of information. He looked after all the reports and telegrams sent between Java and Sumatra.

But the problems for the PDRI in acting as a national government are illustrated by its inability to get information about, let alone to direct, the revolutionary struggle in other parts of Indonesia. What, for example, did you, in your Sumatran headquarters, know about events in Kalimantan, Sulawesi, and so on?

We didn't know anything. We could only guess that in those places, too, there was substantial sympathy for the Republic of Indonesia, but in practice the republic at that time consisted of Java and Sumatra.

The very existence of the PDRI and the opposition it organized meant that the Dutch were finally ready to hold more negotiations. Talks were held between Roem and van Royen, and an understanding was reached between the two. According to the Roem-van Royen understanding or agreement, Yogyakarta would be returned to the Republic of Indonesia, and further negotiations would be held to discuss the transfer of sovereignty. Thus after the Roem-van Royen negotiations were settled, Yogyakarta was returned, and Sukarno and Hatta and the other ministers who had been detained were returned as well. So the government could start working again and there was no longer any reason for the PDRI to carry out its duties as an emergency government. Hence it was our duty to return our mandate to Sukarno, although we ourselves did not agree with the Roem-van Royen agreement. This was because we felt its contents were too weak and didn't reflect the strength of the PDRI struggle, because we really were far stronger than the people in Bangka (where Sukarno and Hatta were held by the Dutch) suspected. The people in Bangka didn't really know our situation, but we were convinced that the Dutch would never defeat the PDRI. On the other hand, the PDRI could never hope to defeat the Dutch militarily. In the long run, the Dutch simply wouldn't be able to bear the burden of such a long war; they had to lose in the end. So, seen from that angle, the truth is that the Dutch were probably keen to negotiate with us. And the fact of the matter is that if we had rejected these negotiations, in the long run we certainly would have won. But Sukarno and his friends didn't see it that way, because as prisoners, naturally they wanted their freedom as quickly as possible!

After the mandate was returned, a new cabinet was formed and I was appointed second deputy prime minister, the first deputy prime minister being Sultan Hamengku Buwono, who was based in Yogyakarta, while I was based in Banda Aceh. While most of the cabinet joined in the Round Table negotiations in The Hague, in the Netherlands, I myself was sent to Banda Aceh, with the intention of making me "goal keeper." The plan was that if the negotiations with the Dutch failed and we were forced to continue the struggle, then I would already be "in position." In fact, I was rather stupid, I should have asked to join the negotiations, because that would have been great fun! Anyway, I don't believe they seriously entertained the possibility of failure!

36

*

A Dutch View of the Struggle

A.J. PIEKAAR

At last, on 15 August 1945, the long awaited hour had come. The nightmare was over. Japan had surrendered unconditionally. After three and a half years the end of the Japanese occupation of Indonesia was finally in sight. The Indonesian people saw the Japanese depart with feelings of great joy. Not for nothing was there a saying in Aceh that "the dogs [the Dutch] have been driven out for the pigs [the Japanese] to be let in." The strain of the Japanese occupation had been nearly unbearable, especially in the last years of the war.

Two days later, on 17 August 1945, the Republic of Indonesia was proclaimed in Jakarta. To most Dutch people this declaration of independence came as a total surprise. This was true for those who had been trapped in the Netherlands East Indies at the time of the Japanese invasion, approximately 100,000 of whom had lived under excruciating circumstances, as civilian internees, and 37,000 as prisoners of war. But it was equally true for the Dutch in the Netherlands themselves, who hadn't had the faintest idea of what was going on in the Far East during the years of German occupation so there was a general tendency to view the republic as a Japanese creation, as well as an implicit faith in the possibility of picking up the threads in Indonesia where they had been dropped at the outbreak of the war. No one realized that the relevant hopes and aspirations had, in fact, been overtaken by the course of history. The developments in Indonesia did not occur in iso-

Courtesy of ANP-Foto.

Dutch marines give first aid to wounded Pemuda after a battle in September 1946.

lation, after all, but formed part of a broader process which, stimulated by World War II, was manifesting itself in other Asian countries as well. The fact is that the Dutch weren't ready yet to see the republic as the exponent of Indonesian nationalism.

The circumstance that the Japanese occupation had not only accelerated this historical process, but had also exercised a markedly anti-Western influence on it by means of systematic propaganda did not help to make the situation any simpler. The less so as a large number of Indonesian leaders had collaborated with the Japanese authorities—either under coercion or from what we in the Netherlands saw as opportunistic motives—during the occupation. Dutch resentment about this subsequently served to complicate relations with prominent Indonesian politicians. This was especially true as regards Sukarno, who at the proclamation of the Republic of Indonesia had been appointed president, and Mohammad Hatta as vice-president.

Dutch policy had been laid down long before this in a radio speech given by Queen Wilhelmina from exile in England on 7 December 1942. In it the Dutch ruler linked up with previous radio speeches, in which she had indicated the possibility of a Round Table Conference being held to deliberate upon a political structure for the kingdom and its territories that would be adapted to the changed circumstances. The structure she had in mind was that of a federated kingdom, of which the Netherlands, Indonesia, Surinam and Curaçao would take part as equals. Each would be allowed to manage its own internal affairs independently, using its own resources, but each should at the same time be prepared to assist the others. This conception represented a logical continuation of the so-called Ethical Policy professed in progressive circles before the war. Indonesia's future status was envisaged as that of an internationally recognized, self-governing, economically independent nation, in which all the different ethnic groups would coexist peacefully and which would freely decide on its position vis-à-vis the Netherlands.

This government standpoint was fully endorsed by the joint resistance movements in the Netherlands, including the communists. They had testified to this in a statement drawn up by a committee chaired by the prominent socialist politician and later Dutch prime minister, Professor Schermerhorn, that was published in the underground paper *Vrij Nederland* in April 1945.

We civil servants, like most of the other ex-internees, could hardly restrain our impatience to get back to work and get on with the job, re-constructing, together with the Indonesians, the heavily ravaged country. We were well aware that this would be a different Indonesia from the prewar one, an Indonesia that would be run by Indonesians them-selves and would have to decide independently on its own future, in conformity with the queen's statement, as soon as possible. Our task would be to prepare for this transfer and to help the Indonesians with its implementation, more especially as advisors in the administrative and economic fields. To many of us this meant a very great sacrifice, as we felt we could not spare the time for the necessary recuperation after our gruelling experience during the war years.

How was the situation in Indonesia developing, meanwhile? The South East Asia Command under Mountbatten had been given the re-sponsibility of supervising the surrender of the Japanese military forces in Indonesia. With respect to East Indonesia and Borneo, this task was taken over by Australia. As a result, the strategic areas of Borneo and East Indonesia were occupied by Australian troops as early as Septem-ber 1945. The great majority of the 170,000 Japanese in the area was disarmed and concentrated in around fifteen places. On 29 September 1945 the first SEAC detachment was put ashore at Tanjung Priok, Ja-karta. Medan, Padang, and Palembang were likewise occupied, fol-lowed in the second half of October by Bogor, Bandung, and Surabaya.

It was to be a long time still before Dutch forces were allowed to take over from the British and Australians. On 14 July 1946 the trans-fer of authority with respect to East Indonesia, Borneo, Bangka, and Billiton took place. Java and Sumatra remained under British Allied rule till the end of November 1946, however. Here, too, the approxi-mately 150,000 Japanese troops had been shipped off by that date. In this connection we should pause to remember that by 1 July 1946, well over 35,000 Europeans were still left in republican territory, most in Indonesian internment camps. For them the nightmare of war still was not over. The fact that the Allied occupation of Java and Sumatra had to remain restricted to a few towns and cities, in contrast with East In-donesia and Borneo, had major repercussions for subsequent political developments.

The factual transfer of the administration in East Indonesia, Borneo, Bangka, and Billiton had been effected without too many hitches. The proclamation of the republic here had met with relatively little response from the population in most areas. The inhabitants were on the whole quite prepared to accept Dutch aid for the political and economic reconstruction of the country. From 15 to 25 July 1946 guidelines for the future state structure were laid down in consultation with representatives of these areas at Malino, South Sulawesi. Here a federal structure was decided on for Indonesia, in which the units would not be too small, but so that the specific character of each different area could be done full justice. A transitional phase under Dutch sovereignty was believed to be necessary for the proper organization and equipment of the new state. After the transfer of sovereignty a permanent bond was to be maintained between the Netherlands and Indonesia.

This federal structure appealed to Dutch politicians of both the more progressive and the more conservative parties. The accusation that the idea of a "divide and rule" policy was responsible for this should be categorically refuted here. I myself have wholeheartedly devoted every effort to the realization of this federal structure, first as secretary of the government agency charged with the further working out of the Malino plans and later as secretary to High Crown Commissioner Beel.

Malino was followed up with the conference of representatives of the populations of all the regions of East Indonesia at Den Pasar, Bali, from 19 to 24 December 1946. Agreement was reached here on the formation of the State of East Indonesia. Tjokorde Gdé Rake Sukawati was chosen president, and his republican opponent, Tajuddin Noor, chairman of the provisional parliament. In the first half of 1947 definite plans for the political structure of the autonomous areas of the different parts of Borneo and of Bangka, Billiton, and the Riau Archipelago were completed, pending the combination of smaller areas into larger entities. The representatives of these areas were, like their republican counterparts, guided by the thought that they should do what they judged best for the people and the country under the circumstances.

However, the situation in Java and Sumatra was different altogether. Here the declaration of independence had met with considerable response, in particular among the younger generation. The republic's sphere of influence was rapidly expanding, a development for which neither public opinion nor the government in the Netherlands was prepared. The situation arising from the proclamation of the republic had in one stroke wiped out all existing Dutch conceptions of the future development of Indonesia, and entailed a new reality which had not been anticipated. That it should have provoked fierce opposition from certain conservative groups, who under the motto "the loss of the Indies will only bring disaster" wanted to see a continuation of the prewar situation, goes without saying. But even in progressive circles people initially reconciled themselves to the reality of a republic under Sukarno's leadership with only the greatest of difficulty. The first meeting with republican leaders, including Sukarno, of Lieutenant Governor-General Dr. Van Mook soon after his return to Indonesia from Brisbane in October 1945 was, in fact, so much resented by the cabinet led by Schermerhorn that it might have cost Van Mook his job had it not been for Queen Wilhelmina's a priori refusal to give her consent for his discharge.

The developments in Java and Sumatra on the one hand and in East Indonesia and Borneo on the other were diametrically opposed. Where Sukarno and his associates advocated a single Republic of Indonesia encompassing the whole of the territory of Indonesia, the federalists together with the Dutch government favored a federal structure based on the model of the United States of America.

Many attempts were made to reconcile these different standpoints. But neither the talks held at Hoge Veluwe in April 1946, with Sir Archibald Clark Kerr as mediator, nor the negotiations conducted in November 1946, with the assistance of Lord Killearn, produced any results. The latter discussions did, however, culminate in the Linggajati Agreement, initialled on 15 November 1946, whereby the republic, as de facto ruler of Java and Sumatra, was to be assigned its rightful place in the United States of Indonesia, which would cooperate with the Netherlands in a Dutch-Indonesian Union. But soon differences arose about the interpretation given the agreement by the Upper House of the States General of the Netherlands at its ratification.

The republic, too, was in an extremely difficult predicament. The republican army, the core of which was made up of members of the Japanese-created "people's army," composed wholly of younger men, had little inclination to observe the agreement reached. Accordingly the violations of the cease-fire increased rapidly. Further discussions were fruitless. So the Dutch saw no alternative but to impose law and order themselves.

Two military actions, in July 1947 and December 1948, resulted in an extension of the federal state structure to large parts of Java and Sumatra. Social and economic life gradually returned to normal, even in

the recently occupied areas. It was possible for the people's most pressing needs to be met. Production at European agricultural and mining
enterprises was resumed. By April 1948 Indonesia had a trade surplus
again. With this achievement a foundation was laid for the independent
state of Indonesia to continue building on after the transfer of sovereignty.

Notwithstanding the occupation of Yogya and the internment of the
principal republican leaders during the second Police Action, the republic's spirit remained unbroken. As a result of the repeated intervention of the United Nations Security Council, it was possible to keep
the road to a solution through negotiation open. The first Police
Action was followed on 18th January 1948 by the Renville Agreement,
and the second by the Van Royen-Roem Agreement of 7 May 1949.

This second agreement provided for the return of the republican
government to Yogyakarta, the formation of a provisional body to represent all the regional governments in the archipelago, and the holding
of a conference in The Hague to discuss the speedy, unconditional
transfer of power. This Round Table Conference finally brought agreement on 2 November 1949, and the transfer of sovereignty took place
in Amsterdam on 27 December 1949. The resulting federal state was
replaced on 17 August 1950 by the unitary state of the Republic of Indonesia.

I personally regretted this latter development, even though I recognize that it is up to the Indonesian people themselves to choose the political structure they consider most fit for their country. Fortunately
they have realized the need for the possibility of deviation from the
centralistic model of the unitary state. Of this the granting of the status
of *daerah istimewa* (special region) to Aceh, which was not put into effect
until after the necessary conflicts, is unequivocal proof.

Later the New Guinea issue poisoned the relations between the
Netherlands and Indonesia for many years. It prompted among other
things Indonesia's renunciation of the Netherlands-Indonesian Union.
The total restoration of the relations between Indonesia and the Netherlands since then may be considered illustrative of the mutual understanding, respect, and appreciation which have continued to exist
between the two nations in spite of everything.

Looking in retrospect at this struggle, which lasted well over four
years, and which I am inclined to characterize almost as a fratricidal
war, the question as to the "why" of it immediately arises. The repub-

lic, the federalists, and the Dutch all had the same aim in view: the creation of an independent Indonesia which would be free to shape its own destiny. What kept opinions divided was only the question of the way and the time in which this goal was to be achieved. Looking back now it is scarcely possible to understand why the two nations had to be made to suffer so much misery before they could be brought to cooperate together on a basis of mutual understanding. We can only be grateful that this has eventually been achieved, in spite of all the suffering we have caused the Indonesian people, for which we can do no more than hope to be forgiven.

37

*

Several Indonesian Views of the Struggle

AN INTERVIEW WITH FOUR PARTICIPANTS

Why was the struggle for independence successful? Was it due mainly to the tenacity of the armed forces, the determination of the pemuda, *the skill of Indonesian diplomacy, the support of other nations of the world, or perhaps something less concrete, some particular quality or feeling?*

Syafruddin Prawiranegara: Ah, now, that's a very good question, and most people have probably never answered it as I shall: it is quite clear, it is God's will. Indonesia's independence is the decision of God the Almighty, because if it had been left up to the Indonesian people, we would never have defeated the Dutch. In the period before World War II, Indonesians tried time and time again to free themselves from Dutch colonial power. One of the last attempts, Pangeran Diponegoro's rebellion, was put down by the Dutch. And the last time we rebelled was in 1926, when communists, and Muslims who knew nothing of communism, cooperated to try and free themselves from Dutch colonialism. But the Dutch put down that revolt very easily, and later on, many people were exiled to West Irian, to a place known at that time as Boven Digul. Sukarno was exiled to Flores. So, if it hadn't been for World War II and the defeat of the Dutch by the Japanese, we would still be colonized by the Dutch. I don't see how we could have freed ourselves from Japanese domination, because I don't believe that the Japanese could have freed us, or ever intended to free us. How on earth could we have freed ourselves from Japanese domination if the Japanese hadn't been defeated by the Allies? It was because Japan was defeated by the Allies that we were freed from the Japanese. But just supposing that then the English had arrived in time to accept the Japanese surrender, we would have been handed straight back to the Dutch! But we were given one month's grace: the British troops were late in coming, and we were able to use this delay to proclaim our independence, organize our government, organize troops for our defense, and by the time the Allies arrived, we were ready to defend our independence. In my opinion, as one who has faith in the One God, Allah, I see this clearly as God's will. So all this talk about man's self-determination is not true, in fact it's nonsense. It is God's determination. God had decided: "It's time you were independent!" Otherwise, it would have been impossible. And if we had had to fight for our independence physically, just with weapons, we would have found it impossible to win against the Dutch, but one thing that did help us was sympathy from the democratic world. They were really fed up with war. In fact, even the Dutch were fed up. We were able to defeat the Dutch in part because they were tired of war, but the main reason is because the United States withdrew its aid to Holland. Without this help from other countries who sympathized with us—help from Australia, help from the United States, help from India, help from the whole democratic world—we could never have become independent.

So, if people say it was all because the Indonesians were so fantastic, it's nonsense! Of course we worked for it, but if you look at all the lucky coincidences and chance events, that's how we became independent. If it had all just depended on Indonesia's efforts, we probably still wouldn't be free today. That's why I believe that it was divine will that we should become independent, and God willing, we can settle everything with His help, as long as we remember Him.

Adam Malik: Actually, the most important thing of all was the feeling of our independence returning with the proclamation, after having been colonized for such a long time. It was that spirit which was important. There was no political spirit, because there were no political parties. There had been some political parties, with Japanese policies, which were pro-Japanese, but they were no longer of any account. So this spirit of independence existed, and obviously its growth accelerated because of the preparations made by the *pemuda* for such a situation.

Just as this spirit could not have arisen without these preparations, nor could the proclamation have taken place just like that. So the very night before the proclamation, we printed pamphlets with simple printing equipment—a mimeograph and a hand printing press—and millions of these were distributed.

Australia played the most positive role in supporting us. Australians supported the struggle of the proclamation by organizing strikes just to demonstrate their sympathy for Indonesia. Later, when the matter was brought before the United Nations, in fact it was the Soviet Union that helped Indonesia, as the Soviet representative at the United Nations expressed support for us. At that time, America tried not to take sides. As for Britain, she carried out her responsibilities as one of the victors of the war and was obviously closer to the Dutch. This was the mistake of the British! Around that time, many British intelligence operations were indeed going on hand in hand with the Dutch. This was a mistake. If the British had been neutral, and hadn't helped the Dutch, there wouldn't have been any incidents at all. But it's all over now, history just took its course.

Sri Sultan Hamengku Buwono IX: Military action without the people's support would not have worked at all. So, this will of the people, this is what was essential, what was important; but it also meant that problems arose when the people's spirits fell. The other very important thing I see now—having read several books, some of which give the Dutch side of the story—is that apparently in New York at the United Nations, the Dutch were probably using the wrong tactics. I don't know for certain, but it so happened that while they were saying in New York that the TNI had been wiped out and so on, by pure coincidence in Yogyakarta it was our intention to prove that the TNI was still very much alive. Of course at that time, I didn't even know what the Dutch tactics were, I had no idea. But some books do in fact say that the Dutch tactic was to convince everyone that the TNI had vanished. So because of this, the general offensive in Yogyakarta opened the Security Council's eyes to the fact that the TNI was certainly still alive. That was very important, I feel.

I do feel that if everything hadn't been focused on the twosome of Sukarno and Hatta, it would have been very difficult, because they were our one and only hold at that time. If we from the republic hadn't aimed our sights there, I think we would have splintered. This was so strongly felt that later on, even the Dutch-sponsored Federal Consultative Assembly was directed towards Sukarno and Hatta. Nothing else would do. At that time, nothing else would do.

General T.B. Simatupang: As an example, let us look at developments in the Indian subcontinent where they were unable to reach a consensus on a foundation for the nation. Thus the movement for independence was followed by the birth of two countries: one nationalist and secular, India, and one based on religion, Pakistan. And then Pakistan split up again into two countries, Bangladesh and Pakistan. We are lucky in that we succeeded in building a nation based on a national consensus, namely Pancasila. When we consider the struggle for Indonesian independence between 1945 and 1949, we see that Pancasila was central to that struggle. Sukarno and Hatta also played a very central role. They were the two key figures in the independence movement. Thus it was only natural that they should have been the "proclamators," and that they should also have been the symbol of our unity in the years following the proclamation of independence. The problem that we had to face after the proclamation of independence was that we had to settle a fundamental conflict with the Dutch, because the proclamation inevitably created a conflict about the sovereignty of Indonesia. We believed that with the proclamation of independence, we had sovereignty over Indonesia, while the Dutch still considered sovereignty of the Indies to be theirs.

Thus a clear problem arose: how to settle that fundamental conflict. Right from the beginning there were three approaches. The first was that we could achieve a solution through negotiations, through diplomacy. This view was based on the belief that since World War II had ended with the Allies, the champions of democracy, as the victors, then the world would surely be sympathetic to our independence movement, especially when they saw how democratic we were by not wishing to settle the conflict with war. The second view took the opposite line, namely that imperialism, colonialism, and especially capitalism, would never be prepared to reach a settlement with revolutions and independence movements. The proponents of this view held that the only way was to conduct a radical revolutionary struggle, and reject all negotiations. The third approach, which was my personal view right from the start, was that in 1945 neither we nor the Dutch had the capability to force our will on the other using military means, because we were both militarily weak in 1945. That's why negotiations lasted over four years, interspersed with military struggle. That's why we built up our armed forces. I believe that if we hadn't done so, we would never have reached a settlement in our struggle against the Dutch.

Thus ended a fundamental conflict born of the proclamation of independence: who had sovereignty over Indonesia, the Dutch or us. But this conflict was only settled after a final battle in the military arena, and this final battle we conducted as a people's war. This automatically brought consequences for development after the acknowledgement of sovereignty, not only in the military field but also in development in the fields of politics, psychology, and other matters, throughout the whole of society.

Glossary
of Frequently-Used Terms and Abbreviations

BKR   Badan Keamanan Rakyat, People's Security Force.

Budi Utomo   An early Indonesian nationalist association.

bung   Revolutionary appellation meaning something like "compatriot" or "comrade."

bupati   High-ranking Indonesian official in the native civil service. Also called a regent in Dutch.

Hokokai   Japanese-run mass mobilization organization.

Indonesia merdeka   An independent Indonesia.

kenpeitai   The Japanese military police.

kiyayi   A Muslim religious scholar.

KNI   Komité Nasional Indonesia, Indonesian National Committee, a kind of governing body during the early revolution.

KNIL   Koninklijk Nederlands-Indische Leger, Royal Netherlands [East] Indies Army.

Muhammadiyah   A Muslim association, originally anti-colonial in purpose, concentrating on education and social services.

Nadhatul Ulama   A Muslim association contemporary with and with purposes similar to Muhammadiyah but having a different outlook in many matters of Islamic doctrine.

NICA   Netherlands [East] Indies Civil Administration.

pamong praja   Postwar form of *pangreh praja*.

pangreh praja In the Dutch colonial system, members of the indigenous civil service.

Parindra Partai Indonesia Raya, Greater Indonesia Party.

Partindo Partai Indonesia, Indonesian Party.

pemuda Youth, particularly a politically aware and highly patriotic youth of the revolution.

pergerakan The prewar Indonesian independence movement.

Permi Perhimpunan Muslimin Indonesia, Association of Indonesian Muslims.

Peta Pembela Tanah Air, Defenders of the Fatherland.

PKI Perserikatan Kommunist di India (Indies Communist League), later Partai Komunis Indonesia (Indonesian Communist Party).

PNI Perhimpunan (later Partai) Nasional Indonesia, Indonesian National Party.

priyayi Elite class of native officials.

Putera Pusat Tenaga Rakyat (Center of the People's Power) a Japanese-sponsored mass organization.

resident A Dutch colonial official, presiding over the administration of the unit known as the residency, a component of the province.

romusha So-called "volunteer worker" under Japanese labor mobilization programs.

Sarekat Islam Muslim Association, an early political, anti-colonial organization.

TKR Tentara Keamanan Rakyat (Peoples' Security Army), interim title for what came to be called the TNI.

TNI Tentara Nasional Indonesia, Indonesian National Army.

ulama Muslim scholar and religious leader.

Volksraad People's Council under Dutch colonial rule.

wayang The traditional Javanese shadow puppet theater, chief vehicle for expressing Javanese values.

Suggestions for Further Reading

There is a large literature on the Indonesian Revolution, and as might be expected some of the most useful material is written in the Dutch and Indonesian languages. References to such specialized works, accessible only to those with the particular language skills, may be found in the bibliographies of many prominent English-language works on modern Indonesia. A very brief listing of the more readily available and valuable of these is presented below.

Abeyasekere, Susan, *One Hand Clapping: Indonesian Cooperating Nationalists and the Dutch, 1939-1942* (Victoria: Monash University Centre for Southeast Asian Studies, 1976).

Abdullah, Taufik, *Schools and Politics: The Kaum Muda Movement in West Sumatra* (Ithaca: Cornell Modern Indonesia Project, 1972).

Anderson, Benedict R. O'G., *Java in a Time of Revolution* (Ithaca: Cornell University Press, 1972).

Anderson, Benedict R. O'G., *Some Aspects of Indonesian Politics under the Japanese Occupation, 1944-45* (Ithaca: Cornell Modern Indonesia Project, 1961).

Benda, Harry J., *The Crescent and the Rising Sun* 2nd edition (Dordrecht: FORIS, 1983).

Benda, Harry J. and Ruth T. McVey (eds.), *The Communist Uprisings of 1926-1927 in Indonesia: Key Documents* (Ithaca: Cornell Modern Indonesia Project, 1960).

Coast, John, *Recruit to Revolution* (New York: AMS Press, 1973).

Dahm, Bernhard, *History of Indonesia in the Twentieth Century* (New York: Praeger, 1971).

Dahm, Bernhard, *Sukarno and the Struggle for Indonesian Independence* (Ithaca: Cornell University Press, 1969).

van Dijk, Cees, *Rebellion under the Banner of Islam* (The Hague: M. Nijhoff, 1981).

Furnivall, J. S., *Netherlands India, A Study of Plural Economy* (New York: Macmillan, 1944).

Geertz, Clifford, *The Religion of Java* (Glencoe: The Free Press, 1960).

Hall, D. G. E., *History of Southeast Asia* 4th edition (New York: St. Martin's Press, 1981).

Hatta, Mohamad, *Memoirs* (Singapore: Gunung Agung, 1981).

Ide Anak Agung Gde Agung, *Twenty Years of Indonesian Foreign Policy, 1945-1965* (The Hague: Mouton, 1973).

Ingleson, John, *Road to Exile: The Indonesian Nationalist Movement, 1927-1934* (Singapore: Heinemann, 1979).

Kahin, Audrey (ed.), *Regional Dynamics of the Indonesian Revolution: Unity from Diversity* (Honolulu: University of Hawaii Press, 1985).

Kahin, George McT., *Nationalism and Revolution in Indonesia* (Ithaca: Cornell University Press, 1952).

van Laanen, J. T. M., *The World Depression (1929-1935) and the Indigenous Economy in Netherlands India* (Townsville: James Cook University Southeast Asian Studies Committee, 1982).

Legge, John D., *Sukarno: A Political Biography* Revised edition (London: Allen and Unwin, 1985).

McMahon, Robert J. *Colonialism and Cold War. The United States and the Struggle for Indonesian Independence, 1945-1949* (Ithaca: Cornell University Press, 1981).

McVey, Ruth T., *The Rise of Indonesian Communism* (Ithaca: Cornell University Press, 1965).

Nagazumi Akira, *The Dawn of Indonesian Nationalism: The Early Years of the Budi Utomo, 1908-1918* (Tokyo: Institute of the Developing Economies, 1972).

Nasution, Abdul Haris, *Fundamentals of Guerrilla Warfare* (New York: Praeger, 1964).

Noer, Deliar, *The Modernist Muslim Movement in Indonesia* (Kuala Lumpur: Oxford University Press, 1973).

Oey Hong Lee, *Indonesian Government and Press during Guided Democracy* (Hull: Hull University Centre for Southeast Asian Studies, 1971).

Penders, C. L., *The Life and Times of Sukarno* (London: Sidgwick and Jackson, 1974).

Pluvier, Jay M., *South East Asia from Colonialism to Independence* (Kuala Lumpur: Oxford University Press, 1974).

Reid, Anthony J. S., *Indonesian National Revolution, 1945-1950* (Hawthorn: Longman Australia, 1974).

Ricklefs, Merle C., *A History of Modern Indonesia* (Bloomington: Indiana University Press, 1981).

Simatupang, Tahi Bonar, *Report from Banaran: The Story of the Experiences of a Soldier During the War of Independence* (Ithaca: Cornell Modern Indonesia Project, 1972).

Sukarno. *Autobiography as told to Cindy Adams* (Indianapolis: Bobbs-Merrill, 1963).

Sukarno. *Indonesian Accuses!* Trans. Roger Paget (Kuala Lumpur: Oxford University Press, 1975).

Sukarno. *Nationalism, Islam and Marxism* Trans. K. H. Warouw and P. Weldon, Intro. Ruth T. McVey (Ithaca: Cornell Modern Indonesia Project, 1970).

Sundhaussen, U., *The Road to Power: Indonesian Military Politics 1945-1967* (Kuala Lumpur: Oxford University Press, 1982).

Supomo, S., "The Image of Majapahit in Later Javanese and Indonesian Writing," in Anthony Reid and David Marr (eds.), *Perceptions of the Past in Southeast Asia* (Singapore: Heinemann, 1979), pp. 171-185.

Sutherland, Heather, *The Making of a Bureaucratic Elite: The Colonial Transformation of the Javanese Priyayi* (Singapore: Heinemann, 1979).

Steinberg, David J. (ed.), *In Search of Southeast Asia* 2nd edition (Honolulu: University of Hawaii Press, 1987).

Thorne, Christopher, *Allies of a Kind. The United States, Britain, and the War against Japan, 1941-1945* (New York: Oxford University Press, 1978).

Van Niel, Robert, *The Emergence of the Modern Indonesian Elite* (The Hague: van Hoeve, 1960).

Williams, Michael C., *Sickle and Crescent: The Communist Revolt of 1926 in Banten* (Ithaca: Cornell Modern Indonesia Project, 1982).

DUF